My
LIFE
AS I REMEMBER IT

My LIFE

AS I REMEMBER IT

DAVID R. WILSON

To order additional copies of this book, contact:
Xlibris Corporation
1-888-795-4274
www.Xlibris.com
Orders@Xlibris.com
117096

Contents

❧

I dedicate this book to my progeny.
It is my hope that those who follow me will learn
from the ups and downs of my life and that knowledge
will lead them to a more complete appreciation
of the God of the universe and will increase
their fellowship with Him.

❧

Preface

Irretrievable, as it is relentless, one's life weaves its way through the decades, leaving marks in the sands of time as it passes. It is the recalling, recounting, and recording of those events which caused the marks that give a person pause.

Is it really of any importance to anyone that I should devote any part of my life now (which is swiftly being borne along on an accelerating ebb tide) to remembering, evaluating, and writing about some of these events? Strangely, I have an impelling desire to try to part the veil that is drawn across the past. Why?

After giving prayerful consideration to this question for some time, I have concluded it is important for me to focus on my life to see the hand of God throughout it. It might be of some benefit to my children as they venture through life (I wish my father had done something like this for me). I hope to put some thoughts in writing that may be used of God. To know something of the life encounters of the writer can be enlightening to those who read what one writes.

I have had the exposure of reading what others have written, who have tried to describe events, which they and I have mutually witnessed. I realize how differently they saw and interpreted what we both experienced at the same time. I feel somewhat reluctant to put on paper my impressions, which inevitably will conflict with some of my contemporaries. I also am aware that with the passage of time, history is ruminated in the mind, and events can become conveniently massaged. Sometimes the result can be tinted or distorted according to one's biases. Despite these obvious drawbacks, I have decided to attempt the project.

For these reasons, I am titling this undertaking *As I Remember It*.

Chapter 1

Before the Beginning

One comes to life as a tiny bud on a branch of a gnarled and twisted tree, which has weathered the storms of previous generations. There the tree stands obscured in the twilight of the past, providing a source of some clues as to the characteristics that appear in the new little bud.

The little new bud had no say about the type of tree of which he became part, nor did he decide on which branch he would appear, nor did he choose the location of the branch where he would start living. He didn't even realize that he had embarked on the awesome task of building a branch of his own.

As time passed, the bud absorbed the sunshine, soaked up the rain, endured the winters, laughed in the springtime, enjoyed the summer breezes and the spicy fall air. All the while, a branch of his own was trailing out behind him, and there were even fresh new buds starting out!

To a large extent, that was the way it was.

I did not a have anything to do with the fact that I became a child of parents with white skin and who lived in the state of New Jersey, USA. I could have been born in Africa, China, or India into a completely different culture and social background. I did not select but was endowed with certain physical, mental, and probably spiritual attributes derived from those who preceded me on the family tree. To have a better understanding of the qualities of one's parental heritage is to better understand oneself. Therefore, what follows in the rest of this chapter is a review of what I have been able to learn concerning some of my immediate predecessors.

My knowledge of my mother and father comes from my own memory during my lifetime, plus what my mother has told me about some of the events and circumstances before I was born. The information I have about my grandparents is primarily drawn from oral and written communication with my mother and is rather sketchy at best. Nevertheless, it does give a flavor of their history.

John Wilson was born in Kilbourney, Scotland, 4 August 1855, died in New Jersey in 1923. He was married in Scotland and had two children there, Anne and John. I assume his first wife died because he married my grandmother, Janet Stuart (born in Kilbourney, Scotland, died in New Jersey in 1936), and they moved with the children to the USA apparently in the 1890s. They had several children in the USA. As husband and wife, they ran a strict religious family environment arising out of their staunch affiliation with the Plymouth brethren.

Their children are as follows:

Anne (died in New Jersey, 1974) married to a businessman, lived in Kearny, New Jersey, all her life. They had no children.

John (died in 1966) married and moved to California, where he became a lifelong resident. He had three sons and a daughter.

Nettie (died in New Jersey, 1918) was unmarried and died in the major flu epidemic prevalent at that time.

Dan (died in Tucson, Arizona, 1964), my father, more details later.

Effie (died in New Jersey, 1969) married and lived a relatively prosperous life as the wife of a man who worked for one of the larger manufacturing companies. They had two children.

Lillias (died in New Jersey, 1994) married with two children. A substantial corporation employed her husband.

Stuart (died 1995) married and had three children. They lived in the Midwest of the United States and later moved to Florida. He was in sales for a prominent company and later formed his own corporation.

I have no idea how my grandfather supported his family financially in either Scotland or the United States. They owned their home in a respectable part of Kearny, New Jersey, which would lead one to believe that they were reasonably prosperous. One thing I remember is that he had grapevines growing in his backyard. I was told that he made and sold grape jelly and other kinds of preserves. He died when I was in my first year of life, so I have no personal memory of him. I have a warm feeling about him, which I think rises out of the one photo I have of him holding me when I was a baby.

I remember my grandmother Wilson as a person who was very kind to me as a child. I suspect that both my grandparents were upright Christians who were industrious but also had an active sense of humor. I think this because each of these traits was generously sprinkled in the personalities of all of their offspring.

Franklin Doehrbeck was my grandfather on my mother's side of the family. He was born of wealthy German parents in the city of London, England. I do not know his date of birth or death. It appears he was reared in Berlin and turned into an undisciplined child, became a member of the Prussian army, went AWOL, and found his way to the USA. He met my grandmother, who fell madly in love with him and married him. After many years of nonsupport, in addition to playing the part of a handsome, irresponsible, cane-carrying dandy, my grandmother divorced him. Sometime later, the family learned that he had died penniless in New York City and was buried in a pauper's grave—a very sad story!

I never saw him. I never saw a picture of him. No one ever spoke of him. There was a gaping hole in the family ranks. It was a silent conspiracy of shame!

My grandfather's one redeeming feature, in my mother's eyes, was his exceptional ability to cultivate and nurture a magnificent display of flowers and shrubs in the front and back yards of one of the many places they lived during her childhood.

Louise Bergrisch was my grandmother on my mother's side of the family (born in Graz, Austria, 1872, died in New Jersey, 1961). Her birthplace, Graz, was and is an historic city surrounded by the beauty of the Alps. My grandmother's father (Frank Bergrisch) was a well-to-do person who lived in a large home, which employed several servants. Her childhood in this environment left her with many pleasant memories. (Her picture in Austria is on the right.) Her father, apart from his business activities, was an active and talented artist who had been awarded many prizes for his paintings, many of which graced the walls of their home. She had a sister named Rose Bergrisch (whose place and date of birth I do not know) and a brother (Frank Bergrisch, born in Vienna, 1874, died in Rye, New York, 1963). For some reason, which is not clear, her father became at odds with the Prussian Empire and was hounded by them until he finally escaped to the USA. After he left, all their property was taken over by someone (who that "someone" was is not clear). Subsequently her father sent tickets for the family to join him in the United States.

In 1880 they traveled by ship in steerage class, the poorest accommodation available. The weather during their trip was extremely stormy, causing constant motion sickness for the entire family. My grandmother remembers seeing icebergs and a sinking ship. All in all it seemed to be a harrowing experience!

Her father met them at the pier and took them to a cheap tenement flat, which was all he could afford. Being dropped from the height of opulence and cultural vantage to the bottom of the ladder economically and socially was more than her mother could bear. She died within a year after arriving in the United States. Her name was Ursala Beyer. (Died in 1881 at the age of thirty-five and was buried in a Lutheran cemetery in Long Island, New York.)

Following the tragic death of the mother, the father tried to cope with the raising of the children and found that it was more than he could handle. He left them in the care of a Roman Catholic convent. Eventually he remarried and took them back into his home. However, there was not harmony between the children and the stepmother. At a young age they all took jobs and found boarding accommodation.

Rose soon married and became pregnant. She died giving birth to twins, who also died.

Frank, my grandmother's brother, went on to be an outstanding entrepreneur in the city of New York. At age eleven he worked for a jeweler in the Bowery in New York City during the day and slept on the floor of the premises at night. A difficult beginning! Later he got a job with a realtor in Maywood, New Jersey, with which he also lived.

He went into business for himself, building homes and selling them in Maywood Park, New Jersey. In the course of doing business, he met a girl named Lilly whose mother had bought one of his homes. They married in the year 1900. According to the information I have, that would make him twenty-six years of age.

He soon turned his attention to New York City and built numerous apartment and office buildings in the Bronx and Manhattan, which resulted in wealth and prestige for him and his family. Successful though he was, he kept in contact with his sister Louise (my grandmother), and every Christmas there was a gift of cash for her, her children, and her grandchildren. I can remember well as a child getting money from someone called Uncle Frank. He seemed to have been an industrious, thoughtful, generous man.

He had a son Frank Jr. (born in 1902, died in Rye, New York, in 1974). In 1925 he received a civil engineering degree from New York University. He was presented with the university's meritorious Service Award in 1953. He was very active in many community service projects during his life and seemed to be highly regarded by a variety of organizations. When he died in 1974, his funeral service was conducted in an Episcopalian church in Rye, New York.

Now back to Louise, my grandmother. When she was in the convent, the nuns taught her to sew. She was employed by a manufacturer of fur coats. The owner was impressed with the quality of her craftsmanship and offered to teach her the trade. She was a willing learner. She became knowledgeable and skillful, which resulted in an extensive clientele. She used this occupation as a means of livelihood for the remainder of her financially productive years. She was a lady who faced great financial and emotional hardships throughout her life with outstanding tenacity, durability, good humor, and personal dignity. I remember her being full of energy and at the same time attentive to individuals, even to a little kid such as I was at the time.

Since her husband was not a "breadwinner" by any stretch of the imagination, she became the sole provider for the family. They had ten children: Helen, William, Maude, Charles, Anna, Louise, Lulu, Viola, George, and Alma.

Maude (died 1987) married and had four children. She lived out her life in New Jersey. Her husband died early in their marriage during the flu epidemic in 1917.

Charles (died 196—?) married a schoolteacher. They had one stillborn child. As far as I am aware, they lived a happy life together in New Jersey.

Anna (died 1973) happily married and had two children. She resided in New Jersey all her days.

Louise (died 1899) fell out of her high chair as an infant and died from her injuries.

Lulu was my mother. Lots more about her to come.

Helen (died 1952) married and moved to Seattle, Washington. She died prematurely but had two boys, Maine and Jack Tonkin, who are still residents of Seattle.

Viola (died 1996) married and had a successful life in New Jersey. She had one daughter.

William (died 1962) became a "singing waiter" and traveled with the sun between points in New Jersey and Florida. He married, but it was not a pleasant adventure. They had one adopted daughter.

George married and had one daughter. He was a homicide detective in Newark, New Jersey, and spent his life in the state of New Jersey. He is still living at Toms River, New Jersey, at time of writing.

Alma (died 1999) enjoyed a long life with her husband in Phoenix, Arizona. They have one daughter and one son. Alma was about ten years older than I, which would make her birth year 1912.

Lulu Frances Doehrbeck (born in Hoboken, New Jersey, in 1899, died in Tucson, Arizona, on May 1, 1989). She was my mother. Having been born into the middle of a large struggling family, she had little of the carefree joys of a normal childhood. Since her father was irresponsible and her mother had to work all the time, it fell to the older children to care for the younger ones. As a result she became sensitive and responsive to the needs of others at an early age. These characteristics became part of her nature for the remainder of her life.

Her mother was going to name her Louise (after herself) to take the place of the daughter who had died after falling out of the high chair. Someone told her that if she did, this child would also die. Therefore she decided to call her Lulu, which became a source of embarrassment to Mom through her youth and early adult years. (But it became something in which she took personal pride later in her life.)

The extent of her formal education was limited to about grade six. However, she acquired a deep hunger for books and became an avid reader for the remainder of her life. She also learned to have a keen appreciation of poetry. Collecting poetry, which was meaningful to her, became a hobby throughout the years.

During childhood she attended a German Presbyterian church in Newark, New Jersey, in which she
was confirmed in 1914. After she and my father

Mom at Confirmation

Grandmas Doehrbbeck & Wilson

Grandfather Wilson

met, they attended the Brethren Assembly in Kearny. She maintained this association all of her life. Her demeanor was one of high moral and ethical standards, underlined by a sincere love of the Lord Jesus Christ.

When she was about sixteen years of age, because of cramped living quarters, her mother made her leave home and find permanent employment in the workforce and to locate a place to board on her own. Her older brother Charles was still living at home, and she thought that he should have been the one to go first. I assume all the older girls were already launched into the stream of life in some capacity. She felt quite abandoned by this action because she really had no knowledge or training to be thrust into this experience. She didn't know where to go or what to do. Fortunately she had a girlfriend whose mother had some accommodation she could use on a temporary basis. She found a job working for DuPont in the printing department. She became allergic to printing ink and was transferred to shipping. She got along well and received some encouragement and promotions from her supervisors.

Daniel Fotheringham Wilson (born on February 28, 1900, in Kearny, New Jersey, and died in Arizona in 1964). He was my father. I am left with the impression that he was an energetic, mischievous, venturesome child with a wide-ranging sense of humor. He helped with the production of the preserves his father made when he was a youth.

He attended school until grade six and stopped for reasons I do not know. Although his formal education was short, he was a very bright individual who learned quickly and possessed an innate quality to assess and influence people.

In 1916 there was a revolution in progress in Mexico, and as part of the outcome of that activity, Pancho Villa crossed the border between the United States and Mexico and attacked some towns in New Mexico. The United States retaliated by sending troops to the area. My father lied about his age (he was sixteen), joined the army, and was sent to the border of Mexico. He was only there a short time when my grandmother informed the authorities that he was underage. He was immediately discharged and sent back home.

Upon arrival back in New Jersey, he found employment at DuPont in the shipping department! The plot thickens!

One day, my father was telling a fellow worker that his sister Nettie was looking for a copy of the poem "The Face on the Barroom Floor." Did he know where he could get one? My mother overheard the conversation and mentioned that she had a copy, which she would lend him if he would be sure to return it to her. She did, and he did, and that was the start of their romance! They were both about seventeen years old.

It wasn't long before their attraction to each other resulted in them "going steady." My mother's temporary boarding accommodation came to an end when her friend's grandfather came home to claim the room my mother was occupying. She had to return to her mother's flat while she searched for another place to stay. My father was not happy about her having to go from one boarding house to another and asked her to marry him so that they could both find a place where they could live. My mother agreed, and so they made arrangements to be married.

My father was supposed to tell his mother, but he didn't, and so his family knew nothing of their plans. The day arrived, and the only people involved in the wedding celebration were the bride, the bridegroom, and Mom's girlfriend and her boyfriend, who became the witnesses at the ceremony. The knot was tied in an unostentatious manner in the home of the pastor.

My mother's family chose to ignore the whole proceedings and was not represented at the gala occasion at all. Lulu wore a white dress, which was made for her by her girlfriend. Mom's girlfriend's mother prepared the "reception," and a table was set at her home for the four of them to commemorate the union. They had little money, and they had no place to go. So my father took my mother back to her mother's flat, and he went home to his mother!

A bleak beginning to a love affair which was to stand the test of time and the vicissitudes of life for the next four or five decades (until death parted them in 1964).

Someone put a notice in the paper announcing the details of the wedding. (I suspect it was my mother's girlfriend since she seems to have been a very active player in all of this!). In any case, the information was seen by one of the parishioners in my grandmother Wilson's church, who dutifully congratulated her the following Sunday morning! My father still had not informed his parents! All of this did not augur well for achieving warm in-law relationships!

So the young couple started life together without the blessing or support of either of their families. They found a two-room place to live as the first of many dwelling places they would jointly occupy. After a while they moved to a flat, where tragedy nearly brought their lives to an end. My father woke up to go to work (he was a conductor on the streetcars at that time), and he fainted a couple of times, and my mother had a terrible headache. They didn't know what was wrong. On his way to his job, my father phoned Grandma Doehrbeck and the doctor. Mom's mother lived close by and was there quickly. She immediately realized the place was full of coal gas. She threw the windows wide open, and the fresh air rapidly revived my mother. The doctor arrived soon after and said they would have been dead if they had been exposed to the gas for much longer.

My mother was pregnant when this episode happened; within a matter of weeks she gave birth to a son at the local hospital. The date was February 23, 1921. It was a difficult birth, requiring the use of instruments. This new person was welcomed into the world and was named Daniel, after my father. He was my older brother. In the short span of three weeks he died of undetermined causes. My mother lived with the belief that something happened to him at the hospital, which resulted in his untimely death.

There was no money for a professionally run funeral. The baby's body was placed in a small casket, which was held on the laps of my father and of my mother's brother Bill. I assume some acquaintance provided the transportation to the cemetery for the forlorn tiny group of mourners, where they buried Daniel.

It was a devastating, heartbreaking experience! However, I sense that out of this tragic event, a healing process began with their families, which tended to bond them throughout the succeeding years.

This completes the overview of the environment and the condensed inventory of genes that greeted the "little new bud" (David Robert Wilson) as he emerged through the bark of the branch of the family tree to begin his time in the sun.

Chapter 2

The Beginning
(1922-1929)

Digest of the Times and Circumstance:

The dramatic repercussions of World War I were beginning to recede, and the United States was entering into a period of prosperity that permeated the whole American society. The "machine age" was rolling on with ever-increasing momentum propelled by the thrust it received by the need for weapons of war in 1914-1918.

The automobile was fast taking over the country as the major means of commuting within localities and also for short distances between towns. Although there were still horse-drawn vehicles employed, they were rapidly becoming replaced by cars and trucks. The need for better and longer roads became essential as the automobile became affordable for the ordinary person.

Over land, the steam-driven railroad train was the major transport for goods and people. On the seas and on the large rivers the steamboat provided the mass transportation. The sailing ships had faded into history. Airplanes were not yet a dominant means of conveyance, but they did carry the mail between principal cities on a regular basis.

There was an aura of excitement that emanated from the victory experienced in WWI, the advancement of scientific achievement, the pride of patriotism, and the belief that the USA was by far the best country in the world and that indeed they really didn't need anyone else. Congress refused to have any part of the League of Nations, even though one of the main people to conceive and promote the idea was their own President Wilson (no relationship!). To emphasize their desire to be isolated from the rest of the world, high tariffs were placed on all goods imported from other countries so that products produced in America would have a greater price advantage in the U.S. consumer market.

Arizona and New Mexico had been added to complete the forty-eight states under the Stars and Stripes ten years before, and although the Civil War had been fought a few decades previously, there were still many people who kept the embers of discord glowing. By the standards of world history, the United States was still a young inexperienced nation who, in the opinion of the older nations, had better listen to its "elders" in the matter of diplomacy and trade. Since the States had financed the Allies in WWI and was owed hundreds of millions of dollars by them and had succeeded in building a strong industrial base, it had no intention of taking a backseat to anyone.

These were also the days of "prohibition." It was illegal to manufacture, sell, or buy alcoholic beverages. This situation induced bootlegging across the Canadian and Mexican borders. It spawned the speakeasies, where people went to consume illegal alcohol secretly. It spawned the Mafia and the Elliot Nesses. It spawned gang warfare and corrupted politicians. An underground subculture was formed, which became epitomized by booze, jazz, Basin Street blues, and flappers.

The daily newspaper was still a major dispenser of information, and most of the population depended on reading the paper to keep abreast of current events. The radio was fast becoming another means of spreading information to the people. The domestic use of the telephone was becoming more commonplace, although a large percentage of the population was still without this equipment in their residences. Television was nonexistent.

Christianity was the predominant religion in the country, and the Judeo-Christian ethic was perceived to be the guiding moral compass for socially acceptable behavior by the general public. Attending church on Sunday morning at one of the standard denominations was a usual and fashionable thing to do, even if it was a mere formality. In addition to the staid denominations, there were other religious Christian activities more fervent and evangelical, typified by the enthusiastic preaching of Billy Sunday. At that time, the USA was still known as a Christian country.

My father and mother were two young people who had been through the heart-wrenching experience of losing the firstborn son. They had to face making a life together in the environment of the day. While they only had minimal conventional education, they had the will to work. Dan was employed as a taxi driver. He was determined that he would be the one in the household to earn a living and my mother would be the homemaker. My grandmother Wilson had encouraged my father to be a mechanic and had provided him with tools and access to training; however, it was not the type of employment that suited him. He was more inclined to work with people rather than machinery. By nature he was a salesman and a leader.

I was born into this little family on 24 February 1922. It was one year plus one day after my brother Daniel had been born. Since my brother's death, my mother had a great distrust of hospitals; consequently, I was born in the flat where they lived, at lA 5 Forest Avenue, Kearny, New Jersey.

The economy was buoyant, and wages were high; many people became interested in summer places. The nearby Atlantic Ocean provided a coastline that was increasingly popular, particularly with easier access by car. My father became a salesman of bread and cake, and we moved to a small town on the beach about sixty miles from Kearny. Its name was Avon-by-the-Sea. From there he was able to service the many stores up and down the coast that had sprung up because of the growing tourist industry. He remained in that business for most of the rest of his working life, with the exception of part of the Depression years.

I was about two years old when this major change in environmental surroundings occurred. It was to have a profound effect on my life. We settled in a little bungalow on Marine Place in Avon-by-the-Sea, where we remained for the next four or five years. It was there that my first recollections of life began.

Personal Thoughts and Memories

Avon-by-the-Sea:

Avon was typical of many small municipalities strung along the New Jersey coastline from Asbury Park to Atlantic City. Each of them had a strip of sandy beach frontage on the Atlantic Ocean. Wood-frame hotels were sprinkled along the waterfront, which catered to the flood of tourists, mainly from the interior cities, such as Newark and New York City. The first six to eight blocks adjacent to the beach were composed of summer-style bungalows with well-kept gardens and neatly manicured lawns and shrubs. The sidewalks were paved with cement, but the roadways, which crisscrossed the residential area, were covered with clean gravel, scrupulously graded every day. Then came Main Street, running parallel to the shoreline, where the shops and the all-important streetcar line were located. The streetcar linked many of the coastal towns together. Avon was a tidy picturesque village where there was freedom of movement, a friendly atmosphere, and virtually no crime. The police force was minuscule. As far as I can remember, there was just one intersection where there was a traffic light.

Marine Place, the street where we lived, had an exotic sounding name, but in reality, it was a lane that ran adjacent to and alongside Main Street. Although Main Street was composed of commercial properties primarily, our little bungalow backed onto a large residence, which faced onto Main Street. I came to know Marine Place as "the alley." There were a few other similar cottages on the alley where other young families lived. This provided nearby companionship in safe, friendly surroundings for me to begin the discovery of the wonderful world into which I had come to dwell.

Directly across the alley from our home was the playground of the local public school. This afforded a huge expansion of my domain. Not only did it provide play equipment plus space to run and learn games, but as I watched the behavior of children, it also made me discover at an early age

Me Mom and the dog
that went mad

The house where we lived
on Marine alley

that society is made up of a variety of personalities. I assume the neighbors in the large house also owned the house we lived in, for there were no fences in between. There was a garden of many colorful flowers and a most impressive overhead latticework arbor supporting a vigorous grapevine. When ripe, the grapes were a deep purple in color. They emitted a heavy, enchanting fragrance, which remains etched on my olfactory to this day.

My remembrance of those neighbors is of warmth and friendliness. They were always kind and attentive to me. They were immigrants of recent vintage (from Italy or Greece I think). The most notable thing about them was their pet! It was a jumbo brilliantly feathered (yellow, green, and red) parrot who could say all the bad words in several different languages. He surveyed his estate from his perch, framed in a bay window overlooking the garden. We kept an eye on each other, I from my back porch and he from his bay window!

After reviewing some of the available photos, a more knowledgeable and critical observer might conclude this was not an ideal place for a child to begin to find his way. To me, it was, and still is, a paradise, which is now tucked away in the folds of my mind.

Mom and Me:
Alongside a picture of me at about age two, in an old album in which my mother kept memorabilia devoted to me, there was prayerful verse written in her own handwriting. Here are a few of the lines:

> "It is a wonderful thing, a mother.
> Other folks can love you, but
> Only your mother understands,
> She works for you, looks after you,
> Forgives you anything you do."

Those few words encapsulate my mother's attitude toward me all the days of her life. She always loved me. She always believed in me. She always did anything she could for me. She fought anyone who would want to hurt me. She turned a blind eye to any of my faults. She was always proud of me. She truly loved me as unconditionally as one person can love another. And it showed!

Being enveloped in love of such degree has to be the best emotional climate that can be provided for any child starting out on the pathway of life. I was very fortunate!

Because my mother remained at home with me, I had her full attention and devotion. She was young, healthy, endowed with a venturesome spirit as well as having an insatiable appetite for walking. This combination was a perfect mix to explore the coastline of the nearby ocean edged by a boardwalk extending for mile upon mile upon unbroken mile.

According to pictures taken before the move from Kearny to Avon, my mother had long hair, which flowed over her shoulders down her back

Mom on the left with long hair and on the right after cutting it

to her waistline. Pictures taken after moving to the shore show her hair having been cut into a kind of long bob, earlobe length. This is my earliest remembrance of her hairstyle. To cut her hair must have been traumatic given her religious connections and conservative influence of her mother and mother-in-law. Somehow it demonstrates an early trait toward independent thought and decision making, which characterized her personal actions all of her life. She was never a crowd pleaser or crowd joiner but took action resulting from what made sense to her. Personally, in my mind, I hold pictures of the wind blowing her shortened hair in every direction as we walked the boardwalk or strolled the sandy beaches. It seemed that we found our way to the beach more days than we did anything else whether it was winter or summer. In the summer, the warmth of the sunshine and the glistening of the sunlight on the water provided a welcome sense of well-being. The untamed winter storms sent howling wind, which drove the wild waves crashing under the boardwalk. Each of the seasons offered dramatically different images of that magical terrain where the end of the land meets the beginning of the sea.

In the summer, the sand and the surf were crowded with people, which generated its own brand of excitement; but the time I liked best, as a small child, was in the late spring or early fall. During those periods the beach was relatively empty for miles, with the exception of a handful of locals. Mom and I felt that it all belonged to us.

It was warm enough to toss off our shoes and be barefoot. On to the soft sand we would run, slipping and sliding, until we reached the hard-packed part of the beach, which had been saturated and smoothed by the constant caressing of the rhythmic motion of the surf. Once on this surface, we had a racetrack stretching out before us as far as our energy would carry us. It was great fun dodging in and out as the waves would chase us on the sand and then drain away. The sandpipers would play the same game, but in their case they were looking for bits of food washed up by the water, which they would snap up with their pointed beaks.

When it was low tide, more of the beach was exposed, and we would look for shells of many shapes and sizes, which were sculptured by the motion of the ocean. We took the more interesting ones home to add to our collection. At various points along the shoreline there were jetties constructed of very large rocks jutting out to the sea. They were placed there to keep the sand from being washed away. They also provided habitats for myriad types of crabs and related sea life that became fascinating exploration sites for a curious little boy.

When the winter came, it introduced the storms. The placid waterfront became a war zone where the powerful Atlantic Ocean attempted to dismantle the East Coast of the North American continent. The wind whipped the waves into hordes of white-mane lions charging into the beach in the attempt to devour the sand and drag it out to sea. Some storms sent the crushing wall of water down the streets and into nearby homes and hotels. My mother would take me to see these stunning spectacles from a safe viewpoint. From my early youth I learned to respect and hold in awe the might of the sea.

The full-blown heat of the summer drove the city dwellers out of their cramped, airless neighborhoods to the breezy expanse of the ocean. There they also had the opportunity to wade, bathe, or swim in the refreshing waters of the Atlantic Ocean, which was tempered by the offshore flow of the Gulf Stream. Often during the months of July and August, at the warmest part of the day, it was nearly impossible to find a spot on the beach the size of a blanket that was not occupied. The sun worshippers were out en masse! To find the way from one's own territorial claim to the water without throwing sand on or stepping on a prostrate body could become a major strategic hopscotch maneuver.

This time of year had a different charm than winter, spring, or fall. It was then that I had the most exposure to my aunts, uncles, cousins, and grandmothers. My parent's home became the gathering place our relatives used to invade the beach. It was a great arrangement for me because I was the "prince" and got all the attention I could manage. It became somewhat overbearing for my mother, though, because of the number of bodies coming and going.

Mom had a couple of friends that came along on some of the adventures we had. They were people her age who had children about the same age as I was. Sometimes they were with us on the seaside expeditions, but mostly they joined us when we took trips into the city on the streetcar. As I mentioned before, a streetcar line that ran down the center of the Main Street of each of them connected the municipalities along the coast. The largest of the nearby towns was Asbury Park that became the destination point of these jaunts. It was there that the major emporiums were to be found, such as Kresge's and Woolworth's (competing five-and-ten-cent stores!). There were all kinds of toys on display, and once in a while, I even got to take one home. However, the crowning activity of those tours came when we sat at the Woolworth lunch counter and devoured a ten-cent hot dog smothered with mustard, slurped down with a five-cent mug of Hires Root Beer.

It was on one of those safaris that I received my first lesson on racial discrimination. In those days and in that area, white-skinned inhabitants were predominant. One day, while riding with my mother on the streetcar, a black person got on board and sat in plain sight of us. I stared for awhile and then stood up, pointed my finger, and in a loud clear voice said, "Mama, look at that burnt lady!" The atmosphere froze among the passengers. The lady ignored the remark, and my mom quietly explained to me that God had made some people different from others.

My mother tells the story of entering me in a baby parade held to create interest in the boardwalk entertainment facilities at Asbury Park. She had looked forward to this event for some time. My wagon was decorated; my clothes were chosen; everything was ready to go. The day before the event somehow my light blond hair got soaked with salty seawater while playing in the ocean. The bright sunshine reacted with the seawater to turn my hair green! She put me in the parade anyhow, but much to her chagrin, instead of the people remarking how beautiful her baby was, they laughed at her baby's green hair! (That was before green hair was fashionable!)

Dad and Me:

My father was a hard-driving, intelligent, personable young man who was determined to support his family as well as make his way in the world. He had imagination and was well received by people in general. With these qualities he soon built up a clientele of storeowners who were interested in promoting the bakery products he placed on their shelves. The overall result was that he began to prosper.

Because of the amount of time that I spent with my mother at this stage of my life, I was much closer to her than I was to my dad. However, I have stimulating memories of being with him one or two days a week when he made his rounds up and down the coastline. I felt like a somebody when I climbed into the cab of the truck and drove off to faraway places.

After a while the customers expected me and put on a royal welcome when I entered their premises. More often than not, there was a gift for me, ranging from ice cream to candy bars to balloons! My mother was in despair because I was eating so much junk food and reprimanded my dad for letting it happen. A compromise was reached whereby I brought the assorted goodies home. There was a controlled dispensing of the edibles over time and divided among other people who cashed in on my good fortune.

It pleased him to have me with him on these expeditions. A relationship was established between us, which was different from the one I had with my mother—more man to man! It gave me a sense of importance. I believe these encounters with the public on an individual basis contributed to the ease I have experienced throughout my life in meeting with anyone, anywhere, anytime.

Since my father was working five or six days a week, he wasn't part of the ocean escapades that I had with Mom. However, sometimes after he finished work during the summer, he liked to go down to the beach after dinner before dark to have a refreshing swim. Often he would take me with him. He would rush into the surf with me in his arms or on his shoulders, and we would frolic in the waves. It was during these times that he taught me how to swim and how to manage myself in the swirling currents as the waves formed and broke into the beach. By the age of four I could swim.

During the summer weekends when my aunts, uncles, and cousins arrived for a day or two at the beach, we had hilarious sessions of water and beach games. My dad became the chief organizer and fun maker. He was an activist and a ball of energy.

In late November or early December of every year, a phenomenon occurred. It was the coming of the frost fish. It was a type of codfish that appeared in large schools and bunched together in the breaking surf all along the coastline. It always happened after dark. As the waves broke on the shore, the fish would be washed up on the beach and would flop around until they found their way back into the water. The locals watched for their arrival, and when they came, hordes of people, armed with flashlights and bushel baskets, invaded the landing area. The technique was to spot a fish struggling to get back into the sea, kick it onto the dry sand, and plunk it into the basket. My dad got us into the action as a family. He and I would kick the fish to my mom, who was in charge of the plunking into the basket. Excitement? I guess! The fish were about fourteen inches long and very good to eat.

At one point during this period, my dad bought a model-T Ford car. It had a brake pedal and a clutch pedal on the floor. A lever controlling the supply of gas was mounted on one side of the steering column, and another lever that controlled the amount of spark was mounted on the other side of the steering column. The balancing of the amount of spark in relation to the supply of gas determined the speed of the car. I don't remember how it was put into reverse or forward, but I believe it involved the manner in which to depress the clutch pedal. In any case, it was a vastly different vehicle to operate than the automobiles we have today in 1998!

My mother wanted to learn to drive this four-wheeled monster, and my dad agreed to teach her! I sat in the backseat while all this instruction took place. It was the closest thing to a fight I ever witnessed between my mom and dad! The climax came when we arrived at the only important intersection in the town, where the only traffic light was located. My mother panicked and said, "Dan, I can't cross that street!" My dad said, "Lulu, you cross that street or your driving days are over!" My mom gritted her teeth, gripped the steering wheel, pulled the gas lever, and we went flying across Main Street and landed safely on the other side! My mom drove a car from that day until the year of her death at the age of eighty-nine!

Somehow that incident remains with me as being symbolic of the relationship they had. They were two strong-minded people with mutual respect for each other, who deeply loved each other; the combination helped them to resolve the challenges of life together.

After we got a family car, we made trips to Kearny to visit our relatives on festive days such as Thanksgiving, Christmas, and Easter. These were gala events in my life. I got to participate on their turf, city dwelling.

Although the journey was only about sixty miles to travel, these excursions lasted for the better part of a day. It was unusual to complete the trek without having at least one flat tire and often as many as three or four! My dad carried a hand air pump and a repair kit to patch the inner tubes as necessary. Once, when passing through one of the small towns en route to Kearny, we struck a large dog who ran right in front of the car. The steering mechanism broke. My dad lost control. We vaulted the curb and found ourselves suspended in midair on top of a fire hydrant! That was my first experience with a car accident.

Action in the Alley

There were a few events that stand out. One of them had to do with one of my playmates along the lane from where we lived. We often played together amicably. However, one day we both wanted the same toy and were insistent to the point of having a row about it. I grabbed it and held on. In desperation he clutched my arm and sank his teeth into it! Screams of pain and indignation! Mothers rushing to the defense of their respective offspring! Trip to the doctor! The result was a long cooling-off period between families. The four-year-olds had struck again!

We had a hound-type mongrel when we lived at Marine Place. I can't remember his name, but I do remember chasing him and playing with him in the yard. He was black and white and friendly. One day he started running around the grape arbor in a circle. He sped faster and faster and started to froth at the mouth; he wouldn't stop for anyone! Finally someone decided that he had gone mad and contacted the police. The policeman came, shot him dead, and took away his body. It was a harrowing experience for me. It was my first contact with death.

My recollections of those early years are filled with happiness and light for the most part. However, one time I caught the measles; there was supposed to be a high risk of permanent eye damage if one were exposed to bright sunlight. For the duration of my disease, I was confined to my room while it was daylight; heavy blankets covered the windows to provide protection for my eyesight. For a young boy who was accustomed to the freedom of the sun, sand, and sea, it was a severe and an unusual punishment, tantamount to being place in a dungeon. The treatment seemed far worse than the disease!

During our stay at Marine Place, my mother's twenty-seventh birthday arrived. I don't specifically remember it, but after she died, one of the things that I kept in remembrance of her was the flyleaf of her Bible. The inscription said the following:

"To my dearly beloved wife Lu on her twenty-seventh birthday Oct. 23, 1926. 'And all these blessings shall come on thee, and overtake thee, if thou shalt hearken unto the voice of the Lord thy God.' (Deut. 28:2)"

It was written in my father's handwriting. All of the rest of her days she consistently read that Bible. One of the strongest impressions I have is of Mom and her open Bible at every phase of her life. Her personal relationship with God and His Son, Jesus, was the joy and anchor of her soul. This fellowship set the tone for our family. Over time it produced the type of blessings promised in the verses that come after verse 2 in Deuteronomy chapter 28.

Neptune City, New Jersey

When I was about five years old, we moved from Avon to Neptune City. Neptune was a small town, more rural than urban by nature, with plenty of open fields. The street layout was random and nondescript when compared with Avon. It was acreage, which previously had been farmland and was removed from that status. It was situated only slightly west and inland from Avon and literally on the other side of the railroad tracks, which ran parallel to the coastline.

The southern boundary of the municipality was a body of water called Shark River, which was more like a basin than a river. It was approximately round in shape and was about three miles in diameter. It was connected to the ocean by an inlet, which, as one would expect, was dubbed Shark River Inlet. This body of water played a key role in stretching me from childhood through boyhood. It became to me what the ocean was for the previous three or four years. It was an expanded, exciting vista of adventure and learning.

There was very little commercial enterprise within the confines of the town. It was consisted mostly of scattered homes and small vegetable-garden farms. Nearby there was one general store, a forerunner of the modern-day convenience outlet. The heavy grocery shopping was accomplished at Avon. A few blocks away, the other major structure of note was the public school. It was there that my infamous academic career had its beginning.

10 Bradley Street:

The accommodation at Bradley Street was a step up from Marine Place. It was in a proper residential neighborhood, and the house itself was more spacious. Bradley was a dead-end street; it was only one block long and emptied into a thorough street, which ran the length of the town.

There were several happenings that I clearly remember during the short time we lived at this address.

It was from this location that I started school. I had had the experience of living across the alley from the school in Avon but was not old enough to enter into the mysteries that transpired among all those children within the confines of that red brick building. Now I was to enter my own red brick building with my own set of peers and learn what it was all about! I attended that school until grade seven. My mother kept my report cards from those days and gave them to me before she died. The one thing they proved beyond a shadow of a doubt is that her son David was not a genius. Despite my inauspicious grades, I have only pleasant memories of the period of my life that I spent with the kids, the teachers, and the principal of that school.

The thorough road to which Bradley Street connected ran in front of the school a few blocks away, thus providing a direct route from my home to my place of learning. The highway department decided to pave this particular roadway, which placed in motion events that were to lead me to painfully learn one of the important lessons of life.

I walked along this project every day and watched the cement segments being added to each other, evolving into a hard surface extending for blocks. It dawned on me that this was the perfect place to ride the short two-wheeled bike I had been given. No traffic, no bumpy gravel—what could be better? I had a chum who also had a little starter bike; we decided to give it a try one day after the workmen had finished their shift and there was no one around to stop us.

It was a most exhilarating experience as we flew back and forth on such a long unhindered raceway. There was no harm done until we decided to have a go at the sections that had been completed that afternoon! The cement was not yet set, and as we drove over it in a zigzag fashion, the wheels left marks in the fresh paving! No one had seen us, so we kept the details of our adventure to ourselves.

Nothing was said to us the next day, and we didn't discuss it with anyone either. The following day was our school assembly, when all the pupils gathered together in the gym to sing songs, to learn how our athletic teams were doing, and other relevant current events; it was generally an upbeat time. In the middle of this particular assembly, our principal, Mr. Somerville, stood at the front and asked for quietness. He then solemnly told us that the highway department had told him that there were wheel marks made by two bikes on the new pavement, and that they wanted to know who did it!

The ax had fallen! Doomsday had arrived! It was "hollow-stomach-time"! Mr. Somerville went on to say that he wanted whoever was guilty of this deed to report to him in his office some time during the day.

Then began the turbulent struggle of our consciences. Nobody saw us, so could we get away with it? How much would it cost for damages? Who would pay? What would our parents say? The teachers and kids would look down on us as bad guys! In the end, we decided that the only thing we could do was to come clean, no matter what the consequences.

After lunch my buddy and I walked timidly down the school corridor, heads hung low, stomachs churning, until we reached the Great Door, which was the entrance to Mr. Somerville's office. With trembling hands we knocked. A voice said, "Come in." We entered the holy, hallowed sanctuary of the reigning figure of our world. With quivering lips we told our story, said we were sorry for any trouble we had caused, and waited for the judgment from "on high." Mr. Somerville looked at us carefully with his piercing blue eyes then said that he would contact the highway department after which he would be in touch with us.

I told my mom and dad that night, and they didn't seem to be overly upset about it. I, however, was having internal mental fits about the shame of it all, coupled with the dreaded forthcoming punishment, which was being determined by the authorities.

Nothing was said for several days, until in one school assembly, Mr. Somerville called my friend and me forward to stand before the entire student body. The fateful moment had arrived!

Mr. Somerville told the story and then turned to us and said that after consultation with all the people involved, it was decided that we meant no malicious harm. The most impressive thing to them was that even though we could have gotten away with it, we had come forward and told the truth. Not only would there be no punishment, but they were going to honor us for being honest! He gave each of us a glossy, crisp, new one-dollar bill (which was a lot of money in those days for a seven-year-old!). Our peers all clapped, and we were treated as heroes instead of being treated like villains as we had anticipated.

Our consciences were cleared, and we had learned some of the benefits that can come from being truthful and forthright.

My mother and father continued their association with the Brethren assemblies after they were married and moved to the coast. A group of these people (about six to eight families) met in a small storefront a short drive from where we lived. The church met faithfully three times every Sunday. The morning service was conducted around the breaking of the Bread, which was a communion observance; the afternoon gathering was for the children, and the evening event was dedicated to evangelism. There was not an official pastor; the male members took turns preaching the Gospel. One Sunday evening a man by the name of Mr. Hart was the speaker. He also was the manager of the local A & P store where we bought our groceries. He was a tall man who had a pure-white full head of hair, and I knew him as a kind and gentle person. His message was centered on the Bible verse John 3:16. He emphasized that God had given His Son Jesus to be our Savior and Friend, and that all we need do was accept Him into our hearts just as we would accept any gift. I believed that night in the truth of that message. I invited Jesus into my life. He has been my constant companion from that time until now (about seventy years later).

Bond Baking Company employed my father at that time. During the winter, part of their uniform was a dark-green cord coat with large pockets. One night he came home from work and came into the kitchen. He told me to put my hand into one of his coat pockets. I did and felt something soft and warm. I took it out of his pocket, and there in my hand was a brown-and-white puppy! For the next six years he was my constant and faithful companion. He was named Pal, and he surely was well named, for he was with me every possible moment that circumstance would allow, from morning until night, every day for the next six years. He was a major source of joy and comfort to me throughout my preteen boyhood.

I was seven years old when my mother became ill. One day my father stayed home from work and took me away from the house, and we went for an extended drive around the countryside. After several hours we returned home, and there in my mother's arms, as she lay in bed, was a tiny baby! It was my brand-new brother! He was named Stuart.

The new arrival changed the dynamics of our household dramatically! No longer was I the lone star prince; now I had to share my glory with another prince. It was not easy competing with a sparkling new baby who needed care every hour. I had to learn to move over a notch and to share the limelight. This was not an easy thing for me to do after having had the undiluted attention of my mother up to this point in my life. It all transpired so suddenly that I was completely unprepared for the changes that had to take place, and I resented it.

We required larger living quarters; so we moved to a small bungalow several blocks away, which became to me home in the real sense of the word. It was the base of operations from which I explored the far reaches of Neptune City and its environs as I attempted to gratify the venturesome spirit of a growing boy.

It was also 1929, the year the stock market crashed. We didn't realize it then, but it was to markedly affect our lives—but that is the story of the next chapter.

Chapter 3

Basic Learning
(1929-1934)

Digest of the Times and Circumstances:

During the 1920s, the overriding attitude of the American population was "Let the good times roll." Little thought was given to what the consequences might be. Business was good, and as a result, companies prospered because their products were consumed as quickly as they could be produced. This scenario resulted in the price of their common stock rising up and up and up. The greed factor at all levels of society was triggered. The people bought common stocks of good and bad quality, and in the process of doing so, a huge number of people invested their life savings and the proceeds of mortgaging their homes. To make matters worse, the brokerage houses indiscriminately sold the shares on margin. The result was a large percentage of the ordinary persons of the USA were made completely vulnerable to financial disaster.

When it became apparent that the stock market was vastly over inflated, some began to sell. The word spread, and soon there was a torrent of sales that created a panic among investors, which hammered the price of the shares to rock bottom. This had the effect of destroying the confidence of people in the entire financial system. Those who had some savings remaining rushed to draw their cash out of the banks.

Many banks collapsed, forcing them to close their doors. Companies had overextended themselves and had to curtail their operations; many declared bankruptcy. All of this combined to produce a domino effect that resulted in the total number of unemployed workers rising to fourteen million in the United States and many more worldwide. In reality this figure represented whole families being without income since in those days there was usually only one wage earner per family.

The resultant shockwaves ravaged the country. Homes were lost. Suicides were common. Men wandered from state to state looking for work. Shanty towns, constructed of boxes, mushroomed on the edges of cities where the homeless and hungry huddled together seeking company in their misery. The United States of America that seemed so invincible and invulnerable was brought to its knees by events that arose out of its unbridled excessive use of the fruits of its own success.

The USA entered the period of history, which has been named the Great Depression. It was a phenomenon that spread to all of the capitalistic countries of the world. It happened during the presidency of Herbert Hoover, who undeservedly got most of the blame. Franklin D. Roosevelt became a presidential candidate in opposition to Hoover. He was able to capture the imagination of the population of the United States by giving them hope in the midst of the morass. FDR was inaugurated as the thirty-second president of the United States in 1933.

Roosevelt attacked the problems with what he called the new deal, out of which there flowed a stream of legislation designed to resolve the multitude of weaknesses in banking, in security trading, in employment, in food production and distribution, in home ownership, and in other social issues.

The flurry of activity promoted by this man with the jaunty countenance and cocky attitude, who dared to look at the prevalent overwhelming situation and say "We have nothing to fear but fear itself!" touched the spirit of the common citizen and aroused in the country the confidence to rebuild. Slowly the psychological and financial fabric of the Union repaired its tattered ego and readied itself for the next bout with history.

Europe had not recovered from the bruises of WWI when the Great Depression gave it another beating. Germany, Italy, and Spain were especially hard hit, making them ripe for political incursion. The entire continent was a battleground being fought for the political souls of the population. The fight was between dictatorial communism on one hand (which already had a firm hold in Russia) and dictatorial fascism on the other (which eventually gained the upper hand in Germany, Italy, and Spain). Moderate democratic capitalism was hanging on by its fingernails in other countries, notably England and France.

On the other side of the world, Japan was proceeding to achieve its goal of becoming a world power. It had a small landmass and an increasing population. It had accumulated the technical know-how, which allowed it to build a solid manufacturing base. It did not have an adequate source of raw material within its own country to supply its manufacturing capability. The blend of a large population, small landmass, and the lack of its own raw materials, coupled with its impelling desire to be the controlling empire of the Pacific, plunged it into a series of military conflicts. These actions resulted in the conquest of many groups of islands and eventually Korea and part of China. Japan's attitude and demeanor was a source of concern and agitation to such countries as the United States, Russia, and Great Britain.

The culmination of the combination of the events in Europe and in Asia eventually led to World War II.

There were vast changes in the area of transportation during this era. Highways were constructed, linking distant cities in the United States; the quality and quantity of automobiles was reaching new heights; buses were common carriers of people between cities; regularly scheduled airlines came into their own right; lighter-than-air dirigibles were being constructed and touted as the "wave of the future." Horse-drawn vehicles were becoming an oddity.

The radio increasingly became a major means of disseminating the news as well as being a source of entertainment for the public. Radio shows including music, comedy, drama, and serial fiction commanded a large listening audience since almost every home had a receiving set of some description.

Before the effects of the Depression hit us as a family, we had moved to our new address 67 Ridge Avenue, Neptune City, New Jersey. My dad had bought a different car. It was a Ford model A. It was a far superior car than the old model T. All in all, life was looking up!

However, it was not long before the savage teeth of the Depression sank its fangs into the flesh of our family—my father lost his job! It was a frightening, harrowing outlook for a young couple with a baby and a small boy.

My father was a fighter who did not accept defeat easily. He took any job he could get to earn a few dollars to keep his family intact. He worked at a variety of jobs, from a hired hand for moving companies to delivering telephone directories. During the worst of the Depression, our friend Mr. Hart (the manager of the A & P grocery store) prepared a large box of groceries for us each Saturday, which he allowed my father to have on credit to be paid at some distant future date. The consequence was that we never suffered from hunger throughout this difficult period of economic turmoil.

My father never stopped trying to get back into the business he knew and liked best—selling bakery goods to stores throughout the region. Finally he found a company that baked products and sold them to individuals who in turn would sell them to retail outlets. It was called Mi-Own Bakery.

It was a risky venture because in addition to paying for the products he bought, he also was required to lease a truck from the corporation. His reputation in the business was of such outstanding stature that they agreed to extend him credit to get started.

He was a resounding success! It was not long before he had more work than he could handle and considered hiring someone to work for him on a second route.

Personal Thoughts and Memories of this Period:

67 Ridge Avenue:

This home had three small bedrooms, a kitchen, living room, and dining room with a front veranda and a back porch. There was a gravel driveway alongside the house that led to a garage at the rear of a deep lot; both the house and the garage were constructed of wood and painted a light gray. On one side of the property there was a thick hedge, which separated us from a Spanish family that consisted of adults who were not very sociable. On the other side of our property, behind it and across the street from it, were unkempt empty large fields still displaying the odd pear tree, giving evidence of its recent past. Our backyard was as unkempt as the fields around it. It all added up to an outstanding location from the point of view of a preteen boy.

The street itself was gravel with a cement sidewalk on our side of the road. To the north of us was a rise of land, which was called the ridge because it was elevated about one hundred feet above the surrounding area. On the top of this hill there was a "fresh-air camp," where some of the underprivileged children from the city of Newark came each summer for a time of recreation. On the other side of the camp, at the bottom of the hill, there flowed a large babbling brook embellished by mature trees on both banks. About a block beyond the brook my school was located. This became the route I traveled to and from school each day. It was an ideal path for a young boy with a venturesome spirit.

Within a short distance from my home there were two small forests, some rolling wooded hills named Shark River Hills (about two hundred to three hundred feet high), and of course Shark River itself. The ocean was a twenty-minute saunter away; plus there was a freshwater pond into which the brook flowed. All of this exciting territory provided a large scope to investigate and to learn the secrets of the outdoors.

In addition to all of this, there were plenty of compatible friends of my own age with whom I enjoyed companionship during the whole time I lived at this address. There were all the advantages of small-town living with no disadvantages that were apparent to me.

Mom:

The predominant memories I have of my mother during this period were of her being occupied with washing clothes, cooking, and taking care of my brother. There was some strain that developed between us because she could no longer go venturing with me as she had before, and I was increasingly wanting to stretch her apron strings to the limit as I tested the new and stimulating surroundings. It was the natural course of growing, including the expansion of life in general, but it was a bit painful for me, and I suspect it was for her too.

This is not to say that we didn't have lots of good times together, but they were different because always there would be other people around in the activities. Also I was drawn to the other children my age, and as I will relate later, we got involved in plenty of enterprises.

Because of the unemployment that was rampant, there were men roaming the countryside looking for work. They were hungry and would ask for a meal from my mother. She was always ready to share what she had. As I have mentioned, we were fortunate to receive our weekly supply of food from the A & P grocery store, which my mother turned into delicious soups and stews among other things, which were easier to dish out to these hapless humans. Our back porch was their dining room. Not that she fed hordes of them but about five or six a week and then only one person at a time. It was not a Salvation Army operation but a neighborly thing to do, which many people did during that distressing social upheaval.

My mother did not have an electric washing machine. They were very rare in those days. She washed the clothes in a tub using a corrugated washboard on which she scrubbed the garments up and down with her hands and knuckles. When they were clean, she rinsed and then wrung the water out of them with a hand-turned ringer. When that was done, she took them outside where there were two posts about thirty feet apart with a woven cotton line strung out between them. On this line the clothes were hung and then raised higher into air using a long pole to catch the wind and the sun, which dried and bleached them. It was not an easy task especially since a ready supply of diapers for Stuart was necessary.

One time during one of our disagreements, I threatened to run away. She said to me, "Go ahead and run away then!" I said, "OK, I will!" I proceeded to pack a few things in a red-colored piece of cloth, knotted the corners together, and started out the door. My mother began to panic and started telling me not to leave, but I kept on going.

I planned to stay in the small woods within sight of our home. She couldn't follow me because my brother couldn't be left alone. She called, "David! David! David! Come back!" The farther I went, the fainter her voice became, the darker and more foreboding the woods became, and the smaller my home became!

The audacity and bravery within my heart began to seep into my stomach, down through my legs, into my feet and trail out behind as residue in my footprints. My pace slackened and finally stopped. I turned around and headed back. When I got there, my mother threw her arms around me and welcomed me with tear-filled hugs! All was well again. It was the first and last time I ever tried that caper!

My mother was a berry-picking fanatic, particularly blueberries. She and some of her friends went on expeditions at the appropriate hot days in summer to gather the harvest in the nearby hills where the patches were to be found. The bushes were low and scrawny, and the berries were small. It was not a pleasant task to perform, kneeling or bending over in the blazing heat of the sun.

Much to my chagrin, I was a captive laborer for whom it was a mandatory function to participate in these escapades. It was the only one of my mother's adventures that I can recall that I disliked with a vengeance. It left a scar on my psyche in the berry-picking department that remains with me to this day!

My brother and I were very healthy during this time of our lives with the exception of childhood diseases such as chickenpox and mumps. When these things occurred, though, I remember how well my mother tenderly hovered over us.

She was a great caring mom not only in these conditions but also on an everyday basis. She also was our fearless defender whenever we might get into neighborhood fracases; not that it would happen that often, but she was right there by our side through thick and thin.

Dad:

My dad had the capacity to see some humor in everything and had a positive attitude no matter how difficult the situation might be. These attributes were invaluable to him and to those around him in the depths of the Depression. My mother was particularly buoyed in spirit by his unquenchable approach to the challenges of life. The atmosphere of our home reflected this disposition.

I believe that this demonstration of fortitude in the middle of my formative years had a marked influence on me all the rest of my days. I learned that no matter how bad the circumstances may appear to be, one never quits or loses one's ability to laugh.

Before the repercussions of the Depression struck our family, my father was having problems with his top set of teeth. For whatever reason he elected to have all of them pulled instead of having them repaired. He went to Philadelphia, which was over one hundred miles from Neptune City. He had them all pulled in one sitting and had an upper plate made. When he got home he had the false teeth in place and couldn't get them out because of the swelling in his gums. I can recall him sitting on a kitchen chair in great pain, struggling to pull them out of his mouth. I don't remember how long it took, but he finally got them loose, and eventually his gums healed. It was a dreadful ordeal.

However, he used those teeth as long as he lived. True to form, he turned it all into something to generate laughter. By jutting his upper plate forward and framing the teeth with his open mouth, he created an image that was apelike in appearance. He used this ruse to make people laugh. Children were especially intrigued by this antic.

When my father got the job of delivering telephone directories to the homes that had this equipment, he let me work with him. We filled our car to the ceiling with the books and then would proceed to go house to house and block by block until all of the territory assigned to him had been covered. My inclusion in this operation made me feel important and gave me a sense of being a contributor to the well-being of our family.

One of my favorite memories involving my dad during this period was when we played catch. My mother's sister Alma and her boyfriend, Wassey, used to visit us. They took a liking to me and bought me a brand-new catcher's mitt. It was the pride of my young life. Consequently any chance I got to play catch was a delight.

My dad liked to pitch, and so we spent much of our spare time in the driveway alongside our house pitching and catching, using the garage doors as backstop. I became the catcher on the school baseball team as a result of getting this glove and having the practice with my father.

When my father started working for Mi-Own Baking Company, he got a brand-new Dodge, a covered van truck. It was a beautiful Chinese gold metallic color. It was his pride and joy. Two or three times a week he traveled to Patterson, a nearby town where the bakery was located, to load up with the products he would sell and then drive home with the vehicle filled with goodies. However, this machine was the center of two unpleasant experiences for me.

Dad took my brother and me for a ride in it when he first got it. I think Stuart was about four years old at the time. He was sitting in the middle, and I was on the outside of the passenger seat. We were thrilled! When we stopped in our driveway, I jumped out in a state of elation and slammed the door! Unfortunately, Stu was right behind me and had his hand on the door frame. He yelled in pain. My father ran around the truck and released his bruised fingers from the door jamb then he grabbed me and gave me a thorough spanking accompanied by the wailing serenade of agony from my brother. I can still hear, feel, and see the scene! I have always been mindful of slamming doors ever since!

On another occasion, my dad was going to rearrange some of his cargo. This required backing the van close to the porch. He asked me to stand by the porch and to tell him to stop when he reached the proper distance. He proceeded to reverse toward the platform. I said, "Stop!" He didn't hear me and kept backing, which resulted in a crash into the corner of the porch, making a large dent in this prized possession. He said I didn't tell him to stop soon enough. He administered a sound licking, which hurt twice as much because I felt it was unjust and undeserved.

Often when Dad came home he would invite my mom out to the truck filled with a variety of goodies, throw open the door, and say, "Take your pick, Lulu. You can have anything you want!" My mother always had a sweet tooth, and she would be so excited as she lifted the lids on the different boxes, revealing all manners of palate-teasing treasures. She would make her selection and take it into the house for us all to enjoy.

My father did a considerable amount of preaching. As I have indicated, the Brethren did not have full-time permanent local pastors. They had itinerant teachers and evangelists who would come and stay for a series of meetings and then move to some other place. However, those men who had suitable gifting were used to doing the public preaching or teaching locally on a week to week basis. He was asked to speak at other nearby churches as well as our own. As a general rule this would occur on a Sunday evening, and we would go with him as a family.

We often went to a group of black Christians who lived in a village called Pinebrook. This was always a stimulating event because all the singing was accompanied by enthusiastic hand-clapping and thigh-slapping action. There were no musical instruments permitted (they were too "worldly"), but these folk made up for it by manufacturing their own natural percussion section.

My mother also taught a midweek Bible class after school to the children of Pinebrook, and I used to tag along with her. I have cozy sensations when I think about that place and those people.

Stuart:

The role of big brother in our society has been allotted a high place. It is because he is seen as the one who hovers over the little brother, protecting him from bullies and rescuing him from danger or threat of harm. He is the one who constantly delights in the activities of the littler fellow.

I feel that in some of these categories, I fell very far short of the passing mark. While I wouldn't allow anyone to hurt Stuart, I didn't like to go out of my way to be of help to him. It wasn't that I disliked him; it was the fact that he was a hindrance; he was not part of my agenda. I could do the perfunctory things like rock his cradle (on request), or later on, watch him for my mother but never take a personal interest in helping him accomplish things he wanted to do. As he got to be three or four years of age, he wanted to be with me all the time and this annoyed me very much.

The fact that there was seven years' difference in age between us had a great deal to do with the gap in the closeness of our relationship. Our friends were diverse; our activities were dissimilar; and our interests were unlike. All of these ingredients combined to nullify a potential comradeship that we could have enjoyed in our youth.

A primary example of this remains in my memory bank. One day, my mother took us both along with my cousin James, who was visiting us, over to Shark River to go swimming. James and I had a time of playing while Mom splashed with Stuart in the shallow water then she asked me to watch him so that she could swim in the deeper water. Stu was not old enough to walk steadily but could sit up and dawdle in water six to eight inches deep.

Mom proceeded to go for her swim, and for a short time, James and I paid attention to Stuart. This did not last long until we turned our backs on him and moved into deeper water to follow our own pursuits. Stu tried to copy us and fell over face-down and couldn't right himself. Fortunately my mother saw the situation and yelled at me to get my brother. I got to him in time to avoid a catastrophe, but we were all badly shaken, Stuart most of all! This episode seems to typify the state that existed between me as the big brother and Stuart as the little brother.

The Great Depression, carrying with it all its destruction and devastation throughout the world, didn't leave any lasting personal scars on me. I was aware of the homeless, hungry people and of the shanty towns and of the lineups at the banks. However, because I had a stable family environment and a home to go to and sufficient food to eat and a school to attend and kids to play with, the vortex of the storm went right over my head. I didn't have new clothes or new toys or new anything, but others didn't either. We learned to do with what we had, and we had fun!

We had a coal-burning stove in our house. Cash was sparse, and steps were taken to curtail spending at every juncture. There was a source of coal for heating our home that could be had for the picking. It was near the railroad track adjacent to a swamplike area where the steam engines emptied their ashes out of their fireboxes. Invariably there be would many pieces of coal that were not consumed in the process of heating the boilers. These would be dumped out with the ashes. My father took me with him to the ash dump. We had a couple of burlap bags in hand to retrieve what unburned lumps we could find.

On one of these salvage trips, we came upon a goose with an injured wing sitting on the ash pile. He couldn't fly well enough to take off, and after an exciting chase, we captured him and put him in one of our bags. We would surprise Mom by providing the main entree for a goose dinner!

We arrived home displaying the triumphant air of big-time hunters returning after a victorious safari. After giving us due praise and exaltation, Mom posed the chilling question: "And who is going to kill and clean it before I cook it?" Of course there was only one answer to that question, and that was "My dad."

Down the narrow stairs he went to our low-ceilinged cellar, toting the bag-entrapped bird and followed by his faithful accomplice (me). There was an ax and a block of wood that my father placed into position; my job was to hold the goose in the bag while my father stretched his neck out and struck off his head with the ax. As soon as the guillotine fell and he was decapitated, the goose got out of the bag and started flopping and half flying around the tiny space, up and down and all around, bumping into walls, spurting blood everywhere.

When he stopped his postmortem demonstration, it was time to pluck the feathers and then clean out his guts. As we got halfway through "defeathering" him, our enthusiasm for having a goose dinner (with that particular goose) began to diminish rapidly. My mother was a spectator to part of the spectacle and was eager to make the decision unanimous. We would forego a goose dinner at this time. All the evidence at the scene of the crime was properly eradicated, and life moved on!

One of the foundation stones of my social life was a club composed of about half-dozen boys my age. The symbol of the club was two horseshoe nails that we drove into a tree or wooden plank and bent them so that they crossed each other to form an X. Neither the nails themselves nor the X carried with them any significance that I can recall. However, the name of the club had great significance! It was called the Daredevil Club! That was the whole idea. We wanted to do daring things.

The way it worked was this: Each of us took turns being the leader for a day; the job of the leader for that day was to think of something for the rest of us to do. The more daring it was, the better! Sometimes it took the form of "follow the leader," in which case the leader for the occasion would have to perform the trick or stunt first and then the rest of the members were required to follow suit. Anyone who could not or would not follow the leader relinquished his membership in the gang.

We did such things as jump off the roofs of garages and land on the ground, leap off high banks at the edge of the river and land in sand, catapult on the end of a rope tied to a branch of a tree at the riverbank and land in the water. One of the things I liked to do was playing Tarzan over the brook nearby the school. As I have mentioned, there were large trees on either side of the stream. We would climb a tree on one side and leap through the air and clutch a limb of a tree on the other side. Quite often we missed, which resulted in a soaking in the water! We never broke any bones, which seems incredible to me as I think about it from this distance.

In one of the wooded areas nearby we constructed our secret hideaway. It was a cavity in the earth that we dug. It was about six feet deep and five or six feet square. There was a ladder that led to one corner of the roof to allow entry and exit. The roof was made of branches taken from the surrounding trees and intertwined across the top from one edge to the other edge of the hole. It served us well until we entered the rainy season, when the covering became a sieve and the offending water turned our floor into a quagmire.

Sometimes the Daredevil Club had secret meetings on our front veranda. We preferred to have the sessions after dark so that we could use the special homemade multicolored candles we each had manufactured out of crayons. Our habit was to sit in a tight circle, with head and candles close together as we discussed what outstanding challenges we would attempt. One of our members was a German boy named Frank Vogel. He had blond strawlike hair that hung over his forehead when he bent over. One night (you guessed it!) Frank dipped his hairdo into one of the candles, and phissedt! Before we could douse the fire, Frank had bald spots on his head!

This incident caused an intense parental investigation into the merits of our club. This inquisition carried with it the distinct possibility of the dissolution of our association. However, good sense prevailed in the end, and we were permitted to continue our adventures, which for the most part were deemed to be relatively harmless.

One of our high jinxes almost led to serious consequences. The pond that I have previously mentioned was a center of our activities from time to time. During most winters it would freeze over and provide a skating surface when it became thick enough. However, before it became safe for skating, it presented a marvelous temptation for the Daredevil Club. We called it rubber ice. The surface was strong enough to hold one up as long as one kept an adequate acceleration either running or sliding. The crust moved up and down in an elastic fashion and did not break unless one hit a weaker spot or inadvertently stopped moving.

One time I broke through and had difficulty getting out. The ice kept breaking as I struggled to get onto a firmer surface. I managed to reach the shoreline and safety, but I was thoroughly soaked! I headed for home. By the time I got there, my clothes had frozen solid! My mother had a fit and plunged me (clothes and all) into a hot tub of water, all the while giving me a vicious tongue lashing, admonishing me for being so recklessly foolish. Of course she was right.

I had a deep desire to explore other life forms that I found, which shared the same neighborhood as I did. Besides being interested in birds that I could see, I was fascinated by other creatures that I could capture. These included turtles, tortoises, frogs, tadpoles, and snakes. I set up my own private menagerie in my backyard. I found an abandoned wooden trough that had been used to mix sand, cement, and water during a construction activity.

It was watertight, so I set it up with some stones underneath at one end and poured water into it. One section was dry, and the other had about eight inches of water at the deepest point, which tapered off to the arid portion beginning in the middle. I put some rocks in the center of the pool so that the turtles could climb out and sun themselves. In the dry portion I put grass and pieces of cardboard to provide shade. My collection of reptiles could have dry or wet according to their needs. Some of the larger creatures would escape, but they were easily replaced. My activity was limited to milk and garter snakes—nonpoisonous varieties!

I was also intrigued by the many forms of life to be found in the saltwater of the Shark River basin. The variety was astounding. The species ranged from jellyfish and eels to blowfish and sea horses to several categories of clams and crabs. The tide influenced the basin, leaving behind tidal pools that trapped many of those critters, which allowed me to study them. Not only did I get my curiosity gratified, but I also learned to gather edible crabs and clams, which I brought home for food. They were good too!

One of nature's most majestic breathtaking sights that I repeatedly witnessed was the ospreys swooping down out of the sky and plunging deeply into the river or the lake or the sea and emerging with a large fish or eel. The strong wings of the hawk would lift off the water, having its long sharp talons firmly embedded in the flesh of its thrashing prey. The sight of the flight as the struggle continued across the sky to the large and scraggly nest of the osprey was an unforgettable display.

Our church considered some activities to be worldly and frowned on any Christians who engaged in them. They included such things as going to the movies, reading newspapers or comic strips on Sunday, listening to the radio on Sunday, watching or participating in athletics on Sunday. The use of tobacco, in any form, on any day, was anathema. The reading of novels was considered to be tantamount to skirting along the tenuous edge of the slippery slope that bordered the pit of mental moral depravity.

Our Sundays were filled with meeting going and visiting between families at the church. Since there were other kids my age involved, I didn't find the Sabbath prohibition burdensome. Somehow we were all in it together and, for the most part, found it acceptable.

The one regulation that I found most distressing was the absence of movies from my life. Not that I had seen one to have any idea what I was missing, but all the kids in my neighborhood went to see all those Western cowboys every Saturday. My peers at church didn't live nearby, so the consequence was that for most Saturdays I was left alone to fend for myself. In the end, though, this provided an opportunity for inventive exploration on my own.

The Shark River hills were within about an hour's walk from our home. They provided an ideal place for a boy to wander through rolling woodland to watch the squirrels, rabbits, and birds as they went about their daily activities. This was the way I spent many of my Saturdays. My trusty dog Pal was always at hand, eager and ready to respond at the slightest whistle of invitation. My mom would pack a lunch for the two of us, and we would take off for several hours of pure enchantment in the quietness of the forest broken only by the whispering of the breeze or the chatter or chirp of the squirrels or birds. These experiences taught me to appreciate and enjoy my own company, without the necessity of the constant companionship of other people.

One of the lessons learned in the woods was a bitter one. I wasn't aware that some vegetation was poisonous to the touch of people who may be allergic. On one occasion, I spent an afternoon in a grove of sumac trees. The disastrous result, within a day or so, found me with a swollen face and hands infested with a multitude of tiny blisters oozing pus that congealed into a pebbly crust. My countenance became a large caramel-toffee candy apple rather than the face of a human being.

Any activity that caused my facial muscles to move also cracked my skin—no laughing, crying, or such! To eat, I had to use a wet cloth to soften the encrustation surrounded my mouth to be able to open it sufficiently to insert a glass tube or spoon to eat or drink. The itching sensation seemed like a legion of minuscule worms crawling around just underneath my skin. It was total torture especially because I was convinced within my own mind that I would never return to normal. However, I did recover within a couple of weeks, much to my joy. It was the most agonizing experience of my young life, even surpassing my bout with the measles!

I have since been told that not all sumac trees are toxic, but I have never messed around with any of them ever since. I do appreciate their appearance though; they are among my favorite shrubs, particularly in the fall of the year.

Neptune City Public School was the center of my life. The academic side of this experience was not outstanding, although I liked all my teachers and did not fail any grades. The most significant, lasting contributions this institution made to me was to teach me what loyalty meant and how to be a team player. The inspirational leadership of our principal, Mr. Somerville, established these values, which permeated through the staff and students alike. I participated in football, baseball, and the school orchestra. They were all under his direction and were used to promote lasting values for daily living.

The mention of the school orchestra brings to mind the many hours I spent practicing on a decrepit violin, which I couldn't keep tuned because the keys would not stay where they were turned to maintain the tension of the strings. It was most frustrating! My parents couldn't afford better equipment; it was hard enough finding the fifty cents to pay for each lesson. The exposure to the domain of music was profitable to me even though I didn't turn out to be a world-class violinist.

The summer times were extraordinary seasons. We spent almost every day, Monday to Friday, of every week at the beach, basking in the sunshine and frolicking in the surf. It was a carefree environment even though the world around us was suffering and on the point of collapse. The ocean and the beach combined to be our "oyster." There were about eighteen to twenty of us, a mixture of fellows and girls, who would gather at a prearranged place and time in Neptune City then make our way over the railroad bridge into the town of Avon.

Through the village we would run on the sun-baked sidewalks and across the sharp gravel roads, occasionally dancing off to the side to relieve our bare feet in the cool grass of the bordering lawns. After about twenty minutes, we reached the hot sand, dropped our towels and lunches without stopping, and rushed like a thundering herd into the salty satisfying surf! Exhilarating! Exciting! We then would spend the rest of the day surfing, sunning, loafing, and playing games. It was a tough job, but somebody had to do it!

All of the towns in that part of the country had volunteer fire departments. When there was a fire, a siren sounded and all the volunteers would drop what they were doing and rush to the fire hall, jump on the fire engines, and dash to the location of the fire. One evening, not only our siren sounded but also the sirens in all the neighboring villages did too! Something big was afoot! Word soon passed that one of the large-frame seaside hotels in the adjacent village of Belmar was on fire!

My uncle Bill, my mother's brother, was a singing waiter at one of those hotels, so we had more than a passing interest in the blaze. Consequently, we jumped into the family car and took off in the direction of the firefighting equipment.

When we arrived at the site, it was dark. The entire scene was spectacular! Monster flames were licking up the paint-encrusted seasoned wood. Galaxies of sparks were cascading upward into the blackened sky. At the end of extended ladders, hoses were spouting water into the conflagration, creating belches of steam and smoke. The surrounding streets were jammed with the flashing red lights of ambulances and firefighting equipment. The buzzing chatter of the onlookers, punctuated by the shouts of firefighters, provided an eerie accompaniment. In the end, all that was left was the charred skeleton of what was once a charming white edifice. The episode provided the complete ingredients for a nightmare.

After being assured that it was not the structure where my uncle Bill worked, we returned home in the early morning hours and went to bed. A short time later my mother heard some paper rattling. She traced the noise to our hallway, where I was found on top of a chest trying to climb up the wall as if to put a fire out. I was sound asleep enacting my own private nightmare!

The harbor of New York City was situated along the coast about one hundred miles to the north of where we lived. As a result there was a great deal of ocean traffic that traveled a few miles offshore. It was composed of tankers, freighters, yachts, and passengers liners that could be seen from the beach. One night a ship named Morro Castle became engulfed in fire and burned in full view of land. There were hundreds of people onboard. It was a dreadful sight to watch it drift helplessly. People could be seen hanging out the portholes screaming for help. The vessel came to rest a short distance from a beach that normally was the preserve of tourists. Bystanders stared in paralyzed horror at the floating crematorium. I was not there when it was burning, but I well remember seeing the hapless hulk of steel stranded on the sand. It resembled a gigantic decomposing whale. One hundred and fifty souls lost their lives in the tragedy.

The motto of the state of New Jersey is the Garden State. That once was true, but I wonder if there is any land available for vegetable farms remaining. Because of the development of residential and commercial sites linked by multilane highways, the fertile ground has been smothered by cement. However, in the years of my boyhood, there were still many productive garden farms, which were major suppliers of lettuce, celery, peas, tomatoes, etc., to the large eastern cities of the United States. Some of these producers were not far from where we lived.

This fact gave me an opportunity to earn some "pin" money as I worked alongside my mom when I was about ten. We picked tomatoes when they were ready to go to market. The beef steak tomatoes grown then and there were large, firm, and succulent, possessing a flavor that titillated the taste buds with its exotic blend of acidity and sweetness. It was my favorite food! Part of the deal was that you could eat all the tomatoes that you wanted without charge while you were picking. This was beyond belief!

I showed up for work armed with a loaded saltshaker in my pocket. I picked a basket and ate a tomato, picked a basket and ate a tomato, picked a basket and ate a tomato, all day the same routine on the second day and the third day. The morning of the fourth day I was itching from head to foot. My total body was covered with massive scarlet blotches and raised red welts. I was a miserable, messy, fidgety urchin. Diagnosis: hives (tomato overload). Unlike my incident with sumac poison, I have not relinquished my direct contact with the tomato. It is still one of my favorite foods, though the taste of the supermarket variety of today is a far cry from the reminiscence of my cultivated palate.

Lakehurst, New Jersey, was a U.S. Navy air station located about thirty miles south of Neptune City. This was the site of the moorage for dirigibles that came from Europe as well as other points in the world. Since most of the large lighter-than-air crafts had as part of their route New York City, they had to cross over our heads to arrive at the moorage. As a consequence we got to see those massive rigid balloons floating gracefully through the sky on a regular basis. They did not prove to be the means of transoceanic and transcontinental transportation bonanza it was thought they might become because of their inability to withstand violent storms. The explosive crash of the German Hindenburg at Lakehurst was their coup-de-grace. Many smaller versions called blimps continue to be used for observation for special events.

The most distant destination to which I traveled at that stage of my life was Dingman's Ferry in the state of Delaware. My dad's sisters had a summer place there located on the bank of the Delaware River. This was a special place where I formed a close relationship with two of my cousins, Lawson and Nettie, who became like brother and sister to me.

A major organization in New York City called National Biscuit Company bought Christie Brown Ltd., a large bakery in Toronto, Ontario, Canada. The man, who was put in charge of implementing the transaction, was well acquainted with my father's knowledge and reputation in the business of retail sales of bread and cake. He asked my dad to join him in the development of the Canadian company. After much consideration and conversation, the decision was reached that it was a chance of a lifetime for him. However, for me and for my mother, it was the sound of the death knell. It meant leaving the country to which we had given allegiance. It meant tearing the roots of friendships we had established. It meant departing from the shores of our beloved ocean and its environs. Leave all this for a strange land, strange people, and strange customs?

Digestion of the reality that I was going to have to leave all of the surroundings that meant so much to me was a very painful process. I was about twelve years of age, a time of life when under the best of circumstances is a difficult period of adjustment physically, mentally, and socially. Into this mix was injected bidding farewell to all the people and the institutions that had been my support base and had served me so well. I made the rounds of my friends, lamenting that I probably would never see them again. The future seemed so dark and uncertain.

My father had spent some time in Toronto making the necessary arrangements for our arrival in Canada. Living accommodation and legalities had been settled. His instructions were to take nothing except our clothes and keepsakes. This signified that all furniture and extraneous material was to be left behind. We could take only what we could get into our model-A Ford car. The exclusions included my dog Pal.

This was the bitterest pill of all for me to swallow! Pal had been truly my pal in my ups and downs for years. He was the one who listened to all my childish hurts and grievances. He was the one who loved me faithfully under all conditions. He was my protector. It was he who had shared the magic of the woodlands. He had never asked for anything but a pat on the head, a kind word, just to be with me. Now he was to be wrenched from my life and I from his!

The morning on the day we left, I took him to a neighbor's shed, hugged him, then, with a broken heart and tearful eyes, I shut the door, never to hear him or see him again.

Baseball   ....   Dare devil gang   ....   10 years

I have entitled this section of *As I Remember It* "Basic Learning." I believe that by this time, the groundwork on which the rest of my life was built had been established.

At school I had been taught the three Rs, which paved the way for me to add to them some of the refinements of reading in depth and breadth, of writing to communicate and to create and, through arithmetic, to better understand commerce and science. I learned that honesty, integrity, loyalty, and dependability are primary ingredients for gaining mutual respect and make working as a team possible and enjoyable.

Through church I learned to honor and to read the Bible, the truth of which has been a constant source of comfort and challenge. I learned that God is love and that He cares about me and for me. The lives of my mother and father and the other Christians I knew (despite some of the incidental prohibitions to which they adhered) were full of grace and thoughtfulness. I came to respect the teachings of Jesus Christ.

The exposure I had to the beauty, power, and intricacy of nature established within me a huge respect for the Creator of life and the multitude of life's expressions. This primary introduction to the magnificence of my surroundings has been expanded year by year throughout my lifetime as my knowledge and awareness has increased. It is an unending, breathtaking journey that extends into the vistas of eternity. I am grateful to have had a location where an early start along this path was afforded me. In times of

The friends I left behind

defeat and stress it has always been a source of comfort and peace to be able to stand back and take a long look at the big picture.

And so our migration began. The four of us were packed into our Ford model A along with boxes stuffed into every available cranny. Out the driveway, down the street onto the highway, headed north!

Chapter 4

An Immigrant
(1934-1935)

Digest of the Times and Circumstance:

The United States was in the process of extracting itself from the quagmire of the Great Depression. Part of its plan to achieve this goal was to expand its trade with its neighbors in North and South America. This policy came into direct conflict with the trade aims of the British Empire of which Canada was a part. In 1931 Canada was granted the right to be responsible for its own internal and external affairs. However, its ties remained strong with Great Britain by virtue of the fact that the majority of the population was composed (especially in Ontario) of descendants or direct immigrants from the British Isles, plus offspring of the United Empire Loyalists (who had left the United States when it separated from Great Britain).

Canada had its own economic problems, because 10 percent of its population was on relief and thousands of discontented young men were in government work camps, angry over their plight. This condition brought about the "On to Ottawa" trek, which culminated in a riot in Regina, where the marchers were stopped by the armed forces of the government, climaxing in an infamous blood bath.

Canada was fearful of an economic takeover by the United States and turned to a preferential trade alliance with the British Commonwealth of Nations. This mixture of fear and competition inspired a vicious anti-American campaign. Billboard signs shouted "Buy British!" The message was "Don't buy American!"

It was into this environment our family, fresh from the USA, was to be implanted (for better or for worse)!

Personal Thoughts and Memories:

As we made our way along the highway that led us northward from Neptune City toward the vastness of an unknown land, we considered where we would stop for the night before proceeding to the Canadian border. The route to Canada from New Jersey traversed the state of New York. En route there were some mountains that crossed our path, and my father decided not to drive through them in the dark.

I had never seen anything that could be called a mountain (by any stretch

The car we drove to Canada

of the imagination), so my interest was piqued despite the fact that I was in the process of being extracted from the surroundings that I loved so much. By darkness we stopped at a motel where we were to spend the night. Outside of the motel one could see a menacing large black blob against the slightly less dark skyline. It appeared to be a gigantic wave about to break over our heads, but it remained poised and motionless. I could hardly wait for daylight!

As daylight began to encircle us, I was awake in time to see the blob separate itself from the brightened horizon and become a beautiful huge green hill. It was exciting to spend the next few hours weaving our way through and up and over and down what seemed like monstrous stationary ocean surf as we made our way through the range. Though I have seen more spectacular mountains since then, I have never forgotten this first impression.

After we had passed through the mountainous region, we came upon what is known as the Finger Lakes. It was the first time I had ever seen bodies of fresh water that large. It had a marked impact on me to realize that there were other quantities of water besides the ocean that had some size to them. I enjoyed that part of our journey too.

Soon the landscape changed into cramped and crowded Buffalo, New York, and then Niagara, New York, and then the Niagara River, which was the line of demarcation between Canada and the United States of America. With fear and trepidation the model-A Ford crawled over the connecting bridge toward the immigration officer's bureau. The drawbridge lifted behind us. The heavy doors slammed shut, or so it seemed at the time. The customs officer approached the car. The smiling face of my father greeted him against the backdrop of the glum visages of his family.

The conversation between my father and the official established that we were landed immigrants and that we were entering the country carrying nothing with us other than our personal effects. After finishing the paperwork, the content of the car was inspected. All went well until a large box (which was on the bottom of the pile in the backseat) was found to be full of pots and pans! My father was mortified (after saying that we had brought nothing with us!). "How could you, Lulu, when I said to bring nothing?" My mother calmly said, "I wasn't going to leave without my cooking utensils!" The official laughed and waved us on (pots and pans and all). Destination: Toronto, Ontario, Canada. The Wilsons had landed! It was 9 June 1934.

Our new address was 57 Beaty Avenue, which was an up-and-down brick duplex. We lived in the upper half of the structure, which was by far the best domicile that my parents had occupied since they were married. There were hardwood floors throughout, with the exception of the kitchen and bathroom. There were two bedrooms; my brother and I shared one.

This district of the city was called Parkdale, which at that time, was a middle-income neighborhood occupied mainly by professional types of one kind and another. I suspect that it had been the domain of a few families, earlier in its history, who lived on the outskirts of the city of Toronto. I say this because there were large sandstone homes still standing interspersed among smaller more-modest residences. It appeared that acreage had been divided into smaller building lots as the population grew, and the center of the city pressed itself into the suburbs.

Parkdale had wide streets smoothly paved with asphalt, having sidewalks on both sides. The sidewalks were raised above the road level by about eight inches and were edged with cement curbing. Our avenue was lined with mature English chestnut trees and was bordered by manicured lawns accentuated by well-kept shrubbery. Beaty Avenue was only one block long, extending between two of the main thoroughfares of the municipality, King Street and Queen Street. Apart from some shops along Queen Street, this section of the city was composed primarily of single family homes.

The city of Toronto was a more modest municipality then, in every way, compared with the Toronto of today. The downtown skyline was composed of the Royal York Hotel and the Bank of Commerce building. Now those two structures are indistinguishable among the many skyscrapers. The population then was mostly WASPs (white Anglo-Saxon Protestants). Now there is a preponderance of other nationalities from all over the earth. Then, there were only old-fashioned streetcars linking the extremities. Now there are streamlined streetcars, subways, and buses plus multilane throughways to accommodate the mass of automobiles jamming the center of the city on a daily basis. Then, it was known as Toronto the Good. Theaters were not permitted to be open on Sundays nor were other entertainment events; also alcoholic beverages were prohibited to be served in restaurants on Sundays. Now anything goes any time, any day, any hour of the day or night. Then, the policemen road bicycles or walked the neighborhood streets wearing bobby hats and carrying clubs and whistles or were mounted on stately immaculate shiny black horses. Now, the police are mechanized with motorbikes, automobiles, and armed with modern firepower. Eaton's and Simson's had free delivery service achieved by a fleet of sparkling wagons drawn by sprightly trotting horses and manned by smartly uniformed men. Now, delivery is an extra cost and is supplied by truck.

Toronto is situated on Lake Ontario, one of the Great Lakes, which gave me the feeling, at times, of being back on the edge of the Atlantic Ocean. Our home was a short distance from Sunnyside, an amusement park adjacent to the Lake. Overlooking Sunnyside was an elongated green area, which stretched for several blocks on an elevated prominence where the city had placed some benches. It provided an excellent view over the water. In the early days of settling into our new land, this was to be a sanctuary for me.

When we first arrived, I was in a deep funk caused by the painful mourning of the loss of friends, surroundings, and country, which were near and dear to me. I felt there was an enormous gaping hole inside of me that could never be filled or healed again. During this span it was summer. School was in recess, the kids who lived on my street were away on holidays, and I was alone in my misery. So it was to those benches at Sunnyside I resorted to commiserating with myself during the month of July and part of August in 1934. I presented a forlorn figure as I looked across the water of Lake Ontario longing for my homeland on the other side that held all my chums and my dog Pal.

Occasionally my mother would find me and would join me as we shared the same despair. It was not a happy beginning, but fortunately, it did not last. Interest in the new surroundings soon began to seep into my psyche as the neighborhood families began to arrive back into the city to prepare for the return to school.

It was decided that I should be placed in the eighth grade, the last year in elementary, before entering high school. The institution that I was to attend was named Queen Victoria, which was an antiquated building about ten blocks from where I lived. My experience there was a pleasant one after the first few weeks. However, that introductory period was very trying for me.

Not only were the surroundings and the people unknown and foreign to me, but I was also the victim of the trade war going on between the United States and Canada. The scathing propaganda against the dreaded Americans was in full force and permeated even to the kids in primary school. When it was learned that I was a fresh import from the voracious land that was intent on devouring the Land of the Maple Leaf, I became the target of a barrage of cutting remarks in the schoolyard, and to and from home. It was painful in the extreme when piled on top of my already bashed and bleeding ego suffering from the vacuum created by the loss of all I treasured. I was laughed at and jeered and described by a multitude of adjectives at the heart of which was "You dirty Yank!"

I endured this for some time, feeling more and more depressed and disconsolate, not knowing how to handle it all. There was not much I could do about where I lived because that decision had been made for me, so I had to determine how I was going to survive in this unhappy climate. I concluded I had to fight! Fist fight!

So there came a day when I was going to punch anyone who started this verbal abuse. I soon found out a well-placed punch produced a pronounced silence rather quickly! I became quite good at it. The finale came one day at recess in the schoolyard, when a gang came after me and forced me up against the fence and proceeded to taunt me with cruel shouts. I dared anyone who had the guts to step out and back up his words with action. I pointed them out individually, and everyone shied away. From that time on, I didn't have to put up with any more maltreatment. I had gained their respect and bolstered my own self-esteem. It was a rough beginning, but in the end, I received much that was good and helpful out of the year that I spent at Queen Victoria.

There were two subjects that evoked my attention, formal art classes and manual training (which was the employment of tools to construct useful objects). I had not been exposed to either of them in my previous experience. I found them fascinating. In our art classes I learned the fundamentals of painting with watercolors as well going on field trips to the Ontario Art Gallery, and also to High Park to do some landscape sketching.

I created a couple paintings that my art teacher thought were good, so she got my manual training teacher to show me how to make wooden frames for them. She entered them into an Ontario Art Gallery exhibition for elementary school pupils, and I never saw them again. I am sad that I lost track of them because they gave me a sense of accomplishment at a time when I desperately needed it. I would like to have had them as a reminder of those days.

During the winter, ice hockey rinks were erected in the various parks scattered throughout the city, and it was there that I was introduced to this most exciting game. It was an extracurricular activity that would become part of my high school life that would give me much pleasure and challenge.

One of the first links that we made in this new country was the connection to one of the Brethren churches in Toronto. It was called Olivet Gospel Hall. The church was located some distance from where we lived, which required transportation by car or streetcar. It was a place where we were warmly welcomed and made to feel that we belonged. Although the order of services were quite similar to what we had been accustomed, there were about two hundred people who were members, which made a difference in the number of peers my age with whom I had association. My Sunday school class equaled the total number of kids in the whole church group at Neptune. This church was to have a profound influence on me throughout my teenage years.

One of the early effects it had on my life was in the matter of baptism. On the raised platform at the front of the church was a carpet which covered trap doors, which, when opened, revealed a large metal tank with steps leading down into it. It was here that the ritual of baptism by immersion was performed. There was to be a baptism a few months after we arrived, and it happened that a couple of young people my age were going to be baptized. Upon learning this fact, I determined to find out what it meant to be baptized. I was shown that in the Scripture it was a way of announcing that one had become a Christian. It meant openly declaring allegiance to Jesus Christ; I decided that I wanted to participate. After being satisfied with my testimony relating to my receiving Christ into my life, the Elders of the church agreed, and I was baptized. It was an important point in my history.

My father was sensitive to the disruption his business move had caused to his family, to my mother in particular. He sought for ways to make it up to us. He was determined to find someplace where we could spend the next summer that would assuage our wounds and attempt to replace some of the loss we had incurred in the transplant from the United States to Canada. He heard of a small village on the Severn River in the district of Muskoka, which was located north of Toronto about two to three hours' drive. This area was called the cottage country where the city dwellers maintained their cabins for family summer vacations.

My father rented one for the months of July and August of 1935. It introduced a new environment and a completely different way of life for us all. He spent his two-week holiday time with us and then, for the balance of the summer, commuted every Friday night to Severn Falls and returned to Toronto Sunday evening.

Severn Falls consisted of a general store (which also was the post office) plus a marina accommodation. There also was a whistle-stop railway station to service the CPR line. Spreading out from the village up and down the river

were cottages of varying degrees of refinement. Some were just shacks, but others were winterized and posh. The river was part of the Trent Canal system, which provided a convoluted picturesque link between Lake Huron and Lake Ontario. It was a favorite route for many pleasure cruises, from canoes to large yachts. The raison d'être for Severn Falls was to supply the cottages and voyagers gas and groceries.

The cottage we stayed in was not directly on the river front but was one of four or five that were built in a cluster specifically to be rented to people like us. We were within walking distance of the grocery store and another major part of the community, the government wharf that was a utility for the general public. We had the use of a rowboat, which was a great delight to me. It opened the possibility of traveling the river to visit other kids, to go fishing, and to investigate the bays on either side of the river.

This was the first of several delightful summers we spent on the Severn River. While it didn't obliterate the longing for our homeland, it was a marvelous opiate.

Now it was time to enter the world of secondary education to see what ventures the future would present.

Chapter 5

High School: Junior Years
(1936-1938)

Digest of the Times and Circumstance:

Across the Atlantic Ocean, Adolph Hitler was busy stoking the fires under the caldron of hatred and revenge among peoples on the continent of Europe. He consolidated dictatorial power. He purged the ranks of the military and the Nazi party, eliminating any challenge to his personal authority. He embarked on a program of mass propaganda, which was masterminded by Goebbels, aimed at elevating the German people to a position of superiority over all others, and espoused the concept of degrading the Jews and blacks to the bottom of the racial heap. It was his goal to see Germany control the entire world led by him as the glorious one.

His attack against the Jews caused many of them to leave Germany to seek refuge in other countries. A prime example of one of those who fled, while he had the opportunity, was Albert Einstein, who escaped to the USA. Himler was appointed head of the dreaded Gestapo and was placed in charge of concentration camps where so many Jewish people were to be slaughtered.

Hitler reintroduced compulsory military service, which placed the young men of the country under arms. He then proceeded to build a powerful all-encompassing military machine equipped with the latest weapons of war, including planes, tanks, battleships, and submarines. This war-making capability was solidly sustained by a well-engineered, superb manufacturing base. The revamped German infrastructure redesigned to provide maneuverability for the commercial and military enterprise of the nation. The country had become a bastion of armed might waiting to be unleashed.

The world did not have long to wait until Hitler began to bully his neighbors. He parked his army along the border of Austria and threatened the political leadership of that country with military conquest unless they agreed to be assimilated by Germany. After the Austrian appeal for help from other countries in Europe fell on frightened deaf ears, the Austrians acquiesced, and Germany occupied their country.

The next country on the führer's timetable was Czechoslovakia. There was a portion adjacent to Germany, which was predominantly populated by German-speaking people. Hitler demanded that this territory be relinquished. To enforce his demand, he belligerently strung his troops along the Czech border in a posture of invasion. The Czechs responded by lining up their army in a posture of defense. The whole spectrum became so fearful to the other countries in Europe that they decided to pursue diplomatic intervention.

The result was the Munich pact (signed by France, England, Italy, and Germany), which gave Hitler the immediate territory he demanded, with the promise that this would be the last of his land grabs. This pact became known as the Policy of Appeasement. It provided the fertile ground for the seeds of World War II.

On the Mediterranean side of the continent another tyranny was formed, brutally directed by Mussolini, who rose to power by organizing a group of fascists, numbering about four million Italians. They marched on the government in Rome and scored a coup d'état. He took control of all the major facets of power, effectively becoming the dictator of Italy. He dubbed himself Il Duce. He developed a large armed force and became extremely bellicose to his neighbors.

Italy had colonial territory in Africa, which was adjacent to Ethiopia. Mussolini decided that it was in the interest of Italy to take over Ethiopia. Consequently Il Duce unleashed his military might and beat the tiny country into submission. This action drew the ire of the world community in general and the wrath of the League of Nations in particular but received the approval of Germany.

Adding more poison to the relationships in Europe, the Fascist Party in Spain, led by Franco, began a revolution against the Loyalists. The

Communists gave support to the Loyalists, which Italy and Germany countered by providing military hardware and troops to the Fascists. Germany and Italy worked increasingly closer together, which ultimately evolved into the Axis.

The cloud of acrimonious odor of warmongering continued to rise over the European capitals then wafted over the Atlantic Ocean, striking fear into the wary hearts of Americans and Canadians. President Roosevelt signed the Neutrality Act to indicate that the United States would not participate in any European war. Mackenzie King was the prime minister of Canada at the time, and although for the most part he said nothing regarding the political gyrations in the "Old Country," there was a broad sentiment in Canada in favor of isolationism. North Americans had no stomach to participate in another foreign conflict after such a recent bloody experience in World War I.

Across the Pacific Ocean another witches' brew was simmering, concocted by the territorial aspirations of the Japanese and the contest between Mao Tse-tung (for Communism) and Chiang Kai-shek (for Capitalism) over control of China. Japan invaded China and occupied Beijing, Shanghai, and other major cities. Chiang Kai-shek declared war on Japan, and because their homeland was being attacked, Mao Tse-tung joined forces with him against the common enemy.

News of events transpiring in any part of the world was instantaneously transmitted everywhere by radio. Because the knowledge of disturbing information was so readily available and was accumulated on a daily basis, an increasing apprehension developed among the citizens of North America. There was the feeling that a doomsday was approaching from both ends of the globe over which they had no control and which was about to engulf them. This reality created an uneasiness that permeated every level of society.

Personal Thoughts and Memories:

Although there was an underlying feeling of anxiety in the country, life went on, and people proceeded about their daily chores. In my case it involved getting started in high school. Upon graduating from primary school, a choice was required in the province of Ontario educational system. On the one hand, a person could choose to go to a technical school and learn a trade, or they could select what was called a matriculation stream, which would lead to further education. My father was keen on me becoming a medical doctor and therefore encouraged me to take the matriculation course. The school I was to attend was called Parkdale Collegiate Institute.

For the next three years the main categories in my life were home, school, church, and summer holidays.

Home:

My home was taken for granted by me because it was always there for meals and sleep, never causing upsets. There was stability. My father was very busy carving out his career, which required him to travel a great deal. Both he and my mother had less formal education than I did, so there was no participation by them in my schoolwork. My brother Stuart was in primary school, so our paths crossed only at dinnertime. Mom had accumulated a number of lady friends with whom she shared her afternoons.

Sunday was the only day of the week when we spent time as a family, and that was because we went to church together, followed by a drive in the surrounding countryside in consort with all the other "Sunday drivers." Most of the time, each member of my family traveled in his own circle with the circumferences touching gently in the evenings and on Sundays.

I enjoyed the couple of years that we lived on Beaty Avenue. There was a good collection of boys my own age, and we found lots to do when we

Mom and Dad   David & Suart   Mom

were not at school or doing homework. One of the main activities that I recall was street hockey. It was great fun! It was conducted on the paved road that met the solid curbing on either side, forming the "boards" of our rink. The goals were in the middle of the road at appropriate distances and marked by tin cans. We used regular hockey sticks and pucks, and we were mounted on roller skates of the old metal variety. Beaty was not a busy street, so there was not much traffic to inhibit our games. It was an unofficial playground in our own front yard.

Another major activity at this time was my membership in the Boy Scouts. There was a troupe in the basement of a nearby Baptist church. I learned all the knots and how to make campfires and how to cook outdoors and all of those great things. However, my association with this group led to an episode in my life of which I was not very proud.

Telling the truth in my family was just as natural as breathing. To not tell the truth would be about on a par with choking! It would be a shocking, cataclysmic disaster! To attend a movie show was almost in the same category. Being a Boy Scout created an event that set these two forces on a collision course.

Our troupe was invited to spend a weekend with another group in Buffalo, New York—a big deal since it would be my first time away from home among strangers! We were to go over Friday night and return the following Sunday afternoon. It was interesting, exciting, and enjoyable until Saturday afternoon when the schedule included a movie show! What was I to do? I couldn't be rude to my hosts and peers by not going, and yet—besides, I really wanted to go to see what it was like when I was away from home and no one would ever know! So I went to my first movie! I don't remember what the title was or anything about it, except that I was torn between delight and guilt.

We returned home, and in the course of telling my family about my adventure, my father asked if I had gone to a movie. It seemed like an elevator floor dropped from underneath me, and I was in free fall. I mentally scrambled for a response and finally blurted out "No." At that moment it felt that I had committed my second unpardonable sin. My father had been told what our program was to be, and so he said he knew I had seen a movie. I was caught in a misdeed and a lie all at the same time! My father didn't say anything, he just looked at me. I was absolutely crushed flat. I don't think he cared that I went to a show because he knew beforehand and could have stopped it, but I do believe he was hurt because for the first, and the only time that I can recall, I lied to him.

The emotions and the underlying values of this incident left an indelible impact.

My father prospered in business, and accordingly, we moved to a more prestigious home. It was located on Parkside Drive. This residence was also an upper duplex but much more spacious and elaborate than the one on Beaty Avenue. There were three large bedrooms, an ample open kitchen, a formal dining room, and a dignified living room. To me, the most intriguing element of this new house was the fact that the parking space for our car was under the building and could be reached by a narrow staircase from the interior of our living quarters. One didn't need to get wet to reach the car if it were raining! And by this time we had a brand-new light-green Chevrolet!

475 Parkside Drive

Named Vice-President

Dad's recent promotion

The house stood on a rise of land overlooking High Park. This park was roughly square in shape and was about one and a half miles each way.

It was donated to the city of Toronto for the purpose of maintaining it as a recreation area for the general public. One of the conditions required that a large percentage of the land was to remain in its natural state. The result was that while sports fields, cultured gardens, and even a small zoo were developed, most of the property remained undisturbed and presented a bit of easily accessible wilderness for city dwellers to wander through and find solace. The terrain was laced with unplanned footpaths. They came into being solely by wanderers over the years as they meandered through the undulating woodland. This piece of delightful real estate became part of my life during my high school years, and indeed, I had already begun to appreciate its worth when we had our art out-trips in primary school.

The location of our new home was superb in that it was directly across the street from this fabulous park. However, it did create a longer distance to travel to school. In this situation, a bicycle seemed appropriate, so I was presented with a brand-new one. I stored it in our underground garage beside our brand-new car! My world had dramatically changed!

For the next two or three years that bicycle was my primary mode of transportation through sunshine, rain, and slush. My school was about one and a half miles from where we lived. We had an hour and a half for lunch. Often I biked home at noon. On those days I traveled four times between home and school. I also had an early-morning paper route for part of the time we lived there. It was bike-delivered newspapers right to the porch (when my aim was good enough to hit the veranda!).

My bike was not strictly utilitarian. It was also a primary ingredient for plenty of adventure and fun. Although equipped with only one gear, coaster brakes, and not braced for off-street terrain, we used to race through the hilly footpaths of High Park jumping, sliding, and skidding on our steel chargers. On other occasions we went on bike hikes, which would take a whole Saturday. One of the favorite ventures was to travel north from Lake Ontario, up Highway 27 (which at that time was a gravel road and now is an eight-lane highway) to a favorite swimming spot up the Humber River.

I became sixteen while we lived at Parkside Drive, and that was a magical number because it meant that I could become a licensed driver of an automobile. This resulted in another huge expansion to my geographic and social horizon. My dad taught me to drive, and I was successful in obtaining my permit. This did not diminish my use of my bike, but with the passage of time and the accumulation of experience, I was allowed to use the car on my own to attend events, which normally would have required streetcar transport. This was a big confidence and ego builder.

During the time we resided on Parkside Drive, my mother was taken to the hospital with a nearly fatal kidney infection. This caused a major disruption in our family because she was the reliable center point around which our individual worlds could rotate with stability. My father scrambled to find someone who could substitute for her. His oldest sister Annie, who had no children of her own, was willing to come to Canada to stay with us during Mom's convalescence.

Aunt Annie ruled our roost for a couple of months. I was a growing teenager, and I'm sure I presented her some of the usual problems associated with that age group. I do remember a tension developing between us, which never totally disappeared over the years. Finally Mom recovered, and all was back to normal again!

School:

Throughout my high school years I was the epitome of mediocrity in all things. My classmates and teachers liked me. I got passing marks in most subjects but excelled in none. I was on the football team, the swimming team, the hockey team, and the gymnastics team; but I was not an outstanding star in any one of them. I had no real goal to spur me on to great achievement of any description. I was doing what I was doing because that what everyone else my age was doing. I had no burning purpose in mind to challenge me to excellence.

While I didn't qualify as an overachiever by any standard of measurement either academically or athletically, I retained much of the information presented in both spheres, which proved useful to me in later life. This seems to support the adage "An education is what you remember after you have forgotten what you have learned." I agree with that statement.

Gymnastics was in its infancy as a competitive activity when I was in high school. It was not the fancy razzmatazz that one sees in the Olympic competition now. It was a simpler contest using more rudimentary elements of equipment and style than that which is found in today's sport. Each of the five members on the team had to perform on the horizontal bar, the parallel bars, the mats, the horse, and the rings. Each person was marked individually, and the total of the five people became the team score. To qualify for this team required hours and hours of demanding and dangerous practice that filled most of my spare time after school. It was worth it though because I was on the team for four of the five years I attended Parkdale Collegiate. We won the city championship for each of those four years.

*Gym & hockey teams—David front row 2ⁿᵈ
from left in both pictures*

Although we never won any championships in hockey or football, they were my favorite sports. The first three years of high school I was on the junior teams, and in the last two years I played on the senior teams in both sports. My lasting legacy from these activities is my two banged-up knees, which have plagued me from that day to this.

Part of the problem with being involved in all of these games was that their timetables overlapped during the year. The demanding practice schedules often made it necessary to start with hockey at seven AM, followed by classes from nine AM to twelve PM, then in the gym or swimming pool over lunch hour, and classes again at one-thirty PM until three-thirty PM and finally football practice until six PM. There were always at least two sports to juggle, which was physically exhausting. This left little energy or drive to spend on academics. I was young and strong and enjoyed every minute of it, but my scholastic standing paid the price.

Parkdale Collegiate Institute

Class designation was according to forms. In other words, the first year of high school was called form A and the last was called form F. Each form was composed of several classes, which were assigned letters of the alphabet, signifying one's academic standing. Form 1A would represent the students with the highest marks for the previous year. The lowest in our year was form IF. I was in form IE.

The home form teacher for our class was a man by the name of Leslie Bell. He was our history teacher as well as the conductor, organizer, and inspiration for the school choir, orchestra, dance band, and all things musical. The first year I started at Parkdale Collegiate was also his first year.

He immediately discovered who played any musical instrument of any description. When he learned that I had played the violin in public school, he repeatedly invited me to join the school orchestra. I was much more interested in getting involved in sports.

Mr. Bell was a victim of infantile paralysis, which left him with a badly crippled leg. This handicap did not deter him from a full participation in everything going on around him. He was most interesting and informative as well as being possessed with a low tolerance level for any lack of attention during his lectures. Anyone having a competing conversation or doping off could expect a splattered piece of chalk to explode on his desk. He was a crack shot from any spot in the room. He would not miss a word in his discourse and not say anything to the offending student, but everyone got the message!

I never did perform in his orchestra, but I certainly appreciated his musical talents, both while I was at school and afterward. He went on to become the leader of a professional group known throughout North America as the Leslie Bell singers. Unfortunately for the world of music he died when he was in his thirties.

Many of my high school teachers were characters of note, but the idiosyncrasies of some of them remain in my mind after all these years.

There was a Mr. McInnis, who was an irrepressible Scot. He taught Latin with an incomprehensible Scottish accent. This created a difficult obstacle course for Canadian students to overcome on the way to a diploma.

Mr. Norris was a math teacher and would not allow any shenanigans to take place in his classroom. To maintain order he constantly juggled a small sponge ball in his hand as he paced in front of the room. If the slightest tomfoolery emerged, the ball became a missile catapulted by a *swift* movement of his arm to find the skull of the culprit!

An extreme opposite to Mr. Norris was Mr. Sanderson, who taught literature. He was blithely unaware of anything beyond the sound of his own diminutive voice. There could be complete pandemonium, and Mr. Sanderson would be oblivious to the whole shebang. There was a rumor that Mr. Sanderson couldn't see as far as the rear of the classroom. One of the guys decided to put the rumor to the test. He stood in the back of the room, lit and smoked a cigarette (which of course was prohibited). Mr.

Sanderson performed as expected. He prattled on and on, not recognizing that anything was amiss.

There were three principals during my tenure at Parkdale.

The first was Mr. Moore, who was tall, dignified, and bespectacled. I have an image of him standing in front of his office in between class periods watching the students walking through the hallways. He had his hands clasped behind his back, and with his well-rounded stomach gracefully protruding in front, he looked like an owner of a plantation watching his slaves change shifts.

The second was Mr. McKellar, a quiet large man who seemed to be everywhere and who knew everything about everyone but friendly with no one. He wore soft rubber soles and was constantly on the prowl. Often he would slip in the back entrance of a classroom, sit at a rear desk, and scrutinize the proceedings, unknown to anyone. It was most unnerving.

The third was Major Lamb who was a short slim bubbling bundle of energy with white hair. He was a man who radiated friendliness. He had the knack of making a person comfortable in his presence immediately. He had metal clips on his leather-heeled shoes. When he made his rounds, the whole school knew it from the moment he left his office. The sharp sound of clack! clack! clack! clack! resounded through the corridors as the metal clips beat a cadence on the hard synthetic marble floors. When he entered any classroom, he knocked on the front door, opened it, and said, "Hi everybody!"

The diverse personalities and deportment of these men had a distinctly different influence on the staff and students. This reality demonstrated for me the fact that the attitude of a single leader can influence the entire environment around him for good or ill.

My social life at school was strictly limited because of the amount of time that I spent playing and practicing sports. I wasn't involved in the production of the school magazine or a member of any of the many groups that were available, such as photography, arts, literary, and debating clubs. Periodically there were dances held in the gym, some of them immediately after classes. These posed a problem for me since during these events, sports practices were canceled. This left me with no excuse for not attending. The difficulty lay in the fact that my religious background frowned upon dancing. Consequently I had never learned how to dance. It was also true that I was finding girls increasingly attractive and vice versa.

By the time I reached my third year at Parkdale, I had become infatuated with a petite blonde named Gwen Connell. She was present at the sports competitions to cheer for me; she also encouraged me to go to the dances with her. Swing and the big band sound were the in things of the day. I was fond of that style of music then as I am today.

As a result I went to some of the dances with her even though I was suffering pangs of guilt arising out of my belief that my behavior was altogether too worldly! Our fondness for each other grew as time passed. I was becoming increasingly uneasy because she was not a Christian, and I knew there were potential difficulties ahead.

I was on the junior football team at the time. Our home games were held at the old Exhibition Stadium. The junior teams competed first, followed by the senior teams of the opposing schools. My father never attended any of my athletic matches, but on this occasion, because the stadium was on the way from his office to our home, he decided to drop in. My competition was already finished by the time he arrived. I had showered and was in the cheering section watching the senior team compete. I had my arm around Gwen when his eyes met mine as he stood at the entrance looking up into the stands!

In the following days he began to ask questions about this girl, which culminated in an invitation for Gwen to have dinner with us at our home. This event happened, and everything went well. My parents thought that she was a fine person. However, in the following days, my father pressed the point that even though she was delightful, the fact remained that she didn't have the same beliefs that I did.

Since I knew in my heart that he was right, the entire matter wore heavily on my mind. I decided that I had to do something about it. It was an extremely painful, difficult, and awkward challenge for a sixteen-year-old to handle. I went through weeks of torment before I managed to screw up the courage to discuss it with her.

I finally blurted it all out in not a very incoherent manner, I suspect. I am sure she understood but didn't understand and was hurt by it all. I was devastated and ripped up inside. I felt that I had done the right thing in the sight of God, but I was bruised and resentful that it had to be like this.

Gwen soon found another boyfriend, which intensified the emptiness and misery within me over the whole episode. The sight of her with someone else plus the ribbing of my peers poured salt into my open wounds.

Church:

During the first three years in high school, my association with the Christians at Olivet Gospel Hall became stronger. I was part of a Sunday school class of boys, which translated into a club for me separate from Parkdale Collegiate. I had a Sunday school teacher who encouraged us to participate in the activities of the church, which included such things as church picnics, special magic lantern meetings for children, also lunches and dinners at each other's homes. He was a good teacher who gave us a basic knowledge of the Bible.

Our annual church picnics were outstanding events for me. They were held on the Toronto Islands, which provided a protective arc a couple of miles offshore in Lake Ontario. They formed the harbor, which was a major reason for the existence of the city itself. Privately owned automobiles were prohibited from the Islands, thus creating a fabulous world of pedestrians and cyclists. The general public could reach the Islands only by ferry. The ride over was itself an enjoyable experience. It became even more exciting when there were lots of kids involved. On arrival, we had the usual games and food, after which we were released to explore the territory until it was time to return to the mainland. It was always a long, fun-filled day.

There was a young peoples' organization at the church, which arranged social happenings usually held on Saturday evenings. These activities often were joint ventures with some of the many other Brethren churches in the city. They ranged from rallies to hayrides to corn roasts to ice skating to toboggan sliding. Through these occasions I met an increasing number of Christian contemporaries my age. This helped to provide a balance for me.

The Brethren Sunday morning service has left an indelible impression on me because of the simplicity and meaning that it connoted. The chairs in our church auditorium were movable so that different seating configuration could be achieved, depending on the type of service intended. The purpose of the gathering on Sunday mornings was to remember and honor the Head of the Church, Jesus Christ. All of the hymns, prayers, Scripture readings, and oratorical contributions were designed to that end.

The seating was arranged to form a hollow square. In the center of the hollow square was a small table on which was placed bread, plates, a pitcher of wine, and glasses. The elements required for Communion. Upon being seated, the congregation formed a symbolic unity as they sought to devote their attention to the Person of Christ. Our family sat as a unit during this ceremony, with Mother on one end of the line, my father on the other, and with my brother and me in between. This was the general habit of all the families in the church. This gave a feeling of solidarity and oneness.

They believed that the Holy Spirit would direct the service by inspiring different Christians to pray, to select a hymn or Scripture, or to distribute the elements for Communion. There was no chairman designated to guide the proceedings. Most of the time, the result was a beautiful mosaic of Christ woven on the tapestries of our hearts. As I look back, I have tender memories of those gatherings. The singing of the worship hymns a cappella, with over two hundred people in harmony, is something I still have a special wistful craving to hear.

Summer Holidays:

We had spent one summer on the banks of the Severn River at the little village of Severn Falls that was enjoyed by the entire family. After the close of school in the spring of 1937 my father rented another cottage about a mile and a half from the village. There was no road that reached it, so we had to leave the car at the government wharf and travel by rowboat to the cottage. I was the chief oar operator who furnished the power to propel people and provision between the village and our chalet. By the time the summer was over I had developed a great deal of upper body muscles and strength. My father spent his vacation with us, as he had the previous year, and commuted weekends to and from Toronto.

The little rustic bungalow we occupied was a frail structure consisting of two bedrooms, a living-dining area, a kitchen, and a screened porch that overlooked the river from a five-foot-high embankment. There was no plumbing. We carried the river water up the hill by the bucket, put some drops in it for purification before cooking or drinking it. At the rear of the building was the traditional outhouse. The bathtub was a bar of soap and the river.

There were no neighbors closer than the village. We could walk there or go by boat.

My mother and father became friends with a couple who were year-round residents of Severn Falls. Their names were Ted and Vi Cowan. He was veteran of WWI in which he had his left arm amputated. They received a pension from the government. They had a boat with a one-cylinder engine. It was started by spinning a flywheel by hand. It was not a fast-moving vehicle, but it was quiet and comfortable. They would often take my mother up and down the river for pleasure cruises.

Ted Cowan also became a friend of mine during the week I was more or less on my own. He only had one arm, but he could do just about anything. He could cast a plug on the end of a fishing line and reel it back in, with or without a bass hooked on it. He could bait a fishhook. He could tie the mooring lines on his boat. He could shoot a partridge out of a tree with his rifle. He could even manipulate tobacco out of a small pouch onto flimsy paper and roll it into a neat cigarette.

Ted knew all the good fishing spots, and he showed them to me. He also taught me how to fish for pike, bass, and pickerel. When my father came on the weekends, Ted would take my dad, my brother, and me to some fishing spot or other to the delight of us all.

My mother loved to be out on the boat especially if we were fishing. Most evenings after dinner, when the weather was fine, I would take Mom out in the rowboat and meander along the edge of the river trailing a lure called a spoon. It wobbled as it was drawn through the water, causing movement similar to an injured fish. Its action was designed to entice a pike to have an easy meal. The problem for the pike was that as it bit into this palatable morsel, there were hooks that sunk into his jaws. Instead of having a meal, he became the meal.

She was thrilled when the fish would strike at the tire lure. She would excitedly reel in the trophy but would have nothing to do with getting it off the hook! We caught lots of pike when we summered on the Severn.

The river was slow moving where we were located, which made it ideal for rowboat traveling. One could drift with the gentle current or row against it without expanding any great effort, nor was there the danger of crashing into rocks if one dozed off. Consequently often I would lie in the bottom of the boat and float along, basking in the sunshine. My most memorable occasion took place as I lay in the boat when it was pitch dark surrounded by overwhelming silence and stared up into the endless universe. I was captivated by the magnificence of the creative hand of God. We were far enough north to be exposed to the gaudy mysterious display of the northern lights as they dazzled the dome overhead with living blotches of red and green flames ever flashing and changing their configuration from horizon to horizon. It was truly a wonder-filling vision from the unobstructed front-row seat at the bottom of a boat.

The summer of 1938 found us back at the Severn River. This time, however, we were located farther along and on the other side of the river from the village. This necessitated having a powerboat. My dad bought an eighteen-foot Peterborough cedar hull beautifully varnished and powered by an outboard motor, which made it skip right along. It became my pride and joy because it expanded the parameters of my activity. It meant that I could travel farther in less time. This made it possible to visit other kids in cottages up and down the river as well as bring into range more distant fishing spots.

The cottage was more elegant than the ones we had occupied on previous summers. It stood about fifty feet above the river on an outcropping of rock surrounded by scrubby trees, which were typical of that part of Muskoka. It was a rustic lodge covered with shiplap siding, which was stained dark brown. There was a fireplace in addition to the usual wood-burning stove. This was my first experience with a wood-burning fireplace, and it was something that I enjoyed.

The cottage had an indoor flush toilet as well as running water in the kitchen. There was a well for drinking water. The water for general use was stored in a tank providing a reservoir, which was elevated on a large wooden frame above the level of the taps in the house so that there would be gravity flow. The water was pumped into the tank from the river below via pipes and a hand pump. It was my chore to see that the tank was kept filled.

A boathouse went with the property, which was set in a little cove directly below the main structure. We kept our outboard there as well as a rowboat that belonged to the property. I spent quite a bit of time in that boathouse because in the still water beneath it congregated a colony of perch that were just the right size for bait to catch pickerel and bass. I used a bent pin on the end of a piece of black thread with a tiny bit of dough on the point of a pin. I would lie on my stomach and watch until one of the perch took the dough into its mouth and caught it. I put it in a bucket of water until we went fishing for the big ones. It was time consuming but a pleasurable occupation.

I was so impressed by the way the Ted Cowan handled his .22-caliber rifle my father bought me an air rifle that fired lead pellets. In my imagination I became a big game hunter. I decided that I would bag one of the cheerful chipmunks that pervaded the grounds around our summer home. I locate one and stalked him until I could get him in my sights and then fired. I hit him but he ran off. I shot again and he limped away. Once more I shot and killed him. As I saw him lying there I was devastated. I was filled with remorse that I had cut down a beautiful carefree creature. I picked up his body tenderly and gave him a proper burial, gravestone included.

Chapter 6

High School: Senior Year
(1939-1940)

Digest of the Times and Circumstance:

On September 1, 1939, the infection festered by Adolph Hitler's activity in Germany finally burst like an exploding volcano. Sulfurous lava spewed over all of Europe, leaving death and devastation in its wake. It started with tanks, bombers, and one million soldiers blitzing Poland into submission. It did not stop until most of the continent, as well as North Africa, had come under the dominance of the Nazi swastika.

Great Britain and France declared war against Germany immediately upon the invasion of Poland. Canada followed on September 10, 1939. It was the first time in Canadian history that the country, in its own right, proclaimed war against another nation.

After consolidating their position in Scandinavia by occupying Norway, the German forces skirted around the French defensive Maginot Line, swept through Holland, and by June 14, 1940, they entered the city of Paris. As the Nazi army entered France through the lowlands, the Italians pushed across the borders in the alpine highlands, gaining control of the southeast portion of the country. The Axis had a stranglehold on all of Europe within ten months of the commencement of military action.

The major obstacle to the absolute domination of the entire region was Russia, plus the obstinate islands of Great Britain and their military presence in the Mediterranean and protectorates spread throughout the Middle East.

By the end of 1940 the Axis had occupied the Balkans and were poised in North Africa, planning to control the Mediterranean Sea and the Suez

Canal, thereby locking up the easily accessible trade routes to the near and far east.

By this time the Germans had control of all the Atlantic coastal ports in Europe, from the Arctic to the Mediterranean Sea. This positioned them to release a ferocious naval attack on the ships that were Great Britain's lifeline from North America.

While the German U-boats slaughtered the freighters and tankers en route to Britain by sea, cutting the necessities of life and the instruments of war, the Luftwaffe was attempting to pound the British into a psychological pulp from the air. The combination was designed to condition them for an invasion from the mainland. The Allies were fighting valiantly on all fronts but were reeling from the blows being brought down on them from so many different directions. Freedom of the world from Nazi tyranny hung precariously in the balance.

The United States was producing arms and selling them on "lend-lease," which the Roosevelt administration had developed to facilitate aid to the Allies in their struggle against Hitler. Despite the fact that the United States became the largest arsenal in the history of the world, the fight against the Nazis was being lost. The supply line between Britain and the United States was shredded by the activities of the German submarine fleet harbored in the ports along the coast of France.

Part of Canada's mobilization for war resulted in military training for young men, plus converting peacetime manufacturing plants into munitions factories. This affected every phase of life throughout the nation. Men left the workforce to enlist in the armed forces and were replaced by women in the factories. The entire social structure was reshuffled. The air was filled with a mixture of fervor, transformation, and apprehension. As part of the war effort, Canada became the center for training airmen for the Commonwealth, which resulted in an influx of young men from various parts of the world. Their presence contributed to the shifting mélange of the population.

Personal Thoughts and Memories:

The general sensitivities that permeated Canadian society also prevailed at school. It was accentuated because the male population in forms four and five were either at the enlistment age of eighteen or approaching it. I was seventeen when WWII was declared and found myself among those who were expected to take up arms against the Nazi hoards. Suddenly there was a sense of importance and adventure placed in our immediate future. The horrors of war were dismissed from our thinking. Conversations relating to what branch of the armed service we would enlist were predominant. The air force was number one among my peers, with the key role as pilot of a fighter plane occupying the top spot. The whole idea of fighting for the freedom of the world was exhilarating and challenging to us. Many of the fellows who had been my teammates in sports were old enough to enlist and did so in an assortment of army, navy, and air force venues. They were considered heroes and were the envy of the rest of us who were still cast in the role of mundane students.

Even though everyone felt unsettled in the present and unsure of the future, most of the usual activities took place every day. Classes proceeded according to schedule; sporting events happened; church services continued; shopping took place daily (although as time passed some items were unavailable or rationed).

The primary influences in my life continued to be home, school, church, and summer holidays, with the new addition of work.

Home:

My father prospered in his business adventures and was given the appropriate recognition in advancement in the company and commensurate increases in remuneration. For our family, this translated into another move into an even better neighborhood and house, 198 Geoffrey Street.

This was a two-story brick structure with a kitchen, dining room, living room on the main floor, and three bedrooms and a study on the second floor. It was a well-made house with some class to it. It was situated on an ample lot with a garage in the backyard. Both the garage and the house were embellished with a dignified coating of climbing ivy. It was superior in elegance to anything we had called home in our history as a family.

Our new neighborhood was called High Park. As the name indicates, we were still located close to the park that I enjoyed so much. It was a quiet

Dad, Stuart, Dusty

well-established middle-class section of the city. The roads were lined with mature flourishing trees, which generated an atmosphere of stability in contrast to the instability caused by current world events. Whenever I returned home from school or some event, I always had a warm, comforting feeling when I arrived on the street where I lived.

By this time we were well established in our new country. While the loyalties and memories of our past life on the coast of New Jersey were not expunged, they were being complemented by new experiences and friendships, which were to last for many years.

One of the new friends entering our lives at this address was a happy, responsive floppy-eared blond welcoming cocker spaniel, who was tagged with the name Dusty. I don't remember who conjured the name, but it suited him. He was a delightful dog who became the center of attention at all times in our household. He was just a puppy when he was presented to my brother. Stuart had never had a dog before, and my dad thought he should have the experience.

Although Stuart was the official master of our new family member, I got to play with him a great deal. We ran through the woods and up and down the hills in High Park. We worked our way through the sit-up, roll-over, dead-dog type of tricks that we willingly performed when anyone would care to watch. We would proudly walk along the streets of our neighborhood. Dusty became our precious, precocious family clown.

Although my mother referred to him as the pest, he became her most loyal devoted companion to the end of his days. She loved him dearly.

I had one close friend nearby who also was a school chum. His name was Jack Wheeler. His father owned the local garage-gas station, which also was the distributor of fuel oil used in furnaces to heat the homes of most of the people in the area. They were a well-known and respected family. Jack and his dad didn't get along too well because Jack was a "young whippersnapper" who spent all his time and money on the latest music from the big bands. That kind of music was not appreciated in my home either. It was too worldly.

Jack lived in a large home three or four blocks away. He had some older brothers who occupied the bedrooms on the second and third floors while Jack was relegated to the attic. This suited him fine because he had a record player and a supply of big band records, which he could turn loose with minimal complaints from the other inmates. It was to this lair that I escaped, as often as I could, to have the enjoyment of this kind of music and at the same time beat out the rhythm with drumsticks, which he had on hand for that specific purpose.

School:

The war news became increasingly bad during my last two years of high school, which was a disturbing element in all matters that involved the future, especially as it related to one's career. There seemed to be less reason than ever to concentrate on academics for some of the students. However, there were others who wanted to find a way to escape military duty. The most plausible evasion was to hide in universities for the duration. This difference in attitude caused an invisible yet real division among classmates.

Conscription was not enforced because of internal political reasons involving Quebec. This allowed a loophole, through which many escaped exposure to the physical danger and hardship of war.

During my fourth year in high school I developed a recurring pain in the right side of my abdomen. It was diagnosed as appendicitis. I was promptly shipped off to the hospital for an operation to rectify the situation. It was not any great ordeal for me since I recovered rapidly. While recuperating, I shared a room with a man in his fifties who had a hilarious sense of humor. He kept me laughing constantly, which was tough on the healing process of the incision held together by stitches. He had had a tragic accident some years before when one of his legs was caught between a moving train and a station platform. The result was the loss of his leg from just above the knee. He was left with a stump.

He was a patient at this time because the nerves in his stump were behaving as though his entire leg was still attached. There were times when he experienced the pain of the original mishap all over again. The doctors were to try to remove some of the nerves in the stump in an attempt to eliminate the sensation. He chatted with his stump, which he had named Bessy.

Bessy was most vexing during the night hours. She would begin to thrust around in the most violent fashion. My friend would hold on to her with all his might, but she would slam him flat on his back again. He would plead with her. "Bessy, be nice and calm down." Eventually, after sedation, all would be at peace again. Because he was such a joker most of the time, it was very hard not to roll out of bed with laughter on such a performance with his friend Bessy. He was in excruciating pain. After each session he would talk about how comical the episodes were and have a good chuckle himself.

While I was hospitalized, my classmates bought a copy of For Whom the Bell Tolls by Hemingway and brought it to the hospital for me. I was duly impressed by this expression of their care for me.

The sports programs were continued, and I participated in them with as much enjoyment as ever.

I became eighteen in my final year of school, and the temptation to enlist in the armed services haunted me every day. I was persuaded to stay in school to the end of the year, which was what I did.

Church:

A young man by the name of Bill Conway became the teacher of our Sunday Bible class when I was about seventeen years old. He was only about twenty but had a good understanding of the simple and direct truths of the Scripture. He was a gifted speaker and inspired those of us in his group to be doers of the Word and not just hearers. His example and encouragement had a profound effect on how I approached life in general and direct participation in Christian activities in particular.

It wasn't long before I began to teach a class of boys myself at a place called Markham Street Tabernacle. This necessitated personal study of the Bible in a systematic way that was new to me and which became something that I practiced for the rest of my life. I became part of a male quartet, and I also played a mean harmonica in a musical trio. We sang and played in different churches around the city and had a great time doing it.

My weekends were filled with church activities of one kind and another. During this mix of social and church meetings I met lots of other young people. One of them was Harriet Stewart, who attended Central Gospel Hall. I was astounded to learn that she also went to Parkdale Collegiate and that she had been one grade ahead of me for all the years that I had attended the school. We soon began to go to all the joint church events together as well as seeing each other during the week because of our association at Parkdale. The fact that she lived a few blocks away made it all the more intriguing. Before long we began going steady. My church and school influence had merged in an unexpected fashion.

During the wintertime we went ice skating at many different locations. One of the more spectacular ones was the Varsity Stadium football field. The field was flooded using fire hoses thus providing an expansive sheet of ice. People skated in a counterclockwise circle to music supplied by a live military brass band seated in the stands. Artificial lighting embellished the whole scene.

Another exciting activity we relished with other groups of young people from the churches was shooting the toboggan runs. These were ice slides, which were formed by heaping snow in a U formation from the top of a steep hill in High Park, extending out across a frozen pond at the bottom. The shoot would then be sprayed with water until an ice glaze was formed over the entire surface from top to bottom. It provided one slippery slope!

We generally used toboggans, which carried six to eight people. The speed seemed blinding and indeed caused tears to fill our eyes as the cold air rushed into our faces. It was exhilarating to abandon all control to the pull of gravity as we sat linked together on this laminated, polished strip of hardwood, rocketing out across the pond, stopped only by the slope of the bank on the other side. Sometimes it was made even livelier when we would lose our collective balance as we clung to each other. The toboggan would flip over, and we would find ourselves swirling down the trough like a cluster of wildly spinning tops propelled onto the frozen surface of the lake. Once stopped we had to scramble to get ourselves and the toboggan out of the way of the next group of thrill seekers pressing right on our tail. Then came the trudge up the hill to get positioned for another electrifying rush down the bank.

Another winter outing we found most enjoyable which we did two or three times each winter was going on hayrides. This activity would take place at one of the farms north of Toronto, which still had horses and long wide flat sleds with no railing on the side. Hay would be stacked onto them to the depth of about two feet, and we would all pile on. Sometimes there would be three or four of these contraptions following one behind the other depending on the number of young people involved.

The horses would take off under the guidance of the drivers out into the snow-covered fields. Often there was a magical atmosphere. Sometimes there would be the fluttering of gentle snowflakes; at other times there would be the frosty beams of moonlight spreading an enchanting ghostly glow over the pale landscape of snow-blanketed fences and trees; always there would be singing, laughing, and jostling. It was great sport to push someone off the sled into the snowbank without finding oneself in a similar plight! The evening would be capped with toasted marshmallows and hot dogs around a rousing fire.

One of my good friends at church was Gord Mitchell, who also was a member of the quartet and music group in which I participated. Harriet had a close friend in her church named Mary Turnbull. We became an inseparable foursome, doing all the church things together. This became a relationship that was to be of significance in the years to come.

Unfortunately, a healthy relationship did not develop between Harriet and my family. They tolerated each other because of me, but there was an underlying feeling bordering on outright dislike. This made an awkward and unhappy situation. I was caught in the uneasy position of wanting parental approval for my friendship and my determination to continue seeing her regardless. I was still smarting from the experience with Gwen Connell (the little blonde that I had cut off because of my Christian principles), and here was Harriet who was a Christian but did not have acceptable personal qualities in the eyes of my parents and vice versa. I did not know anyone with the maturity and wisdom to counsel me in the circumstance, so I stubbornly continued the path I was on.

Summer Holidays:
The summer of 1939 found us in a new location. It was north and east of Toronto in a district called Haliburton, which was a patchwork of farms and forests bejeweled with sparkling lakes linked together by shimmering rivers and streams. I can't recall how we came to find this spot, but it was to have a lasting imprint on our family, particularly on my mother and my brother. While the sequence of events escapes my memory, the result was the purchase of a building lot owned by a family named Harrison. It was situated on the west side of Lake Kashagawigamog.

This venture began with the renting of a cottage near a village named Ingoldsby, which was located on the southern tip of Lake Kashagawigamog. Just to the south was another small lake whose name I forget. The two bodies of water were joined by an isthmus, wide enough and deep enough to allow travel by small craft. Our cottage was positioned on the small lake on the narrow strip of land between the two lakes. We had our outboard motorboat with us, which provided a means to take advantage of the opportunity for wide-ranging exploration throughout the many connected lakes.

We did lots of exploring that year to get to know some of the fishing spots around the area. There was a different type of fishing from my previous experiences. In these waters were lake trout, which were larger fish than I had caught. The water was deep, and this species thrived in deep cold water. The technique used to take them was to place a lure on the end of a line made of finely threaded copper. It had to be trolled a long distance behind a boat in order to reach a depth of a few feet above the bottom. Since they are a fighting creature, hooking and landing one provides a thrilling experience. Lake trout are a grand-looking fish, and as far as my palate is concerned, they are equal to or better than any other piscatorial delight I have had the pleasure of savoring.

This was the last summer that I was to be full time in cottage country. Stuart was old enough to provide the manpower to serve my mother's needs, and I was hankering to spend the summers working in the city.

That summer was also a milestone of sorts. The peach fuzz was getting so long and thick on my face, it drove my father to the point where he couldn't stand it any longer. He presented me with a razor, shaving cream, and brush, insisting that I begin the lifelong male ritual of managing facial hair. My uncle Bill and aunt Annie were visiting with us. He was the joker of all jokers. He made a huge scene of the whole process. He gathered everyone around and gave blow-by-blow instructions to the last stroke of the razor, much to the howling amusement of all present, except yours truly, who was mortified. However, it was an event I have never forgotten!

My parents built a comfortable cottage, which became a large part of their lives and Stuart's life for many years to come. The Harrisons, from whom they had bought the lot, owned a farm adjacent to the property across, which one had to pass to reach the cottage. My mother and father and brother became very friendly with them. This bonding was strengthened by the fact that the Harrisons and my family were Christians and attended a Brethren church at a small village a few miles away named West Guilford.

Eventually Stuart settled in West Guilford and established a Christian camp for children called Medeba. He and his wife, Jackie, gave a large portion of their lives to this endeavor that continues to be a fruitful work for God to this very day.

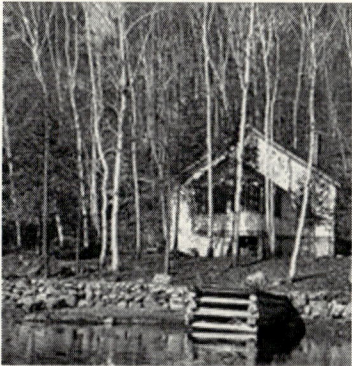

The summer of 1940 found me working in the city during the week and traveling to Haliburton with my father on the weekends. We would finish work on Friday afternoon then rush to the grocery store to do some wild and frantic shopping for weekly supplies for Mom and Stu.

Jump into the car and dash to the highway to join the mass of other frenzied drivers in the preposterous pursuit north to rest for Saturday and Sunday, only to put the whole operation in reverse on Sunday night. Stampede back to Toronto in time for work on Monday morning. Once safely at the lake, it all seemed worthwhile. It was so peaceful. The quiet grandeur of the water mingling with the sensual scent of the verdant forest and circulated by wafts of gentle breezes produced a serenity of spirit that was completely lacking in the metropolis.

Summer Work:

My dad insisted that I work in the same company as he did, which was Christie Brown and Company. They were the purveyors of biscuits, bread, and cake. Since my father was the head of the bread and cake departments from production right through sales to the stores, there was no question about being able to get a job. The placed that he lined up for me was in the shipping department. Salesmen using trucks in the conventional manner serviced the larger centers in Ontario. However, he was not satisfied with only the places of easy access; he sought after the "out of the way" stores, which were strung out along the various railway lines weaving across the province. Since many of these increased their business in the summertime, additional help was needed at that time of year. I worked in the section that was responsible for packing and shipping the cakes to small outlets.

The company had a large ordering pad on which all of the cakes that were produced were listed. The operator of each store indicated how many of the various items he wanted delivered to him, and then he mailed the sheet to Christie's. We filled the orders and shipped them back to him. The cakes were packed in cardboard boxes and then placed in cartons and loaded on the trucks that transported them to the railroad station. It always was a source of amazement to me how few times there were complaints about damage to the contents upon arrival at the other end of the line. My dad had had a hand in the design of both containers and was duly proud of the fact that they protected the contents so well even though the handling was rough and merciless.

My fellow workers were older than I was. By and large, they were from different backgrounds to which I had not been exposed. Their language was courser and cruder than my ears were in the habit of hearing, so it required some effort on my part to be accepted by them and still honor my lifetime of training. To complicate the situation a bit more, I was the son of the big boss and might provide a direct pipeline to him if something went wrong.

It didn't take long to win their respect, confidence, and friendship, but I had to consciously work at winning them over one by one. It provided another great training ground for me to learn how to deal with all types of people under various circumstances.

Chapter 7

Decision Time
(1941-1942)

Digest of Times and Circumstance:

Germany and Russia had signed a non-aggression pact, mutually agreeing that neither country would invade the other. For some reason Hitler postponed his attempt to invade England. Apparently he feared an attack by the Russians. His attitude regarding any pact that he signed was "it is only a scrap of paper." He had no intention of keeping any treaty beyond the point that suited his own purposes. He had decided that it was necessary to remove the threat of an attack from Russia before he attempted to invade Great Britain.

Consequently, in June of 1941, the German army, under his direct command, Hitler crossed the borders of the USSR. The Nazis expected that Russia would be conquered within a matter of weeks or, at the most, four months. The reality was that by the end of November, they had not been able to topple Leningrad or Moscow. The German armies were stranded hundreds of miles inside the Soviet Union. They were ill equipped for the early and ferocious winter that struck them as they occupied land that had been "scorched" by the retreating Russians.

The British began a counterattack on the Italian and German armies in North Africa, which delayed the Axis plans for control of that part of the world.

The United Kingdom signed an agreement with the USSR pledging mutual support against their common enemies. The United States gave Russia one billion dollars in credit so that they could purchase munitions from the United States.

Meanwhile, in the Pacific, the United States and Japan were having major difficulties sorting out their roles in the region. The Japanese accentuated their belligerent posture. This resulted in their occupation of more and more territory possessed by other nations. In the fall of 1941, Japanese diplomats were in Washington DC, negotiating with the U.S. administration in an effort to settle their differences. The military forces in Japan had already concluded that they had to wipe out the United States as a military force in the Pacific if Japan was going to prevail as the dominant power. With the conflagration in Europe absorbing immense concentration and energy in the United States, the Japanese decided it was the opportune time to strike. On December 7, 1941, Japan unleashed an aerial assault on Pearl Harbor, the major U.S. naval base in the Pacific Ocean. The U.S. Pacific Fleet was decimated.

The United States declared war on Japan, Germany, and Italy. The whole globe had become engulfed in armed conflict!

In Canada people were very concerned because the conflict had spread into the heart of Russia and across the expanse of the Pacific. Redoubling the effort in the private sector as well as the military became the paramount thrust. Food, fuel, and other items were rationed as production for the war effort heightened.

Personal Thoughts and Memories:

This was a time of uncertainty and bewilderment for me. On the outside was my healthy red-blooded youth ready to fight for the freedom of the world, and on the inside there was the Christian spirit of forgiveness and nonviolence. This was the plight of many Christians. The leading elders in the Brethren assemblies of Toronto decided to hold a conference for an open discussion of the issue.

The seminar was convened. A mature panel, well versed in the Scriptures, provided input for discussion in front of a large mostly male audience. Questions were posed, which covered all aspects of a Christian's responsibility and obligation during times of war.

The general consensus was that in the present instance, the freedom of the world was under attack and that everyone had the right to repel anyone who was perpetrating such aggression. Christians should be free to take up arms or free to be conscientious objectors as they felt led individually.

This helped me to make my decision. I really wanted to fight. My first choice of where and how was to be a fighter pilot flying a U.S. Navy corsair dispatched from a flight deck of an aircraft carrier.

After finishing high school, I was faced with some decisions. In what service should I enlist? And when should I enlist? I had tried the Canadian Navy, but at that particular moment their complement was temporarily filled. In the meantime, I decided to go to work for Dominion Bridge Company, which manufactured shell casings for three-inch guns.

This was a completely new experience for me, firstly because it was shift work. There were three eight-hour periods, and each shift started at a different time of the day. We had to rotate one week at a time on each shift. Secondly, it was a very noisy place because of the clanking metal, the pounding of the presses, the humming of the lathes, plus the sputtering of motorized carts that scampered back and forth carrying product from one location to another. Above all this cacophony was the shout of human voices as people tried to communicate with each other. Thirdly, I had not worked with so many people in one large congested spot before. And fourthly, the air was polluted with oil fumes from the machinery and burnt chemicals from the metal being heated in the ovens.

All of these things combined together to create an aura of intrigue for me rather than something that was distasteful and difficult to endure. There was the sense of being involved in history even if it was a small part of the entire effort. I worked there for several months while I sorted out what would be my next step.

I had not worked for Dominion Bridge long before the Japanese attacked Pearl Harbor. This changed everything from the standpoint of where and how I would serve. Since I was an American citizen and the United States had entered the war, I had to register as a person eligible to be drafted. My father was also required to do the same. This necessitated a trip to Kearny, where we were both born.

The trip lasted about four days. It turned out to be the most intimate time of comradeship I can ever remember having with my dad. We were alone in the car for hours at a time, away from the pressures of his business and all family matters. I am sure the seriousness of the situation weighed heavily upon him, and he wanted to make up for some of the lost time that had slipped by while he was so busy earning a living for us all.

I did most of the driving and listening while he talked. He told me some of the things he did when he was a boy, some of his ideas relating to business, politics, and life in general. There was nothing earth shattering, but it was a sharing that I appreciated. It was the first occasion that I can recall that he seemed genuinely interested in my opinions. The fact that he accepted my thoughts as valid and important gave me a feeling of maturity.

When Harriet finished high school, the Toronto Dominion Bank employed her. She was working and I was working, but we managed to see each other often in the evenings and weekends. Many times we went with my family to the cottage in Haliburton. We also continued to be involved in church activities of one kind and another.

Chapter 8

Joining Up
(1942)

Digest of the Times and Circumstance:

The Japanese lost no time in advancing their cause in the Pacific. They captured Guam, Midway and Wake islands, which were U.S. military outposts; at the same time they invaded Burma, the Philippines, Hong Kong, and Singapore.

The Germans counterattacked the British in North Africa. While the Nazis still retain large portions of the area, their advance was halted.

The German move on Moscow was stopped by Russian retaliation. They caused disastrous losses to the Nazis as they were thrown into a full-blown retreat. However, it was at the cost of enormous damage to Russia's resources in equipment and manpower.

The United States was faced with an overwhelming challenge. Their position in the Pacific had to be defended with a crippled fleet. They had to provide the USSR and Great Britain with supplies to defend themselves against the Axis powers. All the while, U-boats were sinking tankers and cargo ships in the North Atlantic and along the coast of the United States between New York City and the Caribbean. Added to this already impossible mix, the decision was made to storm North Africa to help the Allies push Rommel out of that continent. This would clear the way for an attack against the Axis position in Italy.

Personal Thoughts and Memories:

I knew that I did not want to serve in the army. I felt that the sea was second nature to me because of the exposure I had in my early childhood. I wanted to fly. It seemed to me that the logical place to serve where all of these desires could be fulfilled was the U.S. Navy. I went to a recruiting station in Buffalo, New York, to inquire whether these goals were possible to achieve. I was assured they were. I returned to Toronto to make arrangements to leave my job and to say farewell to my friends and family.

On June 22, 1942, I joined the U.S. Navy.

I was given a transportation pass for Newport, Road Island, where upon arrival I was to report to the naval training station. As I boarded the train, my family gave me a tearful good-bye but one which was also filled with pride.

As the train pulled out of the station, I was apprehensive, excited, and fearful as I anticipated the future.

There were other new recruits on the train, but we traveled as individuals and kept our own counsel as the steel wheels click-clacked along the rails. It was an overnight trip, and we were assigned berths. Before retiring, however, we were invited to go to the dining car where we were presented with a menu. Among many other choices there was something called Salisbury steak. I thought it was a thick juicy piece of meat, and so I ordered it. Much to my chagrin, it turned out to be a glorified hamburger! I felt I had been duped! It tasted very good despite my misgivings. I was more embarrassed inwardly because of my ignorance than anything else. This was my first hesitant step into the vagaries of life.

Chapter 9

The United States Navy
(1942)

Boot Camp, Newport, Rhode Island:

When the train pulled into the station at Newport, there were two or three trucks waiting to pick up the latest batch of recruits and transport them to the naval training base. I jumped in the back of one of these vehicles along with the rest of the greenhorns. It was an open truck with a high guardrail around the perimeter, much like cattle are transferred from one place to another. As were drove through the gates we passed thousands of sailors in white uniforms and gob hats. I had the feeling that I was a complete novice. I could hardly wait to plunge into the activities of this new life.

We disembarked in front of what seemed to be an administration building. Our names were called out, and we were assigned to platoons and marched away in a ragtag fashion to the barracks, which would become home for the next eight to ten weeks.

The next item of business was to go to the barbers who shaved all the hair off our heads. We then were directed to the supplies depot. We were issued our equipment: from seabags to hammocks, from skivvies to P jackets, from dungarees to dress blues, from shoes to dress scarves and, of course, a copy of the bluejacket's manual (which was the last word in the realm of all things nautical). Everything we owned had to be packed into the seabag with the exception of our mattress and canvas hammock, which were rolled together and carried separately. The theory being that we personally could transport everything we required anywhere, anytime at a few moments' notice. To achieve this packing feat demanded intensive folding and stuffing instruction, which was the first course on the curriculum. This being accomplished, we were marched back to our lodging and allocated spaces to hang up our hammocks.

After we were established in our allotted space, we were told to remove our civilian clothes and head for the shower. When we were cleaned, dried (and bare as our shaven heads), we were told to put on our new uniforms. Sailors at last!

Next on the list of our induction ritual was to discover where to eat. There was a large mess hall seating hundreds of people, all of whom had to get in line and take a metal tray in which there were indentations that served as receptacles for the different types of food (instead of having individual plates for each item). We then moved along in front of a line of cooks who doled out everything from meat to cake. We loaded up and took our place at one of the many tables available. The menu was good, but the noise of so many people talking and clanking knives, forks, and cups left much to be desired in ambiance.

That night was the first time for most of us to sleep in the same room with so many other people and certainly the first time to sleep in a hammock instead of a bed. There were four steel pipes that ran the length of the dormitory suitably supported by upright stanchions at intervals of about eight feet. There was a clear space of about five feet providing a walkway in the middle from one end of the building to the other, on either side of which were strung hammocks between the steel pipes, fifteen on each side. All of a sudden this was home for all thirty of us!

The hammocks were hung about shoulder high. At the end of each of them, there was a piece of wood, 1×1 square inch, interlaced in the cords that were attached to the canvas hammock. The one at the head was about two and a half feet long, and the one at the foot was about two feet long. This gave some shape to the canvas, stretching it so that it did not fold right around a person lying in it.

The remainder of the evening of the first night was spent attempting to vault into our beds and learning to lie still enough so that we wouldn't be thrown out on the floor (or what was now termed the deck). A bystander watching the proceedings would have had a hard time distinguishing our performance from that of a bunch of cowboys trying to mount bucking broncos in a corral somewhere.

At ten PM the bugle sounded, indicating that all was to be silent and that everyone on the base was to be instantly asleep. The lights were extinguished, and the boatswain yelled "QUIET!" Gradually the snickering subsided only to be replaced by melodious snores, which covered at least one octave as each one strove to be the dominant soloist. The entire night was punctuated by here a thud, there a thud, everywhere a thud, thud. Would-be sailors, who thought they were rolling over in bed, found that they had turned upside-down and were grasped by the merciless hand of gravity and were bounced off the floor (that is, to say, the deck).

The bugle blared at six AM. The boatswain bellowed "RISE AND SHINE!" I didn't know whether to be relieved that the tense night of trying to keep my balance was finished or to be irate because I had no sleep. There was no time to think about how I should feel because we were plunged into action! We were instructed to wash up and line up in front of the barracks in thirty minutes.

At one end of our building, there was a room composed of a battery of sinks, a battery of showers, a battery of urinals, and a battery of toilets plus a few washtubs. There was not enough of any one item to serve the needs of all thirty of us at once, so every morning there was a mad dash to be first in line to use the facility to meet our greatest need. We had to shave and accomplish all our ablutions, be dressed and lined up within thirty minutes of reveille. Each day began with a mad mingling of bodies, soap, shaving cream, and swearing.

After our boatswain inspected us, we were dismissed to find our way to line up outside the mess hall where we would "chow down." The boatswain's job was to keep us moving from one location to another and to make sure that we and our quarters were clean and tidy at all times. For this he got to sleep in his own little room with a cot, a tiny desk, and a private washroom.

In order to move from one location to another efficiently, it was necessary to learn to march as a group. This required much practice to know what the different commands meant and how to execute them in an acceptable manner. This instruction was also our boatswain's responsibility, which he took on with much bravado and gusto. I am sure it boosted his ego to the rooftops to have us obey his every command. We moved from class to class, usually in double time.

Our days were filled with learning everything, from how to row a boat as a team to how to tie knots and for what purpose. We were taught the traditions of the navy: flags, saluting, discipline, etiquette. We were instructed in the use and carrying of rifles and small arms at the pistol and rifle ranges. We had to become acquainted with the points of the compass and gain a rudimentary knowledge of navigation. In short, we were exposed to a slathering of military knowledge.

We had to march with other platoons in joint operations. In the course of being drilled in these maneuvers, we came into contact with sailors from other barracks in the mammoth training base. One day I saw in a platoon next to us a familiar face. It was Jim Gibson, one of the boys in the Daredevil Club of long ago in Neptune City. I managed to get his attention when we were standing at ease by calling out his name. We chatted over old times on a few occasions in periods when we were not in classes. We were soon dispatched to different parts of the service in different parts of the world. I never saw him again.

On Saturday mornings all of the sailors on the base had to line up, platoon by platoon, on huge parade ground. Each unit was designated to a specific spot. We marched one group after the other until we arrived at that location. On one side of the area was a reviewing stand where the top brass stood in the shade of a covered roof. There was a military band that played marches during the proceedings.

When all the sailors from the entire base were assembled on the grass filed in summer uniforms, it presented an impressive image of a massive immaculate white-and-green patched quilt.

The quilt, however, was composed of humans. Some showed their frailty by collapsing in the summer heat. It was very humid and hot in that part of the country in July and August. After marching for some time to get into our position, we were required to stand in place either at attention or at ease but not move from where we stood while we had various officers inspect us. Anyone who fainted was not to be aided by his buddies but was left to lie there until the medics took him away. The complete process of going on parade was very distasteful to me. It was at the bottom of my list of enjoyable activities at boot camp.

At the top of the list was physical training. I found the drill challenging and invigorating. It included calisthenics, long runs in platoon formation, and a lengthy obstacle course. This course was a most difficult and formidable task to overcome. It tested our endurance, tenacity, and ingenuity. It was composed of ropes to climb hand over hand, platforms to crawl under on our stomachs, ditches to scramble in and out, twelve-foot wooden walls over which we had to get the whole platoon by boosting and pulling each other, water holes to swing over on ropes, large sewer pipes to clamber through, and rows of tires to straddle laid out flat on the ground. They were spaced so that as we ran, we had to extend our legs to be able to place one foot at a time in each ring made by the tire. The total procedure was an exhausting enjoyable session. It was reminiscent of my Daredevil Club days, only on a larger scale. We did this daily. The net result was our condition was top notch.

By the time I finished boot camp, I was at my lifetime peak of fitness.

After I had been in training for about two weeks, I received a message to report to the headquarters building. I dutifully did this and was met by a man in a lieutenant commander's uniform. It was Harriet's uncle, her mother's sister's husband. He was an engineer with the navy and was stationed at Newport Training Base. He and his wife lived in a lovely cottage overlooking the Atlantic Ocean. He invited me to go home with him during some of my off periods. The result was that I got to spend time at their residence, which was a welcome respite in the middle of such intense instruction.

After about ten weeks, we completed our basic training and were declared to be seamen. This meant that we were ready to be posted to our next assignment. There was anticipation and twittering as discussions buzzed relating to our destinations. I was fully expecting to be travelling to Corpus Christie or some other exotic-sounding flight-training location. Each of us received our written orders. Since my surname began with W, I was one of the last ones to get the news.

My eyes eagerly scanned the paper. The unbelievable words told me that I was to report to the other side of the base to attend "visual training school"! It couldn't be! There was some horrible mistake! I had signed up to be a navy pilot! I immediately took off to see the personnel officer.

Upon arrival at the administration building, I lined up behind many other sailors who seemed to be having similar problems. Somebody must have really goofed! I finally got to see the officer in charge, and he dug up my recruiting information. He agreed that I had been accepted into the pilot training program, but Uncle Sam had a greater need for me elsewhere. I protested that I had no desire to go to signal school and that I had not signed any contract to that effect. He firmly pointed out to me the fine print at the bottom of the page: "Or any other place that the United States Government deems best." He explained that there was a more immediate need in the war effort at the moment to man convoy escort ships to keep the supply lines open overseas, and that I should be willing to do what is required to do my part in the war effort. I didn't like it, but there was nothing else I could do. I swallowed hard and moved over to my new surroundings.

Visual Signal School:

I checked into the administration build of the signal school after lugging my seabag and hammock across the base. I settled into my new barracks with a feeling of betrayal, disappointment, and anger, which produced a negative attitude toward my new surroundings. Fortunately the person in charge of the training course was a man of good humor and experience. He was a chief petty officer in visual signals and had been in the navy for twenty-five years. He had a trim white mustache. We called him Scotty (I can't remember why). He was an unusually fine gentleman who showed empathy to us. The combination of the ways of the navy and his understanding of young men brought out the best in his trainees.

There were about thirty in the class. We were officially designated as strikers, which is a term used by the navy to signify a sailor who is learning a specific trade or skill. To separate us from the raw recruits we were issued a white band to wear on our shoulder. It served to boost our ego, making us feel like old Salts compared to the daily influx of civvies. By this time, our hair had grown, which gave us far more sophistication than the skinheads that surrounded us.

Because of the leadership we had in the person of Scotty, it didn't take long for us to plunge into the courses that were presented. Our days were crammed with learning the Morse code, sending semaphore, and the meaning of flags strung up on the yardarm. We sent hour upon hour sending and receiving messages by flags and flashing light until it became second nature. We also had to recognize the national ensigns of the nations of the world as well as the silhouettes of the various types of vessel that sailed the seven seas.

At the end of about eight weeks, we graduated but were still strikers. Our basic education was complete, and we were ready for posting somewhere. I was dispatched to New York City.

Seamen at last—liberty in Newport Rhode Island

Pier 92, New York City:

Pier 92 was a holding pool for those sailors who were to be part of the naval convoy escort ships patrolling the Atlantic. I was once again thrown in with a bunch of strangers, who were as apprehensive as I was as we waited to discover what ship would become our new home. At an adjacent pier, sunk and lying on its side with half of it protruding out of the water, was an ocean liner that had been used for transporting troops across the Atlantic. The enemy had sabotaged it. A catwalk had been constructed on it from stem to stern on the portion sticking out of the water for the purpose of guarding the wreck.

It was the job of the sailors awaiting the arrival of their next assignment to stand watch over this useless hulk of steel. I had the joy of being one of those carrying a rifle on his shoulder walking back and forth, back and forth for four hours at a time. It was the middle of winter, freezing cold and lonely.

I had to wait two weeks before my ship arrived in port.

Chapter 10

USS *Impulse*: PG68
(1942)

Digest of the Times and Circumstances:

After their disastrous winter experience, by midsummer of 1942, the Germans moved forward into Russian territory. Hitler anticipated that Russia would have been defeated by this time. He had ordered a cutback in the production of supplies for the army. Therefore he was not able to give his forces on the Russian front the equipment and the ammunition they needed. In the meantime Stalin was receiving an increasing amount of material from the United States via convoy escorts provided by the United States, Canada, and Great Britain. This enhanced his military capacity.

The United States landed four hundred thousand troops in French North Africa to join the British in driving the Germans and Italians out of that continent so that the Allies could maintain control of the Suez Canal as part of the preparation for the invasion of Italy.

The U.S. Navy began a series of island hopping in the Pacific to start to make some inroads into the huge scope of the Japanese advancement in that part of the world.

The first successful splitting of the atom was achieved in 1942, inspiring the Manhattan project in the United States, which finally led to the construction and use of the atomic bomb. 1942 was also the year that the first automatic computer was developed, which has revolutionized mankind.

The U-boats played a huge part in curtailing the supplies from crossing the North Atlantic into Murmansk for the use of the Russians, and into Great Britain to support the military effort there. Additionally the submarines operated along the Atlantic coast of the United States to sink the shipping destined across the South Atlantic for the purpose of maintaining the armies in North Africa.

Personal Thoughts and Memories:

Corvettes:

I was interested to learn as much as I could about the USS *Impulse* and soon began asking questions. I didn't acquire the information I am passing on to you all at once but over time, as I experienced living aboard her.

Corvettes, traditionally in the British Navy, were smaller and designed to be used for quick infighting among enemy sailing ships. This was the name selected for the type of ship that was constructed to speedily maneuver around a convoy while defending it from attacking submarines. Great Britain and Canada built them.

Before becoming the USS *Impulse*, this corvette had been manufactured in England and had been manned by British seaman in the Mediterranean against Nazi submarine and air warfare. Part of my job was to keep a log of the daily activities of the ship. The ship's log always stays with the ship. Even when this particular Corvette was transferred from the British Navy to the USN, her log remained with her. Therefore, I could read about the HMS Begonia before she became part of the USN. She had already been in a torrent of enemy action both by air and by U-boats.

In the early part of the period after the United States entered the war, the USN did not believe in the tactic of defending tankers and transport ships, which were carrying supplies to the war theaters by the use of convoy escorts. As a result, there were thousands of tons of shipping sunk by the enemy submarine wolf packs lying in wait off the coast of the United States between Cuba and New York. When the technique was finally accepted, they had few ships of the type represented by the corvette to do the job. In order to quickly rectify the situation, some of the old four-stack destroyers of the USN of WWI vintage were traded for British-built corvettes. HMS Begonia was one of them.

The HMS Begonia was about three hundred feet long. It was fueled by oil and had an engine with only one propeller that made maneuvering in tight situations very difficult. It had a top speed of about thirty knots in the open sea. It was seaworthy but was subject to rolling through about sixty degrees from one side to the other. It had an open bridge that exposed all those who worked there to the bliss of balmy weather and the raging blizzards of the winter.

The designers of these vessels did not take into consideration the comforts of the crew but concentrated on getting a fighting ship on the high seas to meet the enemy. Consequently such things as bunks for sleeping, individual showers, and heads were not included in the blueprint. Also there were uncovered steam pipes throughout the ship, most notably in the head, which caused many a burn as the ship pitched and tossed, throwing naked sailors against the hot conduits.

When the United States took over the ship, it was renamed the USS *Impulse*, and some of the creature comforts were installed in between convoy trips. By the time I boarded the ship, bunks had been installed in place of the hammocks, but the steam pipes had not yet been insulated. The overall head situation remained the same. We had fresh water for drinking and cooking, but washing our clothes and ourselves was done in saltwater with a special soap.

The USN armed the ship immediately with its own guns and depth charges. This included a three-inch gun on the forecastle, two .20-millimeter antiaircraft guns, one on each side of the bridge, two eye guns for firing depth charges on the port side and two on the starboard side at the deck level, and two tracks for rolling depth charges off the stern.

The number of men required to man the ship was about ninety. The urgent need for more trained personnel for convoy escort duty demanded that the current ships engaged in this phase of the war carry more men than was needed to operate the vessel. Consequently the *Impulse* had about 115 men aboard when I first joined the crew. In the visual signal department there would normally be about six. There were ten sailors assigned to this job on my first sailing.

Convoys:

The history of convoys can be traced to the days of the camel caravan and before. The idea was simple: "There is safety in numbers." It is far easier to repel an enemy attack with a larger group than a smaller one. This system had been used very successfully against the German submarines in WWI. The British used it in the early stages of WWII with good success; however, the United States was slow to accept the strategy after their entry into the war. When it became mandatory to maintain a supply line to the U.S. troops in Africa and the wolf packs of U-boats were decimating tanker and transport ships off the Atlantic coast of the United States, they were forced to rethink their position. They embraced the convoy tactic with a vengeance.

There were three major ports in North America where convoys were assembled and then sent across the Atlantic to their destinations in Russia, Great Britain, and North Africa. They were Halifax, New York City, and Guantanamo Bay in Cuba.

The transport ships would board their cargoes then gather in formation outside the harbor in columns of three, surrounded by the protective cover of the convoy escort ships. The convoy would then proceed in unison on a zigzag course in the general direction of the next port of call.

The escort vessels themselves would change course every few minutes to zigzag in front of or beside the convoy to establish a fanlike shield between the enemy and the convoy while attempting to detect submarines with their sonar equipment.

The *Impulse* was assigned to the route between New York City and Cuba. Our station was at the port lead point in the convoy where we guarded the convoy day and night, calm seas or wild, summer or winter until the threat of submarine attack was eliminated.

Introduction to the *Impulse*:

The 18 of November 1942, I reported aboard the USS *Impulse*. She was berthed in Staten Island, which meant that I had to go by ferry from Manhattan, across the harbor, past the Statue of Liberty. The weather was cold and bleak, adding to the blend of mystery and history as I thought of what might lie ahead in the current war and reminisced over the events of the past, which these waters had witnessed. There was a small cluster of us transferred together, who were destined to serve on this ship. All but one of the group was a stranger to me. There was one fellow who had been at signal school at the same time I was. We located the ship, made our way up the gangplank, were duly logged in, and then reported to the officer of the day. He turned us over to the various department heads where we were to serve. Mine was a very large Swede from Minnesota, who had been in the regular navy before the war and was indeed an old salt. He was a chief petty officer signalman whose job it was to whip as many of us into shape as fast as he could so that the new ships being produced to meet the crisis would have sailors with some experience to man them.

He showed me where I was to sleep! There were two forward compartments where the enlisted men had their quarters. They were located one on top of the other, directly below the forecastle. There was one hatch in the middle of the forecastle that served as a source of fresh air for the crew below. This was supplemented by forced air miserly circulated via pipes and pump from the engine room.

We descended two metal ladders to the lower chamber through two layers of foul air that had been recycled many times through human lungs then spiked by body odors. From the deck to the overhead was about seven feet. The bulkheads and all the available space between them were lined with bunks, stacked three-feet high on top of each other. There was about three feet of space separating each column of suspended cots, which allowed access to one's bunk.

I was informed that all the bunks were taken and that I would have to sleep on the deck between columns of bunks in the lower compartment. The ship was overfilled, and many had to sleep in odd places. This was not a very pleasant morsel of information! I left my seabag and hammock in the place where later that night I was supposed to sleep. I followed my leader back up into the light of day to continue my introduction to this small island of mobile steel, which was to be the center of my life for the next two-and-one-half years.

He took me from the engine room to the bridge and all points in between, explaining things as we moved along. Most of what he said went right by me, but I was left with an impression of the overall location of the various functions that I would need to know to find my way around.

We were to cast off at ten PM that evening, and I was informed that I would be standing watch from midnight to four AM. We were to have chow at about six PM, and I was advised to get some rest somewhere before I had to be on the bridge for duty. That seemed an impossible feat to accomplish, given the place I had been allocated to sleep plus the excitement of anticipating getting underway for the first time in my life on a real ship headed out into the Atlantic Ocean. It was the same ocean that I had surveyed in wonder from the beach as a little boy. I made my way to the bridge where I could watch the proceedings as last-minute preparations were accomplished before leaving port.

USS Impulse—PG68

My First Night at Sea:

It was cold and clammy with a slight mist in the air. The sparse lighting from the pier mingled with the dull illumination from the ship created an eerie atmosphere. The throb of the ship's idling engine could be felt pulsating through the steel decks. Everything was prepared for departure. At last the captain took his place on the bridge, ready to give the final command to shove off. When he gave the word, the handlers on the wharf dropped the thick mooring lines into the water, and the deck hands on the *Impulse* pulled them onto the ship and coiled them on the deck. The captain gave the order "Slow astern," and we were on our way!

To move in and out of New York harbor requires a pilot who is familiar with the traffic and channels. Before we departed, one of them came aboard to guide us to the open sea. Along with the other escort vessels assigned to this convoy, we made our way along the line of buoys that mark the exit of the harbor. There were five naval ships that set up a protective shield around the convoy. Three were placed in front and the other two on each flank. The escorts assumed their position at the mouth of the harbor; then the convoy came out and formed behind them.

As soon as we reached the open water, all the lights on all of the ships had to be extinguished to deter the enemy from learning our position, course, and number of ships. This brought into prime importance the radar technology that kept track of each ship as we moved slowly through the increasing groundswells of the ocean. A boat, deployed for the purpose, picked up the harbor pilot. We were on our way to Guantanamo Bay, Cuba!

It was somewhat intimidating to stare out into the darkness not knowing what was lurking below the water, trusting the navigational skills of someone to place us on the right course and, at the same time, wanting to believe that this ship was able to withstand the harsh buffets of the ancient Atlantic. The mighty Atlantic had swallowed so many mariners over the ages.

My introduction to standing watch at sea began at midnight during the formation of this first convoy. It was a "keep your eyes wide open and your mouth shut" experience for me. I had no specific duties to perform except to write down some of the messages that the chief petty officer received, which were transmitted in Morse code via flashing lights from the bridges of the other ships. It had been an exhausting draining day, crammed with new adventures, and by the time four AM arrived, I was ready to lie down somewhere. Salt spray was being tossed over the bow as we moved head-on into the sea, which was becoming more restless as the moments passed.

I left the bridge and made my way down the ladders to the sleeping area I had been shown. I spread out my hammock and mattress on the deck between the rows of bunks and tried to go to sleep with the hope that the guys in the bunks above wouldn't land directly on me if they got up during the night. It wasn't long before the ship was pitching dramatically as the size of the waves continued to increase. Soon I became aware that there was water sloshing around me, soaking my mattress. The seas that were being thrown onto the forecastle were coming down the only hatch that was kept open and accumulated on the deck that was my bed! I dragged my wet belongings up the ladder and found my way to the mess hall. I parked there and drank coffee until I was too seasick to handle any more.

The constant rolling and bucking motion made me dizzier and dizzier. Soon I made rapid trips to the head, throwing up again and again. Not only was it debilitating, it was demoralizing and embarrassing to be found to be such a sissy to succumb to such a weakness as this! Motion sickness was to be my fate for the next three months! All in all, it was not my dream prescription for my first day at sea!

Seasickness:

When the light of day came, I learned that I was not the only one who had been struck by this wretched illness. All of the new sailors just out of training camp had been stricken as well as many others who had been at sea for some time. As the days went by I continued to feel sick to my stomach, and I vomited regularly. However, I was not as badly off as some of the others. It affected my digestive apparatus but did not affect my mental state. Some were so ill they didn't care whether they lived or died and would just as soon have rolled over the side and ended it all.

After my malady had lasted a couple convoys, I began to get recipes for recovery from some of the old salts in the crew. One of them came from the chief boatswain, who told me the thing to do was to down a bowl of tomato soup along with some soda crackers and make straight for my bunk and force myself to lie down and not think about being sick. I followed his advice and rushed to my bunk (I had been allocated a bunk by this time—hallelujah!). The bunks were really layers of springs on which each sailor spread his canvas hammock and mattress. When there was a sailor in the bunk above, the spring sagged down so that there was barely enough room to turn over.

I lay flat on my back, clutching the sides of my bunk, all the while mentally instructing my stomach to keep the lid on the soup. Suddenly a volcanic eruption belched from my mouth in Vesuvius-like fashion! Red tomato lava spurted straight onto the bottom of the bunk above. It clung there momentarily and then began to plop back into my face! How messy! How inglorious!

After cleaning up, I searched out the boatswain-cum-doctor and told him what I thought of his remedy. I finally did become immune to this dreadful disease, and ever after I have been able to cheerfully go through any storm anytime, eat anything, and hold it down with the greatest of ease and pleasure. I had become an old salt!

Becoming an old salt entails more than getting over being seasick, which is the story of the next chapter.

Chapter 11

My Corvette Life
(1942-1945)

Standing Watch:

Each division of the ship was organized so that all responsibilities were covered at any time. This included engineering, deck hands, radio, radar, sonar, signals, and officers. This was true whether the ship was at sea or in port. Generally one had a four-hour period on watch and then an eight-hour period off watch during which time one took care of sleeping, eating, washing clothes, and personal things such as writing letters. The system worked pretty well as long as the person replacing one on watch was on time. Occasionally someone would sleep in and be late. When that transpired the tardy person would have to make up the lost time on the following rotation.

My watches took place on the bridge of the ship. There was a standup type of desk, covered by a metal hood, to afford some protection from the weather. In a cabinet under the desk there were books dealing with navigation, flags, flares, etc. One of the key functions of the signalman on duty was to keep the log of events that took place on his watch. This would range from nothing at all to general quarters alarm to fight off a submarine attack.

On the forward part of the bridge a door opened into the sonar operator's equipment room, and to the rear of the bridge there was a door that opened into the radar room. There was a lookout posted on the starboard side and one posted on the port side. The duty officer's position was just forward of the signal desk in the center of the bridge where the compass and all means of communication to the wheel house, engine room, radar, sonar, chart room, and gunnery stations were located. I was in a good spot to know what was happening at any given moment when I was on duty because all the information relating to anything vital flowed through the officer on duty.

The bridge was open to the weather with the exception of a tarp that was strung over the spot where the officer's station was located, so when it was sunny and hot we had some shade, and when it was raining, we could get out of the rain. The people on the bridge who had it the most difficult in inclement climate were the seamen who were lookouts on either side. They had to remain exactly where they were placed, rain, shine, sleet, or snow. Their time on duty was the toughest of all when the weather was foul.

Route Traveled:

For all of my time on the *Impulse*, we guarded convoys on the route between New York City and Guantanamo Bay, Cuba. It was a path where the U-boats lay in wait to sink tankers traveling from the Gulf of Mexico to New York City, from there to the Allies in Europe, and freighters reloading in New York City and returning to North Africa. It was a lucrative spot for the Germans to knock off supplies right at the source. The easiest opportunity for them was just after we had passed through a storm. Some of the convoy would not be able to keep up. There would be ships straggling out behind the escort vessels and out of the protective range of sonar. They would often be blown up one at a time. It was mandatory that the escort ships stick with the main part of the convoy that was still intact so that the majority would survive.

Each trip took about two weeks, depending on conditions. We would have about four days on either end to resupply, and then we would return. The round trip usually took between four to five weeks. During the winter we would leave New York City in blustering freezing temperatures, and gradually, day by day as we moved southward, it would get warmer and warmer until we reached the balmy air of the Caribbean. When the seas were calm, the storms abated and the subs silent, it was almost like being on a pleasure cruise, except the meals and the sleeping accommodation were in vast contrast. Of course it was also true that it wasn't pleasant to leave the warmth of the islands to move into territory that, day by day, got more frigid and foreboding as we moved north.

This oscillating environment created a need for a range of clothing to be ready for use depending on the temperature where we found ourselves on any given day. For winter wear at sea, we were issued overalls, jackets, and hats with earflaps, all of which were lined with synthetic material that we called monkey fur. It was warm and comfortable when we had to stand watch in the freezing cold. We also had a large thick woolen parka, which was left over from the days when the British had the ship. There was one for the officer of the day and one for the each of the lookouts and one for the signalman on duty. These were used only in times of windy, frigid conditions. On the other end of the scale, we had cotton skivvies, T-shirts, and trousers to wear in the hot and humid climate in Cuba.

Weather:

The Atlantic coast from the Gulf of Mexico to New Jersey was the track the hurricanes used to vent their fury. Today we have satellite pictures to let us know when one of them is on its way. In those days we had very little warning about what was coming. It would not have mattered anyhow because we had to keep the forces on the front lines in Europe and North Africa equipped to do their part of the job, and we could not let the weather deter us no matter how bad it became. And it became very bad at times!

A violent Atlantic storm lasting a week or more is one of the most apprehensive, exhausting, enervating encounters that I have personally endured in my entire life. They were fearsome and yet captivating at the same time. They seemed to have a vicious savagery, mixed with frolic, as they tossed us around like a cat playing with a mouse.

It was a constant ride on a rollercoaster. One minute we would be perched on a high surge overlooking the whole convoy. Ten seconds later, our ship would be plunged into a deep crater. All the other ships had disappeared. We were left alone staring at an angry sky framed by gray-green ragged ridges of rough water. The episode would be repeated again and again, hour after hour, in daylight and darkness, day after day after day. The decks shifted beneath us, tossing everyone and everything from one bulkhead to another and back again. Bruises and broken equipment accumulated as the days passed. Muscles grew sore and tight in the unceasing struggle to maintain one's balance in the simple activities of walking, standing, or sitting. The metal monster beneath us bucked and pranced as the writhing, thrashing sea tormented it. Eating a normal meal was impossible under those conditions, let alone preparing it. Consequently all that we had to eat for days at a time were sandwiches and coffee or some other soft drink.

Storms at sea are bad in the daytime, but the night brings its own special horror. When one can see the monster attacking in all its fury, one can brace for the coming blow. At night, or when in the bowls of the ship, visual contact is taken away. There is the sense of not knowing from which angle one is going to be slammed or which way to lean to keep from falling down. The ship and the sailors on board are at the mercy of the constant, unseen, uncontrollable sway of an angry ocean.

Having a restful sleep was next to impossible. The only way not to be thrown out of a bunk was to lie on one's stomach with arms and legs spread wide and hold on. All of this torture resulted in frayed nerves and short fuses. Disagreements and arguments among the crew broke out. Many friendships were destroyed as harsh words were exchanged out of pent-up frustration and fatigue.

When freezing winds were added to stormy conditions, the discomfort of it all was raised a notch higher. When our course would take the ship head-on into the crest of the breaking waves, the briny sea would be thrown over the forecastle. It would wallop its way over the entire superstructure of the vessel, including the open bridge where we had little protection from this onslaught of the ocean. What made it more dangerous and harsh was the instant gelling into ice. This produced hazardous conditions to be overcome while we stood our watches. Everything was covered with a coat of ice—the deck, our equipment, our clothes. When we changed course, the sea would catch us broadside, causing the ship to roll perilously. The decks became sheets of slippery steel providing no foothold. The only way to maintain one's equilibrium was to grasp something that was fastened firmly to the ship and hang on. Often we would lose our grip and slide along the deck, but for the railing around the bridge, we would have gone over the side. This situation did not cause us to surrender to the sea any of our crew, but in the course of my tenure in convoy escort duty, several merchant-ship sailors were thrown into the Atlantic in this fashion. This meant certain death for anyone who had this misadventure, not only because of the cold water but also because we were under strict instructions not to stop to look for anyone. Our duty was to always maintain our position of protection for the convoy against submarine attacks. Fortunately for us, we seldom had to face these extreme elements for more than a couple of days at a time. The movement of the convoy soon took us into more favorable conditions.

However, there was one instance, when traveling north toward New York City, we took a freezing sea constantly on our port bow for about four days. The persistent pounding coated that side of the *Impulse* with ice to the thickness of six to eight inches all over the topside. The total weight of this accumulation was enormous, causing the ship to list to port about ten degrees from the norm. This put us in jeopardy of capsizing when we were exposed to situations that created extreme rolls from side to side. We limped into New York harbor looking like a Mack truck with all the tires flat on the left side. It was the first and only time that I felt any doubt as to the seaworthiness of the *Impulse*. The ice was removed, and we returned to sea about four days later.

The weather was not always stormy. The sea could be very alluring, seductive, and charming. There were many trips where the gently rolling ocean surface mesmerized us into thinking that it was only a passive pussycat. They were times to be enjoyed and savored. In these sessions we got to see an impressive pageantry of ships trailing behind us, proceeding in an orderly fashion surrounded by escort vessels providing protection according to plan. It also afforded us the chance to observe some of the creatures of the sea.

The porpoises provided great entertainment. They would charge from afar as if they were going to devour the ship then, at the last moment before impact, they would veer alongside and dance around the hull. They would slap their tails on the bow and dash on ahead as if to say, "Come on, slowpokes, let's race!" The waters are very phosphorescent in the Caribbean, and sometimes at night a lone porpoise would swim directly at the ship, resembling a torpedo racing toward us. Many an inexperienced lookout had a conniption the first time or two this happened on his watch!

The Caribbean nights at sea were filled with majestic tranquility when the sky was clear and the winds were calm. Often on those evenings I would take my mattress and pillow to the forecastle to sleep when I was off duty. It was an exotic happening. The satin silence was enhanced by the slushy sound of the bow making its way through the phosphorescent water, accompanied by the thud of the odd flying fish mistaking the deck for a watery landing area. The umbrella of the universe was spread overhead, leaving one poised on the edge of eternity. All the while, the undulating swells moving underneath the vessel rocked one into a sense of peace and security.

It was on such a night I had an encounter with the God of all Creation that was personal, powerful, lucid, overwhelming, and indelible. It has remained an underlying factor in the driving force of my life. My constant deep desire has been to be His faithful servant despite my many shortcomings.

Engaging the Enemy:

Fighting an antisubmarine warfare was a hide-and-seek operation. This was true no matter which side one was on. The convoys tried to hide from the seeking U-boats by zigzagging their courses to avoid torpedo fire. When the subs found their targets, they would try to escape the seeking convoy escort vessels to avoid being destroyed by depth charges. Sometimes the subs won, and sometimes we won. No matter who the winner was, the result would be death to someone.

Sonar was the equipment we used to find the U-boats when they were under water. It would send out a sound like ping! in constantly changing directions from the ship. If the ping hit something solid, it would echo back: ping! Our ship would move in that direction. As we closed in, the length of time between the original ping! and its echo shortened until we were directly over the sub. Our aim was to drop depth charges in a pattern around the submarine, which were set to explode close to the depth of the sub. The idea was to create enough pressure to crack its hull and sink it. We ran many attacks on these enemy vessels. It was hard to tell how many we sank because of the tricks they played to fool us.

One of the ways of determining whether our tactics were successful was the boiling up of an oil slick from the site of the detonation along with other debris, indicating that the sub had been destroyed. However, one of the maneuvers they used was to discharge oil, clothing, etc., out of the torpedo tubes that would float to the surface. Then the sub would quietly sink to a greater depth. They hoped that we would think we had destroyed them and depart. Sometimes we did go away. But sometimes we stuck around and outwaited them until they moved; then we took another run at them.

This was a vicious and deadly game. For the German sailors, to lose was to die. During the year 1942 there were 257 Allied ships torpedoed in the Caribbean. This number was reduced to twenty-two in 1943 and two in 1944. This was largely due to the activity of the convoy escort ships.

The photo here shows the searchlight we used to communicate between ships in the convoy since we were not allowed to have radio contact. The white spot in the water shows the explosion of a depth charge. The spot in the sky above is another charge about to hit the water.

Often we would go to our bunks below the waterline with the knowledge that our aircraft had sighted a wolf pack lying in wait for us. To say the least, it was an uneasy feeling to know that a torpedo could blow us out of the water at any time. I had great empathy for the fellows who had to work in the engine room under those conditions. At least when I was on the bridge, I felt I had a fighting chance.

Ship's Company:

The personnel on the *Impulse* came from every part of the United States and all strata of economic and social levels. There was a rapid change over in all of the departments because of the urgency to train as many sailors as quickly as possible to supply newly constructed convoy escort vessels with trained crews. After the first six months the turnover slowed down somewhat, and the basic complement remained the same for the next year.

It was an interesting exercise to talk with fellows from varying backgrounds and to watch how they fit or didn't fit into the mélange of the *Impulse*. Some of them stand out in my memory more than others.

The first captain I had was certainly one that I will never forget. He was a regular navy type who had spent some years in the service before the war began. His rank was lieutenant commander and had obviously been passed over for more prestigious commands than the one he was stuck with. From the moment he took control of the bridge on the very first night that I spent on the ship, I had the sense that he was incompetent, insecure, and afraid. As soon as the pilots left the bridge to return to the harbor, he went to his cabin and for the most part remained there until we pulled into Guantanamo Bay. Whereupon he surfaced all spiffy in his dress whites. He would be the first one ashore, and we wouldn't see him again until it was time for us to shove off for New York City. It was the same on the return trip with a repeat on the other end. The few times he would appear on the bridge when we were at sea, he would be dressed in long johns. He was transferred after several months, and I never saw him again. Fortunately for us, we always had a good executive officer as second-in-command.

One of the executive officers that we had during my stay on the *Impulse* was a fellow from North Carolina. He and I became as close as an enlisted person and a commissioned officer can be under USN regulations. We spent a lot of hours together when we both shared the same watch. I was interested in learning about the south, and he was interested to learn about Canada. His name was Jim Early.

Jim got the opportunity to get his own command and was transferred to captain a minesweeper. He had his job about four months when they struck a mine. He was blown up along with his crew. This was sad news for me.

Our chief boatswain was an interesting character. He was born and bred in Chicago and had spent all of working life in the police department of that city. Just prior to joining the navy, he was a homicide detective. He was a rough, tough man with vile language and a coarse sense of humor, but he was loyal to his men and they returned in kind. He was a valuable friend but could be a dreaded opponent. Fortunately for me I didn't have to report to him, and where our paths crossed in the line of duty, we had mutual respect for each other.

The closest and longest lasting friendship I had on that ship was with Gary Edwards. He was from Lansing, Michigan. Before joining the navy, Gary was a bass player in a blues and swing band. He was a sonar man aboard ship and sat locked in a small darkroom, listening to ping! ping! ping! for four hours at a stretch. For the most part it was a boring operation until a sub was located. Then he was the focal point of attention. I used to spend some of my time with him while he was on duty listening to him talk about music and the people he knew in the music world. He composed many songs during his lonely hours on watch in spite of the saturation of sound caused by the constant repetitive monotonous monotone ping! I have often wondered if any of his songs became popular after the war. I spent a lot of my liberty time with him in New York City.

Shore Leave:

When we were in port, it was the standard procedure for one half of the crew to be allowed to go ashore for twenty-four hours and then the other half to have the opportunity to leave the ship for the next twenty-four hours. This made it possible for the ship to get underway with enough hands on board to make the vessel operational at all times. It was not mandatory to go ashore on what we called liberty.

Sometimes there was a lot of trading of days off, when sailors would agree among themselves to standby for each other so that a person could get three or four days in a row. This was particularly helpful in New York City, which was within striking distance of many of the hometowns of the fellows on the *Impulse*.

In addition to liberty times, we could request for a leave of absence, which would in effect be a holiday or compassionate time (if there had been a death or some tragedy in one's family). It could be as long as two weeks and was usually tied to the sailor's seniority and length of time at sea. On the duty we had, there were only two ports of call for the most part, Guantanamo Bay and New York City. They were two vastly different liberty ports.

Guantanamo Bay:

Guantanamo Bay—or Gitmo, as the U.S. Navy nicknamed it—fell into the control of the U.S. government during the Spanish-American War. The United States signed an agreement with Cuba in 1903 to lease nine thousand acres on Cuban soil surrounding the bay. It was transformed into a large base for American military operations in the Caribbean. It remains under lease to this day. It is a well-sheltered spacious harbor that can accommodate many ships.

During WWII it was a vital staging area for the formation of convoys supplying the troops in North African and Mediterranean operations. It was a pivotal point for the oil tankers whose destination was the north Atlantic and those carrying manufactured goods from the factories in the northeastern States, heading across the south Atlantic.

I found it to be a very restful place after enduring the clawing of the sea on so many occasions. My days ashore were often spent on airplane patrols over the surrounding waters, looking for submarines. The observers who had to do it every day were glad to be spelled off, and I was thrilled to be able to get aloft in any old aircraft that would have me. Our nights ashore were spent on the base. Usually we were not permitted on Cuban territory, but exceptions were made. Sometimes we were given a tightly supervised liberty in Santiago that gave us a flavor of Cuban society and permitted us to buy souvenirs native to the region. I bought and sent home many articles (everything from purses to picture frames) made of caiman skins, which are a type of crocodile.

When we were in Gitmo we anchored in the middle of the harbor along with most of the other naval ships that were active in that part of the world. When we were at sea we had to maintain total blackout conditions, but when we were in the harbor we could have the lights on. This meant that we could use the yardarm blinkers to talk to the sailors on the other vessels around us. The opportunity was presented to the signalmen who were on watch to chat with the signalmen from different walks of life and geographical origins during duty hours in port. I met many interesting people via Morse code at that time.

We had to engage in periodic training exercises while staying in Guantanamo. This meant that we left port during daylight hours with friendly subs that would submerge. Our task was to locate and execute mock depth-charge runs on them. At the same time we would have friendly airplanes towing targets above us on which we practiced our anti-aircraft guns. The seas were always smooth, and the sun was shining during these events, so it was a bit of a picnic for us to have the odd day just to drift here and there in the Caribbean while we waited for the next friendly attack to be organized.

Fishing for sharks was one of the activities the crew engaged in at those times. Some raw meat was attached to a hook then tied to the end of a heaving line and thrown over the stern to troll behind us. When the shark struck, several sailors would haul it in. They would then drag it alongside the ship and shoot it in the head with a bullet from a .45 pistol. The carcass would be retrieved on deck and skinned. The teeth of the creature would be knocked out. After a slipshod tanning, the skin would be made into wallets. When the teeth had dried, they would be strung together to form a necklace. Homemade souvenirs!

Every evening there was either a movie or a troupe of entertainers at the outdoor theater. This was another diversion that was available to us. So all things considered, our visits to this base became a pleasant oasis after the battering of the sea and the tension of submarine alerts, which often filled our journey from New York City.

New York City:

This city was, and is, one of the great metropolises of the world to visit. We were lucky to be able to spend some time there every four or six weeks when we were doing our job in wartime. Servicemen, especially sailors, were kings in those days. Everyone was so proud of us. They seemed to feel that they could never do enough for us, even to the point of civilian strangers wanting to pay for our meals when we sat down to eat in restaurants. The four days or so that were our usual stay in New York City were prized by all hands.

There were so many sights to see and so many things to do that the time we had ashore seemed so short. I got to see many of the major attractions such as the Statue of Liberty and the Empire State Building. The activity that brought me the most pleasure was being able to see and hear the big bands playing in the name hotels. I had Gary (the sonar man) to thank for making arrangements. He knew some of the musicians and hotel management. We got royal treatment wherever we went. One of the super benefits was to sleep in first-class hotel accommodation on real beds, usually at no cost to us. This was a special boon if we were returning from a rough, sleepless, tense voyage for the previous couple of weeks.

I also spent some time in Kearny visiting my relatives every couple of months. It was about an hour of train ride from New York City. They enjoyed seeing me, and I enjoyed their company as well. It provided a chance to catch up on all the news relating to the movements of some of my cousins who were also in various branches of the military service.

I always phoned my parents and Harriet at the first opportunity upon arrival in port. My mother was a worrier, particularly where her children were concerned. I tried to reassure her as much as I could.

Periodically our ship needed to go into dry docks for repairs. This afforded the crew more time to have for leave. To accomplish the required work generally required about a week or two. Consequently the ship's complement took off for spots all over the USA and, in my case, for Toronto, Canada.

There was always a skeleton crew who remained aboard ship while the rest went on vacation. While I was attached to the *Impulse*, there were three or four dry-dock times. I had to stay on board for one of them. It was a strange experience to see the ship perched up high and dry! It also was a noisy, smelly undergoing. There were blowtorches, welding arc lamps, and rivet hammers going all the time. During the night shift the whole scene was bathed in sea of relentless spotlights. It was a surrealistic setting designed to drive one mad! I was so relieved when that particular period passed.

However, the other times we had dry-docked I was permitted to go home. I also had been able to put two or three days together once in a while to make a fast trip to Toronto. So I kept in contact to some degree. I even got to visit my parents' cottage in Haliburton, which was a rare treat!

On one of those trips Harriet and I became engaged, and on another, we were married. There was no thought given to the responsibilities or consequences of forming such a union. The uncertainty of being alive to enjoy life after the war colored everything. The immediate grasping of passing moments seemed paramount. The wedding took place in Central Gospel Hall. After we were married, Harriet moved to New York City and stayed with a family from the church who had recently been transferred to one of the boroughs. We were able to spend time together in between convoys. She enjoyed her employment with a firm on Wall Street.

After I had served on the *Impulse* for about eighteen months, a directive arrived on the ship ordering me to report for a medical examination before being transferred to a naval station for the training of airplane pilots! Needless to say, I was ecstatic! I reported for the medical, but much to my chagrin, my right eye did not come up to the required standards. I had to remain where I was. I blamed my problem on looking through the telescope so much while on duty.

The face of the war was changing early in 1944, and the need for my services in convoy escort duties had passed. I had worked hard to upgrade myself while on the *Impulse* and had risen from seaman to petty officer, first class. I started out as a striker and finished being in charge of the signal operation on the bridge. The USN deemed that my services were needed elsewhere, and they shipped me off to Little Creek to be placed in a pool of personnel for further assignment. It was near the large naval station at Norfolk, Virginia.

Chapter 12

LSM Flotilla Eleven
(1944-1945)

Digest of the Times and Circumstance:
(Spring 1944)

The Axis powers were defeated in Africa, and the Allies were progressing well in their invasion of Italy. The tide was beginning to turn in drastic fashion against Mussolini and Hitler.

The U-boat strategy of the Germans had been squashed by the combined efforts of the Allied air power and convoy escort vessels. The supply line to Europe from America had been cleared. The mass of troops and military equipment was poised for the invasion of the continent from Great Britain.

D-Day on June 6, 1944, spelled the beginning of what would prove to be the eventual humiliating conquest of the Axis forces. It would take another year to bring it to a conclusion.

The United States was increasingly devoting more of its attention to strengthening its capability to defeat the Japanese. Since there appeared to be a need to invade Japan before this could be accomplished, there was an acceleration of the production of equipment and the training of personnel to achieve this goal.

Personal Thoughts and Memories:

Little Creek Naval Amphibious Training Base:

About one month before D-Day, I was transferred to the amphibious training base where there were a variety of assignments presented to us.

The two that were offered to me were the lead signalman on a submarine or the lead signalman attached to the commodore of a flotilla of LSMs.

Having pounded to death submarines for the past couple of years, the first option didn't seem very appealing! I chose to throw my lot in with LSM Flotilla Eleven. I reported to Lt. Commander T. R. Langley, who was the commodore of the flotilla and was to be my boss for the remainder of my naval career.

The flotilla staff consisted of the commodore, four commissioned officers, and four enlisted men. We each had our departments to oversee. They were visual communication, radio communication, radar, and navigation. We had thirty ships for which to be responsible. Each ship had its complement of sailors. The captain of each ship reported to the commodore. While the commodore and his staff were quartered on one of the ships of the flotilla, we had nothing to do with the day-to-day operation of that particular vessel. The ship that we were aboard was known as the flagship because all the orders for action originated with the commodore.

LSM stands for landing-ship medium. They were designed to carry small tanks and armored cars for release on an enemy beach. LSTs (landing-ship tanks) had been used successfully in other invasions, but there was a need for smaller, more agile units to support the soldiers who were going into the face of enemy fire.

The configuration of an LSM is very different from a conventional ship. It is similar to an elongated steel box with thick sides and no top. There is a conning tower on the right side that sticks up above the rest of the structure, presenting a profile not unlike that of a submarine. The conning tower is where the control of the ship takes place. The stern is where the engine, the sleeping quarters, the galley, the dining room, the head, and laundry is all located. The bow of the LSM is composed of two massive doors that meet in the middle to form a prow so that the ship can plow through the water. There is a large ramp immediately aft of these doors, which is carried in a vertical position when at sea, ready to be lowered through the open doors when the ship is beached. It provides the access to the landing area for the vehicles.

At the extreme stern there was a large winch with a powerful engine. There was a steel cable wound around it to which was attached a big anchor. The purpose of this mechanism was to extract the LSM from the beach after releasing the tanks and armored cars.

Norfolk, Virginia:

We were told that it would take several months to train all of crews of Flotilla Eleven. Some of the vessels were still under construction, and the men were yet to be assigned. This meant that we could send for our wives to live in nearby Norfolk.

Norfolk was truly a sailor's town. The USN had taken over everything. Even the sidewalks appeared to be paved with sailors. Any street downtown was a stream of white gob hats bobbing along in different directions. This mass of military personnel and their families, along with the people connected to supporting businesses, made it difficult to find accommodation for any new arrival in the city.

So when Harriet came, I could barely get a place to stay. The only thing that was available was a room in a fifth-rate hotel. We had a cubicle that was filthy, and to make matters worse, the bathroom was at the end of a long dirty corridor that we had to share with all the other inmates on the floor. It was a most degrading beginning to what turned out to be a pleasant period in our lives.

One of the fellows on the flotilla staff was from New York. His wife moved to the area also for the time that we were running the training operation. His name was Bill Santic. He was a radioman, first class, in charge of that end of our staff duties. We got along well, and so did our wives. The result was that we rented a house that we shared where our wives could live and we could come home when we didn't have sea duty. Because we were attached to the commodore's staff, we didn't have regular duties to perform in relation to any ship or the base at Little Creek.

The Amphibious Base was much like any other military base with its rows of neat barracks assigned to individual units. Our staff had office space and sleeping quarters. However, Santic and I went home most nights when we were not on maneuvers. I enjoyed this a great deal. We could have home-cooked meals and pretend we had a real life for a while. There was a path that ran along behind the houses on the block where we lived. Santic and I usually took a stroll there in the summer evenings. There was different vegetation than we had in the north. Among the variety of new trees was a fig tree. There were delicious ripe figs on it, and the owner encouraged us to help ourselves, which we did with gusto! It was the first time that I had tasted fresh figs. We did a number of things together as a couple of couples. One was going to Virginia Beach and swimming in the surf. It was delightful to be enjoying the beach side of the Atlantic again. I had spent the last two years fighting submarines just a few miles directly offshore.

Training LSM Flotilla Eleven:

The crews of the LSMs performed some shakedown cruises on their own so that they could become acquainted with the general performance of the vessels. When that was accomplished, they joined us to execute as a unit the maneuvers for which we were intended. This required going out to sea and practicing twisting and turning into various configurations without bumping into each other. Flags hoisted from the yardarm conveyed specific orders from the commodore that were to be carried out by the flotilla when we hauled them down. It was a new and interesting experience for me. We trained clusters of five or six at a time, culminating in landing light tanks (complete with live soldiers) on a beach called Rehoboth. As each group finished training, they departed for the Pacific Ocean to wait until our whole flotilla joined them.

The enlisted men who were attached to the
Commodore of flotilla 11

Points of the entire period I spent at Little Creek. The landing area was about one hundred miles north of our base. Every assault was planned as if it were the real thing. Since we had to travel up the Atlantic coast and the timing had to exactly coincide with the landing of the rest of the "invasion," our precise departure and travel time had to be calculated in advance. Sometimes the invasion would take place during daylight and sometimes at night or at dawn. Each one of these forays would consume two or three days and provide a variety of conditions for us to experience.

The exercises presented a formidable sight as the flotilla approached the beach in formation and then split as it fanned out along the shore.

The speed at which we impacted the land was critical. It had to have enough momentum for the LSM to get close enough to the beach so the ramp could reach the land to enable the tanks to disembark, and not so much momentum that it grounded the ship too firmly, making disengagement impossible.

The second most critical part of the landing was to know when to drop the anchor off the stern of the vessel. Just the right amount of cable needed to be released so that the action of the winch and anchor would pull the ship off the land when the engines were reversed.

Some captains of these landing craft were ninety-day wonders. This was a term used for officers who were fresh out of university, with much theory and little practical experience in seamanship. Consequently there were many blunders made and embarrassing situations created. Sometimes the captains would misjudge the speed of the landing and stop far short of the beach. Since it was a "real" invasion, the tanks had to go down the ramps anyhow, which resulted in them submerging into the water. Fortunately for the soldiers the caterpillar treads on the machines kept on churning and dragged them onto dry land. They were soaked but safely delivered, as they cursed the navy for its incompetence.

Other times the captains would have lots of speed but would release their anchors too soon. This was a real dilemma! It meant the ship would ride way up onto the beach and the cable would run out and fall off behind the LSM into the water, leaving it stranded with no way to pull itself back to sea. It had to sit there until high tide floated it or a navy tug came and retrieved it. All the other LSMs in the maneuver would take off for the base and leave the sad sitting duck abandoned and mortified. Sometimes it would require a couple of extra days for it to get back to Little Creek. Upon arrival, the crew of the hapless vessel would have to endure the good-natured ribbing of the other members of the flotilla.

There were other aspects of the training program designed to equip members of the flotilla staff to be prepared to fit in where and when needed. Two, in which I participated, were shallow-water diving and the operation of depth sounding equipment.

Depth Sounding Equipment:

There was a covered launch about thirty feet long filled with all types of gear used to execute a landing without the benefit of visually seeing where one was in relation to the beach. This included a depth sounder, which was employed to determine the contour of the bottom as one approached the landing spot. It was my job to learn how to read and to interpret the readings as they applied to the known contour of the target. It was not difficult, but it was interesting to understand this aspect of one of the many items that had to be coordinated to achieve a good result. The thing that I didn't like about this exercise was that we were shut into a dark confined space for lengthy stretches in choppy water with a dozen people, most of whom who smoked. I came close to reverting to my previous motion sickness malady.

Diving:

The flotilla needed to have some sailors who were able to repair underneath the LSMs should something happen when we were far from port. Consequently volunteers were requested to get some rudimentary training in diving. Since my enjoyment of the water added to the fact that it sounded like fun, I put my name forward.

Our first lesson took place off a barge on a sunny day in Chesapeake Bay. There were about six of us who were students. In addition there was the instructor and his assistant. On the deck lay a full diver's suit complete with a metal helmet with glass visor and lead shoes. Beside it lay a neatly coiled long skinny rubber hose, a long rope, and a thin line. A chair and an air pump powered by a small gas engine stood at the ready. There were two sailors scheduled to go down ahead of me. The water was thirty-three-feet deep. We were to be lowered to the ocean floor to determine if we could tolerate the depth psychologically and physically.

The first guy sat in the chair and proceeded to put the gear on with the help of the instructor. When he was properly suited, the helmet was secured with the hose attached, which supplied a flow of air from the pump. The rope was firmly secured to lower him and to raise him as necessary. The line was clipped to his waist to be used to signal to the handlers on the barge. The most important signal was three short sharp pulls. That meant emergency! "Get me up in a hurry!" He made his clumsy way to the edge of the barge and inched his way down a ladder.

He was slowly lowered. When he got to the eleven-foot level the descent was stopped for a short time and then commenced again until the twenty-two-foot stage, with another pause and then finally to the bottom. We were told the reason for this procedure was to allow for blood pressure acclimatization. He was down there for a while then signaled that he was ready to return to the barge. When his faceplate broke the surface of the water, the inside was covered with blood. His nose was bleeding! It was a most disconcerting sight for a novice to see just before his maiden voyage!

The apparatus was cleaned up and put on the next candidate. The same procedure was followed. He returned smiling and full of enthusiasm. Now it was my turn.

When the helmet was secured over my head and the air was hissing around my ears, I felt a sense of isolation and helplessness that I had not experienced heretofore. It was with trepidation that I took the hesitant steps down the ladder and let go of the last rung. I slowly sank into the depths as the brilliant sunlight was exchanged for a misty then a sultry and, finally, a murky green as my lead boots hit the sandy bottom. I was in a new and mystery-shrouded world.

My apprehension evaporated as I began to test my ability to move around and to visually scan what appeared to be a vast desert of unending sand, lightly veiled in emerald gossamer. I set out to walk as far as I could. I lost all concept of time until I was rudely brought to heel by a sharp tug on my line, indicating that it was the moment to return to the top. My first lesson was a complete success from my point of view, and the instructor seemed to think I could continue, which is what I did.

Diving in those days entailed wearing a full suit as I have described. Skin diving, as we know it today, had not been developed. Cumbersome as it was, it was all that we had. It required quite a lot of practice to move around clad in such unwieldy paraphernalia. One of the procedures we had to master was getting under the hull of the ships, because that was the most likely area that we would be required to perform. On one of these dummy runs I was to go under the stern of one of the LSMs that was moored alongside a wharf.

The diving barge was anchored nearby, and I descended. I was making my way toward the propeller of the ship when I realized that my suit was filling up with water. It reached the level of my shoulders and was rapidly moving up my neck. I didn't have much time before it would cover my mouth and nose. I had to do something fast! I didn't think there was enough time to have them pull me back up, so I made for the cavity that housed the propeller where I knew there was a pocket of air and a steel strut on which I could pull myself out of the water. I just made it!

I sat there contemplating what my next move would be, and much to my relief, the water receded down my torso. I could not figure out what was wrong because it had never happened before. To make matters worse, I didn't have confidence in my handlers on the surface. They were kibitzers who were always joking around, not paying attention to the job at hand. I finally decided that the only hope I had was to give the emergency pull on the line, push off the strut, and pray that they would get me up before I drowned. That was what I did and barely made to the surface as the water covered my mouth.

Much to my chagrin, the sloppiness of the tenders on the barge was the cause of my near fatality. On the diving helmet there is a petcock, which is used to drain excess air or water from the unit.

As they lowered me into the water, one of the ropes flipped the valve open, which invited the sea to fill up my suit. I had not been told about this valve and didn't know to check it when I was in the middle of my dilemma. I was very careful after that experience to have people in whom I had great confidence attend my lines when I went under water tied into that diving suit.

Liberties and Leave:

As I have mentioned, Santic and I were fortunate to be able to spend our liberties with our wives because of the unique situation we had as members of the flotilla commodore's staff. I only got one leave while I was at Little Creek that I can recall, but it was a humdinger!

Christmastime occurred during our period in Norfolk, and I was given leave of absence. Harriet and I decided we would take the opportunity to go home to Toronto.

Our plan was to travel by train. The trouble was that almost all the thousands of gobs in the Norfolk area had been granted leave at the same time. Every means of transportation was jammed to the rafters. There was nothing straight through to Washington DC or New York that we could get on. We decided to try to get part way and hope for the best. We forced our way onto a train that would take us in the general direction. I forget where we had to get off, but it was far from any place we wanted to be. There seemed to be only one hope, and that was to find our way to a highway that would take us to Washington. This is what we did.

Harriet had a fluffy white fox-fur collar on a light green cloth coat. It was cold and snowing. Wet soggy snow made a mess of her collar. The highway was lined with sailors who had the same idea: hitchhike somewhere! The situation seemed to be bleak and hopeless. We put our thumbs up anyway, and soon a flat open trailer truck stopped and offered us a ride to DC. Harriet could get in the cab with the truckers, and I would have to climb on the back with about fifty other sailors! We didn't have much choice. It was cold and wet and windy, but the one redeeming feature was a canvas tarp that we pulled over us. We disembarked in Washington at the railway station dirty, disheveled, and dismayed.

The conditions were no more favorable. Sailors were sprawled all over the floor with no possibility of going anywhere. What were we to do now? It was opportune that Harriet's uncle (the one who was in Newport, Rhode Island, when I was in boot camp) had been transferred to DC.

Harriet phoned him. He and her aunt were delighted that we were in town. They found us and took us to their home, where they pampered us over the whole Christmas season. We saw many of the sights and historic places and had a wonderful vacation before setting off for Norfolk. The return trip was much more civilized. We didn't get to Toronto, but we had a fine vacation just the same.

Chapter 13

The End of the War for Me
(1945)

Digest of the Times and Circumstance:

By the end of June 1945 world politics had undergone an extensive transformation:

Roosevelt died and was replaced by Harry Truman as president of the United States.

The Allied war machine had rolled over the Axis forces in Europe, flattening them to the heart of Berlin.

Italian patriots publicly hanged Mussolini to death.

Hitler committed suicide in a private bunker in his central command post in Berlin.

The Germans surrendered unconditionally. The world celebrated V-E Day on May 8, 1945.

There had been many gains in the war against Japan during the past year. The moment had now arrived when there would be a complete concentration on bringing the Japanese to their knees.

Personal Thoughts and Memories:

Training Complete:

We had finished training all of the ships in our flotilla and had received orders to sail to San Diego with the final ten ships in the early part of August 1945.

When we got the news of our soon departure, Bill Santic and I realized our wives had to go home. Harriet returned to Toronto pregnant with our first child. It was difficult to part because at that point in time it appeared as though our flotilla was headed for dangerous assignments.

We shoved off, all ten ships of us, and headed for the open waters of the Caribbean. Our cargo was large steel pontoons to be used as bridges or docks in the South Pacific. It seemed strange for me to be sailing calmly along in the same waters that I had traveled in convoy escort duty under threat of the subs. Now the U-boats were all gone, and we could proceed in peace. Our first port was to be Balboa on the Atlantic side of the Panama Canal. We sailed in formation all the way, which gave us a sense of pride.

One of the enjoyable activities that I remember from that trip was the huge bubbling warm springs that we had at our disposal. It was fun to be up on the bridge, but down below in our quarters was full of noise pollution and diesel oil fumes. It was a relief to escape to our private swimming pool.

The pool was located just inside the huge doors that formed the bow of the ship when they were closed. They did not shut completely at the point where they joined to form the bow of the vessel. The result was that as the craft moved forward, the water surged through the opening and filled up the cavity that was created by the upright ramp used for disembarking the light tanks and armored vehicles and the sides of the ship. The basin produced was about twenty feet by ten feet in size. It made a perfect spa with warm salty bubbling seawater. Soothing, relaxing!

Panama Canal:

The Norfolk to the Panama Canal cruise was delightful. After a few days we pulled into the city of Balboa on the Atlantic end of the canal. While we were in port, the first atomic bomb was dropped on Hiroshima. This made a huge line of demarcation in the history of the world. It was August 6, 1945. Three days later the second atomic bomb was dropped on Nagasaki. It was August 9, 1945.

During those three momentous days we traveled through the canal. Speculation was rampant among the crew. What would it all mean? Had the Japanese surrendered? Was the war over? Could we go home?

As we made our way through the canal, the rain poured down in a torrent day and night. The progress was slow and methodical. The flotilla proceeded through the locks in clusters and reassembled when we emerged on the Pacific Ocean, where we reformed and began our journey along the coast of Central America and Mexico en route to San Diego.

As we journeyed, excitement filled the hearts and minds of all hands as we wondered what the end result would be for each of us. The Japanese had indicated that they surrendered, but we had not received official word as yet from the navy. On the twelfth of August we had a chapel service. The call to worship began with the words "Our help is in the Name of the Lord, Who made heaven and earth." The Scripture reading was Psalm 124:8. Our executive officer gave a talk on "Be not deceived; God is not mocked; for whatsoever a man sows that shall he also reap" from Galatians 6:7.

On August 15, 1945, a radio message was received from the admiral of the fleet Ernest J. King, which said in part, "The day of final victory has at last arrived. Japan has surrendered. Her fleet, which once boasted that it would drive us from the seas, has been destroyed." On the same day an officer in each command was set aside to determine who would be the first of the enlisted men to return to civilian status.

A point system was established, allowing credit to be accumulated for length of service, amount of time in sea duty, and how much of that was in combat, etc. The result was that I had more than enough to qualify for an honorable discharge. I was elated and couldn't wait to get to San Diego to be dispatched to Toronto!

San Diego:

The sight as we entered the harbor was ominous and awesome in terms of the culmination of military might. It was there that the acme of the naval power of the United States of America was being assembled for the ultimate onslaught on the Japanese empire. But for the atom bombs being used, this force would have been unleashed in combination with the air force and army, and probably would have effected more death and destruction than the bombs had.

We threaded our way past the aircraft carriers, the battleships, the cruisers, the destroyers, and the support vessels of various shapes and sizes anchored in solemn majesty. When we were at sea, on our own as a flotilla, we felt big and important. But here we were overshadowed! At the same time, we had a sense of pride in that we were a part of this powerful ensemble and that we had been trained to play a unique role in the overall scheme. We tied up alongside a wharf, nestled together. We did not know what our future orders were to be, and so we settled in to wait further instructions.

It turned out that Santic and I had exactly the same number of points. When we went to the commodore to arrange for our discharge, he said that he couldn't let us both go. He didn't think it was fair to let one of us go without the other, so he was going to keep us both! It was a matter of several days before the future of the flotilla was to be decided upon. In the meantime the enlisted men on the commodore's staff were to be granted leave two or three days at a time until we received our orders.

Santic and I used our first day to travel to Tijuana, Mexico, which is a small city just across the border from San Diego. It was not very impressive—dirty and disorganized. Another day, we explored the city of San Diego. It is so clean and has real class. We also went to the little picturesque town of La Joya, which was a delight. I found this part of California to be intriguing. It planted a yearning in my heart to return.

For our next leave we decided that we were going to hitchhike toward Los Angeles. We took off and finally wound up in San Bernardino. It was very hot on the way. At one point we stopped at a store and bought something to eat and drink. It was the first time had ever seen or tasted an avocado, but that was our lunch. The menu was avocado, soda crackers, and Coke!

Our excursion took us into the San Bernadino mountains to Lake Arrowhead. It was a magnificent spot. We were told that the lake was a crater of an extinct volcano that had filled with water from subterranean springs. Around the circumference it was scalloped with lush pine trees.

The entire refreshing vista could be absorbed from an enchanting lakeside hotel. We escaped the heat by swimming in the frigid waters. We stayed in the hotel overnight before returning down the mountain to trek across country back to the base.

Our hitchhiking didn't go as smoothly as we had planned, which resulted in a late arrival. Our penalty for being twelve hours tardy was two days off our next leave. As it happened we would be on our way to San Francisco before that occurred anyhow.

I was going to go overseas to participate in the repair and occupation of the territory formerly held by the Japanese. The pontoons that we carried as cargo would be useful for replacing docks and bridges that had been damaged or destroyed. This made me all the more determined to get my discharge so there would be no possibility that I would get stuck on the other side of the Pacific for months, perhaps another year or two. We had our orders to shove off to San Francisco and then to Hawaii.

We sailed out of the San Diego harbor and left most of the imposing ships of the line still at anchor. The trip up the coast of California was pleasant and uneventful except for an interview I had with the commodore.

He called me into his cabin where he set up a heart-to-heart talk. He seemed genuinely interested in me. He told me that I would make a fine officer in the USN and that I should make the navy my life career. He said that he would see that I received a commission and that he would pave the way for me in the initial stages.

I expressed my thanks for his interest and told him that I was grateful for the compliment he paid me by presenting such an opportunity. However, I explained that I was a civilian at the core of my being and would find the overall discipline of the navy too confining and restrictive. And in addition to all that, I was an expectant father and wanted to be home for the birth of our child.

San Francisco:

It was toward the end of August when we approached it: the shadowy outline of the Golden Gate. It became dimly visible in the mystic light of a foggy dawn.

Entering the harbor just ahead of us were four black subs flying the ensign of the United States. It was quite startling for me to see these subs etched against the gray of the morning mist. I had fought their German counterparts for so long. Each of them had several small Japanese flags painted on their conning towers. Each flag indicated a Japanese vessel they had sunk.

We traveled under the bridge and proceeded to Treasure Island, where we tied up to the wharf in our usual clusters.

San Francisco is a fabulous liberty port. It has such a romantic history. I didn't get to see all I wanted to see, but I saw enough to know that I would want to return some day to absorb much more.

Fritz, one of the fellows on our staff, had some friends who lived in the city. They offered to show him around, and he included me. It was an enlightening tour that I appreciated. It gave me a feel for the general layout so that when I went on liberty on my own I was more at ease finding my way around.

One of the places that stand out in my memory is Fisherman's Wharf. I was particularly interested in the restaurant that served all manner of seafood, which I delighted in devouring. It was there that I first tasted abalone. I thought it was delicious. I have tried it a number of times since then, but it never has it lived up to my recollection of how I relished it at that time.

My stay in San Francisco was overshadowed by the pending decision regarding my future. The commodore had it within his power to release me from the navy if he chose to do so. The date we were scheduled to depart for Pearl Harbor was September 13, and the effective date of the point system for release was September 15. The commodore had said nothing further to me since our conversation before arriving at San Francisco. On the morning of September 13, Santic and I were called to his quarters, and he presented to us our traveling papers back to the state of New York, where we were to be formally discharged from active service!

We packed our seabags and stood on the dock and waved good-bye to our shipmates, who had to continue the voyage across the Pacific.

We were assigned to one of the first troop trains to travel across the country after the war was ended.

Because of this, there were crowds to cheer us as passed through the various towns and cities as we moved across the continent. It was an exhilarating experience similar to what might have been felt by the return of conquering heroes in the days of the Roman Empire.

Santic and I shared a private compartment on the train, which boosted our ego tremendously. We were fed the best fare in the dining car as were all the other sailors traveling with us. We were made to believe that a grateful nation valued us.

My naval career began with a memorable train ride, and it ended with a memorable train ride. Those two journeys were like brackets around a section of my life that I would not have chosen, did not want, and would not want to repeat. However, having been through it, I would not trade it for an easier path in that period of world history. There were many lessons learned that created a base for adventures of life, which were to follow.

After receiving my honorable discharge on September 27, 1945, I made my way across the same bridge at Niagara Falls that our family had used when we first entered Canada. Life stretched out before me. How was I to use it?

I was welcomed profusely by my family and Harriet and her family.

Chapter 14

Unlimited Horizons
(1945-1946)

Digest of the Times and Circumstances:

Much of the world lay in a scrambled mess of senseless destruction. The leaders of the major countries were determined to try to prohibit such a catastrophe from ever happening again. Even though the League of Nations had failed miserably to thwart WWII, a similar organization was formed to attempt to achieve a forum where words could replace war as a means of maintaining peace between nations. It got the support of the United States and eventually founded its headquarters in New York City. It was named the United Nations.

The more immediate need was the desperate situation in Europe and elsewhere, where whole peoples were without homes and without the means to restore their economies to a level required to survive. There were displaced persons' camps throughout Europe, where people who had no food and who had no homes were temporarily fed and housed. Many of these people were transplanted permanently to other countries. Some of them came to Canada and became Canadian citizens. The United States was the only nation with the financial base to provide a long-term solution.

The United States granted billions of dollars to participating nations to assist them in a salvaging operation so that there could be some hope for physical survival and economic stability. General George Marshall, who played a major role as an American military strategist and coordinator during WWII, became a leader in the creation of the blueprint for the restoration. Hence the project became known as the Marshall Plan.

In the United States and Canada the spirit of optimism pervaded everything. For years ordinary consumer products had been suppressed, from the building of homes and the manufacture of all the items required to furnish them to farm machinery and automobiles for personal use. The men and women of marriageable age had been away fighting the war, families had not been formed, and children were not born in adequate numbers to maintain the population growth. All this changed. There was a surge of new births over the next few years that infused the demography with so many children that it became known as the baby-boom generation, which was later dubbed the boomers.

In order to satisfy all of this pent-up need and desire, production was put into high gear, which if let to run amok could cause economic disaster because of the shortage of raw materials and the consequential overpricing of those commodities.

During the war years there was a similar problem relating to competition for the basics to produce war goods. In order to have an orderly procedure that would maintain costs within reasonable bounds, the Canadian government formed the Wartime Prices Control Board. A man by the name of Wally McCutcheon was the chairman of this board. He asked my father to be a member. My dad served in this capacity during wartime and until it was dissolved a couple of years after the war. It was kept intact for an additional two to three years to make a smooth transition from war production to peace production.

All the civilian projects that had been inhibited for years burst upon the landscape of the world. Freedom of movement invigorated world trade, world travel, and worldwide airlines. Freedom of publication encouraged more magazines and books (including Dr. Spock's Baby and Child Care, on whose advice the baby boomers were reared). Freedom of enterprise allowed the development of a multitude of inventions and devices (such as television and the photocopier). They would ultimately change the way people communicated.

On the more somber side, the trials of the Nazi leaders who survived the bloodshed were conducted at Nuremberg. After due prosecution they were administered the justice of the court, which amounted to death for some and prison sentences for others. Sometime later, a similar trial was held for Japanese military and political leaders with comparable results.

Canada's participation in the war and subsequent events thrust her upon the world stage as an influential partner in major changes in the world scene.

Personal Thoughts and Memories:

Family:

The relationship between Harriet and my family had remained one of tolerance when I was away in the navy. My return exacerbated rather than mollified the predicament.

I had no personal resources or a job that could allow us to immediately establish a home. We were expecting our first child to arrive within a matter of months, and we required a place to live. Both of our parents offered us accommodation.

Front l—r Faulkner, Ken, Margery, Joe. Back father, mother, Harriet

My father had continued to prosper, and he and my mother bought a new house, where they lived with my brother Stuart. They had an extra bedroom.

Harriet's parents lived in a four-bedroom house at 117 Indian Road. When Harriet returned from Norfolk, she lived with her mother, father, sister, and two brothers (Margery, Ken, and Faulkner). She had another brother named Joseph, who was killed in the closing days of the war.

Harriet wanted to remain where she was, and consequently we began our civilian life together with five other people. Joe and Anne Stewart, Harriet's father and mother, were very gracious and considerate despite the fact that our presence distorted their routine considerably.

We were both strong-minded people with many things to be sorted out between us regarding our approach to life together. It was very difficult to have frank and open discussions between us within the limited privacy we had at our disposal. It became all the more complicated when the baby came, causing additional considerations relative to laundry, meals, and sleep, not to mention differing concepts of child rearing.

Star was born, and she became the center of attention for everyone. I wanted to name her Star to honor her because of the lasting impression made on my mind by the heavenly bodies, which I had witnessed as they shone brilliantly over Northern Ontario and the stillness of the Caribbean Sea.

Church:

The Stewarts attended a Brethren church named Central Gospel Hall. My parents were still members of Olivet Gospel Hall, which was the church affiliation I had since our arrival in Canada. This caused another conflict because each of the families wanted us to become adherents of the church with which they were associated. Since we had no independent means of transportation and because Harriet wanted to maintain her connection with Central, we decided to go there.

Gord Mitchell and Mary Turnbull, who were the couple with whom we had a close friendship before the war, also went to Central Gospel Hall. This was a great plus for us because we were able to rekindle the relationship that had been interrupted by overseas service. Gord had been quite badly burned in a fire in a Quonset hut in England but had recovered and return to Canada before the war was over. He and Mary married.

Gord and I had worked together in the past, and it didn't take us long to get started when we reconnected at Central. We initiated a young people's Saturday night rally that was held at Central. It became a very successful venture with youth participating from all over the city of Toronto.

The same spirit of optimism and adventure that permeated the commercial world because of the freedom that came with the removal of inhibitions that were caused by the war also penetrated the realm of evangelical Christianity. When hostilities ceased, the globe became open to the spread of the Gospel in a manner not seen in the history of the church. This produced an influx of missionaries into the churches in Toronto to tell their stories about the needs in the part of the mission field where their interests lay. It was all very challenging to me. Ever since I experienced the intimate and transcendent majesty and power of God that night in the Caribbean, I felt that there was something specific that God wanted me to do. Consequently I listened carefully as different opportunities were presented.

Emmaus Bible School had its beginning in 1945 in the city of Toronto. It was the first formalized systematic Bible study using an academic foundation that had been attempted by the Brethren. The timing of its inception was opportune in that many were released from military service who were searching for such training. The government provided some financing for ex-military personnel that could be used for tuition and living expenses while attending an approved educational institution. Emmaus had received that government endorsement.

Young men and women came to Toronto for this purpose from all over Canada and the United States. Emmaus Bible School used the physical facilities of Central Gospel Hall during weekdays in their initial year of existence. By the time the second academic year began, the school had acquired a property devoted solely to its activities. The presence of Emmaus in the city, and the students it attracted, had a profound influence on the Brethren churches in Toronto and in southern Ontario.

Employment:

It was imperative that I become employed as soon as possible so that I could assume some responsibility for Harriet and our soon-to-be family. Harriet's father was the purchasing agent for Exide Battery and as such had many contacts within the industry that supplied his company with material that was used in the production of batteries. The Steel Company of Canada was one of those companies.

He used his good auspices to open the door for me to have an interview with the personnel manager. They had a warehouse that was within walking distance of where we lived. They hired me to work as order filler in this warehouse.

The merchandise we handled were metal nuts and bolts. Nuts and bolts of all sizes, from tiny ones to bolts that were three to four feet long. It was a confining, dismal job in dismal surroundings, drenched in an irritating metallic acrid odor.

It was a drastic change from the freedom and expansive vista to which I was accustomed on the open bridge of a ship at sea. I felt like an eagle that had had its wings clipped and was confined to the ground, stripped of the exhilaration of soaring to the heights.

That job experience had some merit, however. The route that I took from home to work led me through my old standby, High Park, of which I had such found memories from my years as a teenager. It was refreshing to travel some of the well-worn paths that had been part of my youth. My route also took me around Grenadier Pond, where we used to ice skate and across which our toboggans scooted over its frozen surface.

After a short time at that occupation, an opportunity presented itself to work at Goodyear Tire and Rubber Company. By this time my father was the president of Christie Bread and Cake Company. They had a large fleet of trucks and bought their tires from Goodyear. He opened the door for me to have an interview. They hired me to work in their statistical department. I knew nothing about statistics and cared less. However, I was willing to learn. The office where I worked was large, bright, and airy, which allowed me to escape some of the phobia of containment that my warehouse position imposed upon me.

The manager of the statistical department was also the facilitator of conventions and the arranger of the reception of company dignitaries when they came to town. He was in charge of an array of cars for use in fulfilling this part of his responsibility. His name was Joe O'Neal. He had a pleasant personality and was one who paid a lot of attention to detail. He was entrusted with the responsibility of providing personal public relations on behalf of the company to major customers.

Joe took a liking to me and rapidly put me into the position of being his right-hand man when it came to meeting people at the airport and transporting them around town. I became a glorified chauffeur. This suited me fine because it permitted me to be out of the office and on my own a great deal of the time. It also afforded me the experience of arranging accommodation with hotels and functions with caterers.

The most important benefit I received was the variety of contacts I had with other people. I met some of the top-ranking entrepreneurs in Canada. I learned they were just people and need not be feared. This knowledge was to be useful to me in later life.

Among the men that I met was P. W. Litchfield. At the time, he was the chairman and chief executive officer of Goodyear worldwide. He visited our operation in Toronto quite regularly. He flew in via company airplanes from Akron, Ohio, which was our head office. I was usually assigned to meet him and to take him to the hotel or directly to the plant in New Toronto. He was a strong, intelligent, quiet, affable person who invariably engaged me in conversation.

Subsequently, my boss, Joe, received a telephone call from Akron stating that Mr. Litchfield would be coming to Toronto the next day. He wanted me to meet him at the airport. He asked Joe to give me the time off to have lunch with him. Joe agreed and passed on the word, bubbling with ecstatic exuberance because of my good fortune.

The following day Mr. Litchfield arrived and directed me to drive to the Old Mill, a posh restaurant on the banks of the Humber River, where he had reservations for the two of us. After making our choices from an elaborate menu, he asked probing questions into my background in a gentle and paternal manner. Over a two-hour period he had explored all aspects of my life. I drove him back to the airport, and he returned to Akron.

A few days later the president of Goodyear Canada met with my boss, Joe, and me, to informed us that Mr. Litchfield had invited me to join him for a couple of weeks in northern Ontario along with several other young men. He named a date two or three weeks in the future when an amphibian plane would pick me up and fly me to Lake Temagami, where the company lodge was located.

Joe explained to me that a major undertaking, in which Mr. Litchfield was engaged, was to travel throughout the Goodyear organization worldwide looking for young men to transfer to Akron to prepare them to assume senior management positions in the company. He told me that I was the first one that he had selected from Canada.

This presented a decision of huge proportions for me.

My Dilemma:

I believed that determinations made at this crossroads of my life would have a long-term effect.

My interest in the aviation industry remained alive. Soon after my discharge from the navy, I had enrolled in a correspondence course in aviation engineering that I studied evenings in a corner of the basement of the Stewarts' home. It was one of the few places where one could have minimal distraction.

The constant flow of missionaries through the city impressed upon me the opportunity of being a voice for God in the world. I was attracted to the work in China being done through John and Betty McGeHee. Increasingly I became positively influenced as I thought about this prospect.

Harriet wanted me to start at the bottom of a large company such as the Steel Company of Canada with a solid job and work my way up the ladder.

My father enthusiastically urged me to accept the offer from Mr. Litchfield because he thought it would bring large financial rewards. It seemed to be an unsought opportunity of a lifetime that was offered to few people.

These were the four roads I could travel:

- The career in aviation (of which I had dreamed for years)
- A messenger of God in the world (which seemed daring and worthwhile)
- This proposition from Goodyear (which seemed glamorously attractive)
- Working my way through the ranks of a large company (which seemed boring and uninteresting)

All were churning in my mind and in my spirit. The need to decide had been made pressing because of the time frame posed by Mr. Litchfield's offer.

I really believed that I could do anything to which I applied my mind and energy. As I struggled with the different alternatives and attempted to look down the individual paths that each might lead, one thought became paramount in my mind: "What is the greatest occupation I could have?" My memory took me back to the arresting experience I had on the deck of the *Impulse* that starry night in the Caribbean, when the God of the universe overwhelmed me with the power and magnitude of His Person. I knew that whatever I did, I needed to have Him preeminent in my life if I were to have peace and contentment. Once I reached that point in my prayers and deliberations, it became apparent to me that I was to work directly for God as one of His messengers in the world.

This left the mission to China at the top of the list.

I discussed everything with Harriet. Although being a missionary was not her first choice, she was willing to cooperate. This presented me with the awkward situation of trying to explain to the men at Goodyear, who were materialistic in their approached to life, how I could possibly pass up such an opportunity that was being offered to me by Mr. Litchfield.

I told Joe, and he went into orbit! He informed the president of the Canadian company, who was equally shocked. The president phoned my father, who asked me to have a meeting with him.

The theme of the talk with my father was a reiteration of the major financial and prestigious opportunity that I was aborting. It was emphasized that the money and the position of influence could be used to do good things in the Lord's work. I explained to my father that I felt that God wanted me to be directly involved in His work on the front line somewhere and that, as far as I could see at the moment, that place was China. He finally agreed with me and believed that I was making the right decision.

I thanked Mr. Litchfield. He was very gracious and sent me a copy of his book *Autumn Leaves: The Reflections of an Industrial Lieutenant*. It is a memento that I have kept to this day.

I continued to work for Goodyear for sometime after. When I finally did leave, the president told me if things did not work out well in China, they would welcome me back with open arms.

Camp Mini-Yo-We:

Some people in the Brethren churches in Toronto had been exposed to Christian camps for girls and boys through intervarsity Christian fellowship. This organization had some successful experience in operating children's summer outdoor activity for a week or two at a time away from city environment. Sports and related activities were mingled with Christian teaching with exceptionally good results. Enthusiasm was built to the point where a number of the churches wanted to unite to try it. A committee was formed to formulate a plan to move forward.

My father-in-law, Joe Stewart, was the secretary of this group. He invited me to participate. Since it suited my interest in sports and spiritual matters, I plunged right in and became deeply involved.

The summer of 1946 was the target date. A property was leased for twenty days during the month of August. It was named the Fair Havens and was owned by the Associated Gospel Churches. It was a small peninsula located on the Trent Canal system near Gamebridge, Ontario (about ninety miles from Toronto). It had an area that could be used for swimming and a building for cooking and dining, but it had no sleeping accommodation.

Tents and tent platforms were found, twelve of them enough to house fifty campers at a time. Just the right number for the trial run we were anticipating.

Since swimming was going to be one of our activities, it was mandatory that we have someone who was qualified to perform the duties of a lifeguard as well as swimming instructor. Swimming had been one of my major interests throughout my life; therefore, it was natural for me to take on this function. Government regulations demanded that anyone performing this duty had to have Red Cross qualifications. It meant a crash course for me. Fortunately one of the people involved in the camp was Lewis Smith, who was a teacher in the physical education department at the University of Toronto. He used his connections to allow me to have a concentrated course at Hart House that qualified me to be the waterfront director at the first Camp Mini-Yo-We.

I was working at Goodyear Tire and had only been there for a few months. I was not entitled to any vacation time, but I asked if they would allow me to have a leave of absence without pay for the two weeks that camp would be in progress. They not only agreed but insisted on paying me as well. I was most grateful.

Les Rickard was the director of the Camp. It was his responsibility to find the people to staff the operation from cooks to counselors and to train us before our big experiment. He, along with all the other people directly associated with this project, were an inspiration to me. Their dedicated, enthusiastic, unreserved commitment to this enterprise was a prime example of what total effort, without regard to who will get the credit, can achieve under the direction of God.

The camp was a booming success both from a spiritual point of view and physical perspective. The campers and the leaders came away with an exhaustion that was satisfying and refreshing. Everyone's attitude exclaimed "Let's do it again!" We had learned a lot and were ready to find a more permanent site on which to build for the future.

Chapter 15

Preparation Period
(1947-1949)

Digest of the Times and Circumstances:

Politics:

The empires that had been established by the tall ships of the maritime nations of Europe during the 1500s, 1600s, and 1700s began to disintegrate shortly after WWII. Before WWII the British empire in particular was a potent force throughout the entire globe. It was said that the empire was so far-flung that the sun never set on its territory. This translated into tremendous power, especially in trade.

Burma was the first to gain its independence from Britain. It had been occupied by Japan during the war. When hostilities ceased, it had no desire to return to British rule. In that same year India removed itself from Britain's yoke. Concurrently East and West Pakistan were established as separate entities.

The British were a protectorate in Israel. The UN divided Israel into Jewish and Palestinian states. Great Britain withdrew its forces, and immediately the surrounding Arab countries attacked the fledgling Jewish nation. Israel survived the onslaught, which in the end resulted in an increase of territory to the Jews.

The USA military occupied Japan. General MacArthur became the overseer of the formation of a democratic government and the reestablishment of an economic base that could sustain the population.

The Treaty of Paris in 1947, among other things, outlined boundaries between countries in Europe. The USSR had schemes for the control of

Europe and began to become bellicose after developing the atomic bomb in 1948. The Communists took power in Czechoslovakia by a coup d'état.

Germany had been separated into two sections. The Allied forces were in the west and the Russian forces were in the east. The city of Berlin was divided in a similar fashion. Berlin was surrounded by territory occupied by the USSR. For the Allies to maintain land contact with its portion of Berlin, a highway corridor was established.

To exert pressure in their drive to extend their control in Europe, the USSR cut off the supplies from the West to Berlin by blocking the flow of traffic through the land corridor. The Allies resisted this chicanery by airlifting food and other essentials into the city and by forming the North Atlantic Treaty Organization (NATO), which consisted of the newly constituted Republic of West Germany plus many other free European nations. The USA and Canada also became members. The Russians backed off and opened the highway to Berlin. This episode presented a major showdown of gigantic proportions. It was the beginning of what eventually was labeled the Cold War.

In 1949 Chinese Nationalists succumbed to the Communists after a bloody civil war. Chiang Kai-shek fled with his army to Formosa and established a government independent from China that eventually was known as Taiwan. Mainland China became the People's Republic of China under the rule of Mao Tse-tung.

The hope for tranquility in the world did not last long after the silence of the guns of WWII. It quickly became evident the problems mankind had with mankind were still boiling underneath. The power blocks were shifting, and the dark swirling currents of political undertow were once more tugging at the ankles of humanity, threatening to suck us into another whirlpool of conflict.

Science and Social:
There had been much speculation regarding what might happen if a person or an object traveled at the speed of sound. Many thought that there would be such violent vibration that the person or thing moving so rapidly would disintegrate. In 1947 an American by the name of Chuck Yeager successfully flew a plane fast enough to break through the sound

barrier without damage to the plane or himself. This opened the way for military and commercial aircraft and rockets to be designed to safely travel at velocities that heretofore was thought to be impossible.

In 1947 three Americans—Brattain, Bardeen, and Shockley, who were working for Bell Telephone—discovered the transistor. This discovery proved to be a revolutionary step in the dramatic evolution in electronic devices such as radios, telephones, television sets, and computers. It was small and efficient, allowing the elimination of bulky vacuum tubes and other unwieldy forms of conductors.

Radar had been used by the military for years, but one of the first civilian applications was a harbor system that was installed at Liverpool, England, in 1948. Since then it has been employed to advance safe travel in all forms of transportation.

The World Health Assembly met in Geneva in 1948. It was a start in attempting to understand and do something about the physical well-being of people in countries who found themselves out of the mainstream and who were unable to cope with medical problems on their own.

The white minority in South Africa became fearful that the black population of their country would take power from them. The white people instituted apartheid as the official government policy. This action had the effect of segregating the people socially, politically, residentially, and educationally. There were four major groups: white, brown (half-white and half-black), black, and Indian. It became a source of violent opposition within the country and a disturbing factor worldwide, which was reflected in the UN.

Religious:
Some ancient scrolls were discovered near the Dead Sea that had great significance in authenticating the historicity of the Old Testament Scriptures. They dated from the period about the time of Christ and, therefore, became a well of information for scholars studying the conditions of society then.

Some of the prominent denominations in the Protestant church formed an organization that included the Roman Catholic church. It was called the World Council of Churches. Its purpose was to provide a semblance of unity on an ecumenical basis.

Billy Graham began holding mass evangelical rallies in large cities across North America and Europe. This had a huge impact on a large segment of the Christian church.

Personal Thoughts and Memories:

Family:

The three years covered by this segment of my story spans activities in five different sections: church, Emmaus Bible School, work, Camp Mini-Yo-We, and Frontier Lodge. In combination, and individually, these activities had a marked effect on our family life. Since we had made the decision to give the extension of the Kingdom of God top priority in our life, everything else had to serve that end. How each of these came into play in our family will be treated separately.

I left my employment at Goodyear in the fall of 1946. Harriet and I decided we would attend Emmaus Bible School while we're waiting for the opportunity to go to China as missionaries. We continued to live with the Stewarts. Harriet's mother babysat Star when we were at classes in the mornings. Classes began at eight AM and finished at twelve PM. Normally Harriet would go home and I would go to work.

By the spring of 1947 Mini-Yo-We had found a property, which they intended to develop into a permanent site for a children's camp. There was a great deal of repair and new construction that had to be done before it could be used that summer. Harriet and I moved up to the site in May along with another couple, Gordon and Isobel Ferris. Gord was a cook in the army during the war. He took over the cooking assignment. Isobel and Harriet were responsible for the dining room and dishwashing. The Ferrises had a son about the same age as Star. They were both toddlers and were a joy and a chore rolled up into two ever-moving tumbleweeds.

Beside the two families there were several men who stayed all week for several weeks. Some were experienced carpenters, and others were willing laborers.

In addition to helping in building and general cleanup, I was responsible for organizing the work that needed to be done on a daily basis. I also planned the work to be accomplished by the many volunteers who invaded the property each weekend.

There were several cottages where the single men slept. The Ferris family stayed in one of the more formal houses. Harriet, Star, and I occupied another one. Everyone had meals together in a separate building. Water had to be carried from the lake by the pail for drinking and cooking because it was not piped into any of the structures. Outhouses were the order of the day.

Black flies are a scourge in that part of the country at that time of year. They viciously attacked all of us from dawn until dark. These insects bite any uncovered spot, drawing blood on each occasion. By the day's end, the children who were particularly vulnerable had caked blood on their necks, in their ears, and in their hair, each bite accompanied by a tortuous itch.

*Harriet's father
and mother*

Boys' Camp was held during the month of July for which I was waterfront director. Harriet and Star returned to the Stewarts in Toronto on July 1. I joined them on August 1. I worked the balance of the summer before returning to Emmaus Bible School in the fall.

Harriet became pregnant in the winter of '47-'48 and had some difficulties. The doctor told her she would have to remain in bed most of the time, which curtailed her activity and affected our family life as well. We were still living in cramped quarters.

This was complicated by the fact that my classes were in the morning and I had to work in the afternoon and needed to have some time to study at night.

In the summer of 1948 I went to Camp Mini-Yo-We again and also for two weeks' Boys' Camp at Frontier Lodge near Sherbrooke, Quebec. Harriet and Star remained in Toronto.

Jonathan was born in October 1948, which put an over-the-top strain on the space at the Stewarts' residence. Something had to be done for the sanity of both families. Fortunately a solution was found to relieve the situation somewhat.

A fellow by the name of Jim Martindale from Philadelphia was attending Emmaus. His wife and two young boys, about the same age as our children, were with him. They were in need of some place to live. Neither family had enough money to rent a house on its own, so we combined forces and found a place we could afford about a half mile past the end of the streetcar line on the eastern outskirts of Toronto.

While this was far from ideal, it was a change for us and certainly a relief for Harriet's mother and father to say nothing of her siblings.

It was not easy for two families of different backgrounds and cultures to be thrust together on a daily basis, especially for the women involved. They had to put up with their individual methods and idiosyncrasies that came into play in the matter of cooking, housekeeping, and child rearing. They lived in close contact all day long while Jim and I had to be at school or work.

Four young children subject to those circumstances under one roof was not easy to manage. It was further compounded by the fact that Jonathan developed a chronic iliac disorder that caused him to have violent stomach cramps and volatile vomiting for protracted periods. His diet consisted of squashed ripe bananas—nothing else.

Despite all of these circumstances, we lived in peace and mutual respect until graduation time in the spring of 1949, when we parted good friends. They moved back to Philadelphia, and we moved to the province of Quebec.

Church:

I continued my work with the young people at Central and helped to band them together with other young people in the city to have an outreach program. At that time in the city of Toronto, the theaters were not permitted to show movies on Sunday. We got permission from the city to rent a theater to have evangelistic meetings on Sunday evenings. We hired a theater and proceeded with our program. It was a great encouragement to everyone who participated.

We had taken the step of offering ourselves to be missionaries to China, but we were not having doors open before us. The McGehees were having difficulty getting their visas to return to China, and the elders of our church were reluctant to issue us a letter of commendation to allow us to have the recognition among the Brethren churches as bonafide missionary candidates. They had good reason to be apprehensive because the civil war in China was giving rise to increasing political turbulence.

We held ourselves in a state of readiness as God would open the way before us. In the meantime, we prepared ourselves by studying Chinese at the University of Toronto and attending Emmaus Bible School.

I began to do a fair amount of preaching mingled among all the other activities in which I was engaged. There was a huge demand on my time and energy. I had to plan my days down to the last ten minutes. Sleep was at a premium. It was exhausting but exhilarating simultaneously. It was an important phase of my life when I learned a lot about discipline, priority setting, and time management.

Over the three-year period, the situation relating to China did not clarify too much. The elders of Central Gospel Hall suggested that it may be a good idea for us to become involved in pioneer work in our own country before going overseas to a foreign land.

We grappled with this idea for a while and were finally convinced that this was a good plan. We wanted to know the blessing of God in a difficult place and prayed that He would lead us in the right direction.

Step by step it became clear that Magog, Quebec, was where we were to go. I had been at Frontier Lodge, a Christian camp, a couple of times and had spent some time in Magog. Dr. Arthur Hill was a major force in Christian missionary activity centered in Sherbrooke and the surrounding eastern townships. He encouraged us and our elders that this was a place that our service was needed and wanted. This resulted in our receiving a letter of commendation to work in this district.

Emmaus Bible School:

Emmaus Bible School was in its second year of operation as a full-time educational institution when I was faced with making choices relating to the mission field. Since the decision had been made to make ourselves available to go to China as missionaries and we were delayed because of circumstances beyond our control, we decided to go to Emmaus Bible School.

We intended to take one year of a three-year course when we started because we thought that we would be released to go to China after the first year. As the situation compounded in China, our delay was protracted. While Harriet just took the first year, I finished all three years and graduated in 1949.

For the rest of my life I have been grateful that I spent that much time formally studying the Scriptures. It was a very difficult thing to accomplish while working at the same time, attempting to support a family, and trying to take some active part in family responsibilities and privileges.

Some of the stressful moments I remember well:

There was no such thing as disposable diapers. Even if there had been, we could not have afforded to use them. The result was that we washed diapers daily. When we lived at the Stewarts, this meant getting up early in the morning and doing the laundry before leaving for school. Since we had no dryer, these items had to be hung up on an outside line by hand. This wasn't so bad when the weather was warm, but when it was freezing, the wet cloth became a sheet of permafrost, and one's finger became literal icicles.

The streetcar was our only means of transportation. Because I had to spend so many hours a week traveling in this fashion, it became mandatory for me to study en route. Almost always one had to stand all the way to one's destination. One had to hang on to a handle or a strap in order to keep one's balance while the vehicle swayed back and forth and started and stopped with sudden jerks. Meantime, one is trying to read a book held in the other hand. When a page of the book that was being held in the other hand needed to be turned, the timing had to perfect between sways and jerks if one were to remain standing. This action had to be rapid lest the strap or handle one had released for this split moment was grabbed by someone else. There usually was a crush of people standing shoulder to shoulder with the resultant "foot on top of foot" on occasion, which didn't make for congenial relations.

I have mentioned that Jonathan suffered from a type of colic when he was a baby that caused him to vomit. When I came home from work in the evening, it was my turn to walk Jonathan back and forth to help comfort him in his pain. Some nights it would be for hours. I had to maintain my studying, and therefore, I would have Jonathan draped over one shoulder while I also juggled a book. This activity was punctuated by periodic volatile vomit, which he could project several feet. Then it was cleanup time!

In between all of this action, we appreciated each opportunity we could grasp to enjoy each other as a family.

Work:

As a veteran of the USA armed forces, I was entitled to ninety dollars per month subsistence allowance while I was attending school. I needed much more money than this to care for my family. Therefore, I had to work as well as go to school. Fortunately for me there were two people who were Christian businessmen who were sympathetic to EBS students and who also were interested in Camp Mini-Yo-We. They were willing to employ me for the time that I was not going to school or busy with camp.

The first job I had was manufacturing living room table and floor lamps. It was a simple operation involving a few lathes for cutting metal. There were bins of different shapes of variously colored glass globes and cylinders with a hole through the middle of each one. Each of us individually selected and threaded the various shapes and colors on a metal tube and strung wiring up the center. Each creation was fastened on a stand then embellished at the top with a glass flange and finally crowned with a shade selected from an assortment of shapes, colors, and sizes. It was a fun group of people with whom to work. Some of the lamps we brought into being were far out! Picasso would have been proud!

The second job I had was teaching people to drive. It was a fascinating experience. I met many interesting personalities, everything from young kids to older men and women. Every day was a new adventure. I was learning to deal with people who were afraid to drive and, on the one hand, others who were overconfident and reckless. It was a challenge! This work was perfect for me and lasted until the time I was ready to leave for the province of Quebec.

Camp Min-Yo-We:

I have mentioned from a family perspective how this camp affected us. Now I would like to go into a little more detail by relating what the camp meant to me personally.

I was encouraged to become part of what amounted to an executive committee for the development of all aspects of the camp. This entailed finding a permanent campsite as well as helping to spread the word throughout the other churches in Ontario who wanted to learn more about this activity.

The search for a place to have a permanent camp began in earnest in the fall of 1946. Newspaper ads were scoured, and personal contacts were explored. Almost every Saturday one or more of the committee viewed one or two prospects personally. I participated in many of those expeditions. On one of those occasions, Walter Howard and I were doing some advanced scouting. Walter was the man who owned the driving school that employed me. In any event it was he and I who examined one of the properties that had been recommended. It turned out to be the site on Mary Lake. We got the rest of the committee to drive up to see it on the following weekend.

They enthusiastically endorsed the idea of buying it. We proceeded one step at a time until the transaction was completed. The money had to be raised for the purchase and development of the property. This meant informing many people about the great possibilities of the project. This entailed traveling to Brethren churches in Southern Ontario. We usually did this on Wednesday evenings, which was the normal midweek meeting for these churches. We would have a slideshow and then answer any questions. Generally we left Toronto about six PM and arrived home about midnight. This continued even after the camp was in operation because the

First dining hall at Mini Yo We under construction

churches that participated wanted to know how everything progressed on each succeeding year.

The time came for someone to give leadership on the site for the final thrust to get it ready for the summer of 1947. The committee asked me if I would consider doing this. That is how and why Harriet, Star, and I agreed to move to the camp.

The few months in the spring and summer of 1947 was a huge learning adventure for me, both in the management of people and the deeper appreciation of explicitly trusting God to meet the needs of those who are engaged in something that He wants done.

Frontier Lodge:

I have mentioned that Les Rickard, who was the driving force of getting Camp Mini-Yo-We started, had gotten his initial experience in camping at Frontier Lodge. He was still in contact with Arthur Hill, who was the main thrust behind Frontier Lodge. Arthur had contacted Les to see if he knew of anyone who could serve on staff at Frontier Lodge during the summer of 1948. Les mentioned my name. That was how I became involved in the work there. I went for two weeks, which was an initiation period that turned out to be a main part of my life for many years.

Summary of this Period (1947-1949):

These few years changed me from a sailor, to a father, to a missionary, to a camp leader, to an evangelist, to a person who was anxious to trust God completely, believing that He could not and would not fail me.

The big test lay just around the corner.

Chapter 16

God's Kindergarten
(1949-1950)

Digest of the Times and Circumstances:

World Politics:

By its actions and words, the Communist regime in the USSR had declared its intention to dominate the entire world. It was well positioned geographically to be a controlling force both in the western and eastern hemispheres. It had already injected its presence in Europe and followed this by creating overt and covert alliances with Asian countries. A major step in this direction was achieved when China and Russia signed a mutual friendship and assistance pact. Vietnam, Cambodia, and Laos gained independence from France and thereby became targets for the infiltration of Soviet-backed political influence. The USA became increasingly fearful of the activities of the Communists, particularly when two of their most powerful countries, China and the USSR, seemed to be acting in consort to force their system of government on adjacent states. In order to counter this threat, the United States developed a policy of containment, which became known as the Truman Doctrine. The effect of this strategy was to provide weapons and personnel to any country that felt it was endangered by armed takeover by Communist ideologues. The first major trial of the effectiveness of the United Nations organization as a keeper of the peace occurred when North Korea invaded South Korea. After WWII, Russia and the United States occupied the Korean peninsula following the retreat of the Japanese. Because of the differences in ideology between the two occupying countries and because of their strained relationship throughout the globe, Korea became divided into two countries, North Korea and South Korea. The United States controlled the South, and the Communists controlled the North. The South became a democracy, and the North became a communist dictatorship.

It didn't take long for North Korea to invade South Korea with the intent of subjugating its people to Communist rule. The situation was brought before the UN with the result that a military force composed of many of the member nations of the UN (including Canada) rushed to the aid of South Korea. The Truman Doctrine came into play, and the United States entered the fray with General Douglas MacArthur in command of the total operation. It was to become a bitter war.

Science and Social:

The development of guided missiles was increasingly a priority. The United States succeeded in launching one to a height of four hundred kilometers, which was a record to that point in time.

The USA began work on the hydrogen bomb, which would accelerate the race between the USSR and the USA to construct ever-spiraling means of mass destruction.

The blacks in South Africa began rioting against the apartheid policy of their government. Many people were brutally massacred. The disapproval of world opinion was focused on this unjust policy.

George Orwell published the book entitled 1984, which depicted life in a completely authoritarian world. It seemed to reflect the fears of the people in western free societies.

Personal Thoughts and Memories:

The Turmoil of Uncertainty:

To complicate matters, we no longer had a place to live. I had closed the door on the thought of climbing some corporate ladder somewhere to earn a living. We needed to know the guidance of God in no uncertain terms. In the meantime, Les Rickard found that he could no longer direct Camp Mini-Yo-We. The committee asked me to assume this responsibility since I was the likely person for the task.
This created a real conflict within. I was torn between these two alternatives, both of which seemed to be a direction that was desirable and which would further the Kingdom of God.

I had already invested some of my life in each endeavor and knew that I could be used in either one but not both. This was the time that I wanted the unmistakable direction of God. It had to be a concrete indication.

The most specific situation we faced was to have a place to live as a family, and so this became the final test. God would provide a place for us to live where He wanted us to be. Very soon after we had arrived at this conclusion, Arthur Hill wrote, saying they had found a place for us in Magog. So the decision was made. We would work in Quebec to await further developments relating to China.

This was to become "God's kindergarten" for us where we were taught many lessons.

We had accumulated some furniture at the last place we lived. We had a moving van pick it up and transport it to Magog. My parents offered to drive us to our new home, which we gladly accepted. We had thirty-four dollars total cash assets to start our new adventure.

Those were the circumstances surrounding our arrival in Magog, province of Quebec.

Chapter 17

The Province of Quebec

When we moved to the province of Quebec, Premier Dupleissis headed a Liberal government that had been in power for a long time. The Roman Catholic church had been a forceful presence from the beginning of the settlement of the French in Canada. There was collusion between the government and the church to subjugate the French population. One of the ways of doing this was to restrict the educational advancement to university level to the very few and to limit these few students to more classical instruction rather than commercially oriented studies. This overall policy resulted in a cheap labor force for business to exploit. The government encouraged this.

Since the English were inclined and educated toward commercial pursuits, they filled the positions of influence in the large corporations that were rapidly being established in the province. It was of mutual interest both to the church and to the government to maintain this balance. Anything that might be a threat to disturb this tacit agreement was met with vehement opposition up to and including the preaching of the clear liberating Gospel of Jesus Christ to the Roman Catholic French Canadians.

Our Latest Address:

Our new home consisted of two bedrooms, a bathroom, and an open space between them that was to be used as a kitchen-slash-eating area although it had no sink or water supply. The furniture we had comprised of two beds, a table and four chairs, a couple of bureaus, a two-burner hot plate, and a refrigerator, plus basic pots, pans, and cutlery.

Since the suite was at the peak of the house, the ceiling followed the line of the roof, creating ample headroom in one part but insufficient clearance in other sections. The floor was covered with linoleum. The walls and ceiling had been freshly wallpapered.

Our landlady was a widow with a young son. Her husband had been killed overseas in WWII. She needed to rent this accommodation to supplement her income. She charged twenty dollars per month.

My parents returned to Toronto. We were left in the hands of our heavenly Father in a strange community with no salary, completely dependent on God to meet our needs through whatever means He chose.

Magog:

The town of Magog is situated about one hundred miles southeast of Montreal and thirty miles west of Sherbrooke. The principal highway between those two points passed through the heart of Magog. This roadway provided the main street of the municipality, on each side of which stores sprouted that satisfied the immediate requirements of the residents. This strip was approximately one mile long. The town is located in what is known as the eastern townships in the province of Quebec, which is just north of the border of the USA.

When the American colonies severed relationship with Great Britain, many of the New England citizens who were loyal to Britain moved north into Canada and settled in the townships. This resulted in a preponderance of English-speaking people mingling with the French population. There were public schools, a hospital with two doctors and, most important of all from our point of view, a post office. The population was about fourteen thousand, and by this moment in history, the French-speaking segment of the municipality had increased to about 90 percent. Anglican, United, and Christian Advent churches served the dwindling English population.

The area surrounding Magog is a peaceful pastoral landscape consisting of woodland and dairy farms. The two dominant geographic features are Mt. Orford and Lake Memphremagog.

Lake Memphremagog is a majestic deep body of water that begins at the town of Magog and fingers its way through high hills for about thirty-five miles where it crosses the border into the United States. Mt. Orford rises out of undulating farmland like an isolated rogue wave. It looks far more imposing than one would expect from its actual height.

Cherry River:

Cherry River was to become the major hallmark of our activities during the time we spent in the province of Quebec.

It was a cluster of houses on the banks of what was a large creek in the spring and a babbling brook in the summer. To call it a river is a misnomer. It facilitates the drainage of the surrounding hills into Lake Memphremagog. It was a delightful stream that meandered through the countryside and was the site of both pleasure and tragedy over the years.

For the most part, the community was a bedroom for the people who worked in Magog three miles away. There were two general stores that supplied basic foodstuff, not only for the immediate residents but also for the farmers who operated dairy farms that encircled the village.

Most of the population, both in the village and the farms, were English-speaking people. It was a pocket of the residue of United Empire Loyalists.

On the highest spot in the locale stood a two-room schoolhouse. At that time only one of the rooms continued to be used for teaching. The other room was put to use periodically when the Anglican or United church ministers provided a service or some other event required accommodation for people to congregate. The room was void of desks. The only object was a potbelly stove in the center of the space. When needed, Mr. Parker Powers, who lived nearby, made seating possible. He stored some planks and wooden boxes that became seats when the crates were set on end and placed at suitable intervals with the planks bridging the gaps between.

Chapter 18

A Brief History of the Work on which We Built

Arthur Hill:

Arthur Hill was an outstanding Christian who placed all his resources on the line to be used of God in accomplishing His work. His background was Brethren from Ontario.

He was deeply involved in the start of intervarsity Christian fellowship from its inception in Canada. Upon graduating from medical school, he devoted his activities full time to this effort. He did this on a trial basis to determine whether this was where God wanted him to serve. After about a year he came to the conclusion that he should continue his medical career. He married Peggy Harvey, and in 1935, they moved to Sherbrooke, province of Quebec, where he set up a medical practice. He became a popular and successful physician and surgeon.

He considered himself to be first and foremost a missionary, whose principal responsibility was to spread the Good News of Jesus Christ. To this end he expended his considerable talents. He was a person of boundless energy and enthusiastic persuasion. He formed a church in Sherbrooke named Grace Chapel, and from there he encouraged the spread of the Gospel in French and English throughout the province of Quebec.

Canadian Sunday School Mission (CSSM):

This organization had the support and backing of Arthur in its endeavors to reach out into various localities to conduct daily vacation Bible school during the summertime. Cherry River was one of the places that had been the recipient of their activities. A couple of young people had become Christians as a result of their work. In 1948, when I spent some time in the province of Quebec, I helped to coordinate (along with Paul Hunt and Spencer Dibble) a continuance of contact with them by establishing a weekly meeting with all the children who would care to attend.

Paul Hunt was a young man from Toronto who came with me in the summer of 1948. He was single and was able to stay in Magog through the winter of 1948-49 so that contact was not lost with the children. Several people became Christians through Paul's effort. Spencer Dibble was an important contributor to the beginning of the work at Cherry River. He was a son of a missionary family that was on furlough from Africa. He also was a student at Emmaus Bible School.

Frontier Lodge:

Arthur and Peggy Hill initiated the first vestige of Frontier Lodge in a farmer's field on Little Lake Magog in 1936. It was a ragtag makeshift enterprise but was sparked by spiritual encouragement that provided the incentive to continue the effort for years.

The summer camp project moved forward at a variety of sites through many interesting and challenging phases. A book written by Jane Blair entitled The Foundations of Frontier Lodge chronicles some interesting stories and events outlining the history of the camp.

In 1944 a man by the name of Arnold Jackson offered some land to Arthur Hill that was located on Lake Wallace, which bordered the state of Vermont. The donation was conditional upon the development of a summer Christian conference-type activity. He, along with the Christians at Grace Chapel, accepted the formidable task even though they already were responding to the cost of establishing a new church.

When I arrived on the scene, the camp had already progressed to the point of having several cabins, a dining room added on to an old farmhouse (which served as a kitchen).

Beside the farmhouse stood a shed that contained a supply of ice that had been harvested from the lake during the previous winter and deposited there. It was then covered with sawdust to keep it from melting until it could be used in the icebox to cool the milk, butter, etc., during the summer. Central to all of this was a building that had a combined use as tuck shop, office, and sleeping quarters for the camp director.

The acreage on which the campsite sat had a moderate incline as it left the shores of the lake. Toward the rear of the property, on the highest elevation, stood a white chapel that was used not only for the camp but also for nearby cottages for Sunday services.

Gord Warnholtz:

Before going any further with this story, I need to tell about my friend Gord Warnholtz. Gord had been a cook in the Canadian army during WWII. His home was in Hespeler, Ontario. He attended a Brethren church there. When Camp Mini-Yo-We was started in 1946, he volunteered his services as a cook. It was at that camp we first met. When the time came to prepare the new site for the camp of 1947, Gord again served as cook for the advance work party and also during boys' camp that followed.

I was impressed with the quality of person he was and his commitment to being a humble servant of the Lord, willing to use his talents wherever God placed him. We formed a solid working relationship that lasted several years through tests of triumph as well adversity. As I review my life, I consider him to be one of the outstanding godly men that I have had the privilege with whom to work.

When we moved to Magog, Gord joined the undertaking by taking up residence in Cherry River.

Chapter 19

The Stage Was Set

A combination of family, Magog, Cherry River, and Frontier Lodge provided the setting for my work that would extend before me for the next several years.

Determining the timing and priority for the engagement of each of these spheres of activity was my primary consideration during the days immediately after arriving in Magog. My presence as director at Frontier Lodge was not required for several weeks yet, so most of my current activities could be centered locally.

The first thing toward which I turned my thoughts and energy was my family. It was not a little unnerving to think that we had no arranged income and my presence would soon be required at camp, which meant that I would have to leave Harriet, Star, and Jonathan because there was no accommodation for them at Frontier Lodge.

One of the things that I thought I could and should do was to plant a vegetable garden. I got permission from the landlady to use part of her yard to dig up and sow some seeds.

We obtained a box number at the post office through which we had an avenue to remain in contact with the people we had left behind in Ontario. We visited the PO daily. We had no telephone to reach out to anyone.

We had made the decision to follow the leading of the Spirit of God. Now was the time to put faith into action. We had to believe and trust His promise to supply our needs whatever they may be.

Several people had become Christians at Cherry River through the efforts of CSSM and Paul Hunt, who had stayed through the previous winter. Arthur Hill and some of the Christians came out from Sherbrooke, and the new converts were baptized in the stream that flowed through the village. It was an exciting event that was attended by a large number of the inhabitants in the district.

The timing to start in Cherry River seemed to be right. One of the young people who became a Christian through the CSSM was George Briar. His mother owned one of the stores in the village. It was not the one that was associated with the dance hall.

Gord Warnholtz and I requested her to allow the two of us to hold a Christian singsong outside her shop some evenings. She agreed. We had hymn sheets prepared and spread the word throughout the neighborhood about the event. Anyone and everyone were invited to join us.

Gord played the accordion, and I led the singing and preached the Gospel. The reception by the people was enthusiastic and encouraging.

The end result was that Parker Powers offered his planks and boxes to be used in the schoolhouse. We accepted, and from that point on, we used it for our meetings.

We held services every night for a week at which we preached the love of God and the salvation provided through Jesus Christ by the power of the Holy Spirit. The schoolhouse was packed. The message the people carried home with them stirred up the whole countryside. The feeling in the community was conveyed in the words of one old man who described their condition before we came as "We forgot there even was a God."

The time came to leave this aspect of what God was doing because of my commitment to be the director of the boys' camp at Frontier Lodge. The days leading up to my departure were full of soul searching related to the necessity of leaving Harriet and the children. We were in the full blush of the blessing of the Lord in what had happened to date in Cherry River. This was an immense encouragement as we contemplated the next step that God was placing before us.

The day before I was to depart, I picked up a scrap of paper from the floor of our bedroom. It had fluttered out of a letter from my mother. (It was her habit to include small excerpts of encouraging articles.) The theme of this particular piece emphasized the Lord conveying to His followers that He would take care of them.

It concentrated on Mt. 6:33-34: "Seek ye first the kingdom of God and His righteousness; and all these things shall be added unto you. Take therefore no thought for the morrow; for the morrow shall take thought for the things of itself. Sufficient unto the day is the evil thereof."

I took this as a direct challenge to exercise the belief that I had declared to others. "God would supply all my needs, no matter the circumstance, if I would fulfill His will for me." It was the defining moment in my life to that point. I believed I was doing His will, and now I looked to Him to keep His promise. I discussed the situation with no one, with the exception of Harriet. I was convinced that Jesus Christ was Who He said He was and that He would hear my prayer and satisfy any requirement we had.

The time came to leave. The few dollars we had were left with Harriet. I packed a couple of changes of clothing in a bag and tied it onto the rack of a small motorcycle that Spencer Dibble lent me. I had no other means of getting to camp. There was very little gas in the tank. I did not know how far it would carry me.

As I traveled over the rolling landscape, the exhilaration of the wind and sun caressed my face. My heart was pumping excitement and joy through my veins as I anticipated what God was going to do next. At the same time I was apprehensive because it was my little family that was being placed in jeopardy, not me.

To some degree, I felt the chill of trepidation that Abraham must have felt as he climbed the mount in the land of Moriah to place Isaac on the altar.

My vehicle performed marvelously over the highways and through the towns and along the country roads and carried me to the narrow track that led to the campsite. Just as I was within one half mile of my destination, the gas tank finally coughed up the last drop of fuel. The carburetor spewed it into the cylinders. The engine sputtered to a stop. I left the cycle hidden in a nearby cottage.

I walked the remainder of my journey with thanksgiving in my soul and a small bag in my hand containing my change of clothes, shaving gear, and toothbrush.

As I descended the driveway into the camp, the weight of the responsibility that I had agreed to undertake suddenly settled about my shoulders.

Although I had been accountable for the activities and welfare of others in varying degrees before, I had never been top dog, and the immediate prospect was daunting. It would be my responsibility to set the tone spiritually, socially, and physically for the staff and the campers. I settled into my quarters and began to prayerfully finalize the programs and policies with which I had wrestled since accepting the proposition to be the director here. A few of the staff had already arrived, and the remainder, along with the campers, was due in a couple of days. Then the action would begin.

My military experience and the exposure I had in the previous adventures at Mini-Yo-We and Frontier Lodge helped me cope with the opportunity. Looking back on my style of leadership as camp director, I feel I was quite regimented and strict but at the same time encouraged the expression of the talents of others. I took very seriously the physical well-being of everyone at camp and had stringent regulations to provide strong safety parameters. My approach was very much hands-on, which was demanding physically and mentally both for my staff and for me.

View of part of Frontier Lodge campsite on Lake Wallace

Every day was long and strenuous, one that commenced with a personal time with the Lord followed by a staff prayer meeting and then reveille for the campers. The daylight hours were filled with meals, Bible studies, sports events, handicrafts, and waterfront activities, culminating with a campfire composed of skits, talks, testimonies, and music. It finished with late-night surveillance after lights out to determine that all was well throughout the camp.

Despite the exhaustive schedule, we had tons of fun. Most important of all, there was a great deal of positive spiritual results among the campers and staff alike. I finished the camp period full of gratitude for the wonderful leaders that were there. Some of them became friends and associates for many years. I was blessed by the privilege of serving God in this way.

On the surface of my subconscious, my thoughts and prayers for my family were predominant regardless of the frantic pace of activity around me. It was a sense of release when camp concluded and I could return to Magog.

Gord Warnholtz, who was also at camp, and I were given a ride back to Magog in a truck that was owned by one of the supporters of Frontier Lodge. My pockets were as light on the return trip as they were when I was outward bound. My wallet was empty, but the rest of my being was filled with enthusiastic expectancy awaiting the discovery of how God had supplied the needs of Harriet and the children.

I was not disappointed. I arrived back in Magog to find that they were healthy and happy.

Although we did not have a set income from any organized source, there were a number of Christians who were aware of what we were doing in Quebec. We had not widely published our address, but it became known among many through word of mouth. The result was that God touched the hearts of people to contact us by mail to carry their prayers and thoughts for our well-being. Most of the letters also contained one or two dollars, sometimes as much as five dollars. Our mailbox always produced enough to supply the needs of the family for each day. This experience confirmed for me that we were on the right track and that God was cognizant of our activities and our requirements.

Harriet was very sociable by nature and had gotten to know some of the people who lived nearby. One of them was the Milne family. They had two daughters about the same age as our children. The father was the general manager of the textile plant that was the main employer in the area. This relationship was to be of importance to us later on when our activities were not understood and came under criticism by some of the townspeople.

There was hardly time to take a deep breath before the action in Cherry River demanded our full attention. We held a daily vacation Bible school there while the children were still on summer vacation. This proved to be very valuable in that some of the teenagers received Christ into their lives. One of the marked changes in them after they became Christians was that their vocabulary dropped the vile words that had been in everyday use around them by adults. Their parents took note of this and were markedly impressed, causing them to pay even more attention to the saving grace of Jesus Christ.

Gord and I started three services on Sunday—one in the morning for the Christians, Sunday school in the afternoon for the children and young people, and an evangelistic service in the evening. It was a task to walk back and forth between Magog and Cherry River three times each Sunday. This is what I did for a while because I no longer had the borrowed motorcycle.

During the week, Gord and I would often work in the fields with some of the farmers to help them harvest their hay for the winter. We accepted no pay for this, nor did we ask for any money at our church services. They were poor people, and we wanted to show them that we were interested in them and not what we could get out of them. In addition we got to know them better by working shoulder to shoulder.

By the time September came, there were eight more people who wanted to be baptized. We had another service in the river, and the banks of the stream were filled with onlookers who had known the ones being baptized for years, some of whom had unsavory pasts relating to the Saturday night dances and other deeds. It was a momentous stand they were taking before the whole community.

Before long, another twenty people confessed Christ as their Savior. The desire arose among all that had become Christians to have a church building of their own in which to meet. A suitable lot was available, which we agreed to purchase for the price of one hundred dollars. One of the Christians donated part of his standing wood lot to pay for the foundation, and others volunteered to cut the wood and sell it to raise the money.

Someone learned of an abandoned lumber camp that could be purchased and torn down to supply the rough material needed to construct the chapel. A work party was organized to dismantle the lumber camp structures and stack the boards in sorted sizes, ready to be transported out of the bush by horse-drawn sleds when the snow came.

The work that the Spirit of God had done in this neighborhood was breathtaking and astonishing. It became obvious that we could no longer continue to live in Magog and carry on the work that was required in Cherry River. A small house became available in Cherry River, and we moved in November of 1949.

I have titled this chapter "God's Kindergarten." I did so because it was the stage in our life that important basic lessons were assimilated as we ventured into personal practical application of the truths of the Scriptures. We found that we could trust God to meet our need. We found that the Holy Spirit would guide us. We confirmed that it was only God's Spirit that could change the lives of people through His saving grace. We learned the wonder of being His instruments to accomplish His work.

Now He had placed us literally at the crossroads of this little village where so much had already happened. The house that we occupied was situated directly adjacent to the land where a chapel for His use was soon to be erected.

Chapter 20

Church Building at Cherry River
(1950)

Personal Thoughts and Memories:

Our New Home:

The first time in six years of marriage our family was to be the sole occupant of a house.

In the war years we shared accommodation. After the war we lived with Harriet's parents, which was followed by confined quarters at camp, student shelter-sharing at school, and rented rooms in someone else's home in Magog. So it was with additional excitement that we moved into this little village setting.

The small house we rented was situated on the main road through town. There was no front yard. The main entrance began where the edge of the road ended. There was a vacant lot beside it that later would be the site of a brand-new church building belonging to the brand-new Christians at Cherry River.

Across the front of the house was a windowed porch that resembled a sunroom of sorts. The main floor consisted of a kitchen-slash-dining room and a separate living room. Across the entire back of the building was an enclosed shed.

There was a stairway, which was so steep and narrow it could almost be called a ladder. It led from the kitchen to two tiny bedrooms, cramped by slanted ceilings.

The backyard was a tangled assortment of wild weeds that merged with the wild weeds in the unfenced lot beside it. A straight path divided the yard. At the end of this path stood an outhouse. It appeared to be a sentry box, guarding the residents against any intruders that may invade from the banks of Cherry River that flowed quietly by the rear of the lot.

The shed attached to the back of the building served a number of purposes. It held a supply of wood to feed the stove in the kitchen. It was a workshop. It was a storage place. It was the location of a toilet seat perched on top of a large bucket tucked away in a corner (the contents of which had to be emptied into the outhouse pit every day).

There was electricity; therefore, we had lights and could use our hot plate. The major piece of furniture in the house was a massive wood-burning kitchen stove. It was a classic, complete with a firebox, a receptacle for heating water, and a large oven. It was the only means of warming the entire house as well as supplying all the hot water required for laundry, bathing, and dishwashing.

We also had a galvanized metal sink with a manual pump and a drain. A small basin sat in the sink that was used for handwashing. The water supply came from a spring situated in the empty parcel of land next door. It was piped underground into a dirt-floored cellar beneath the house and then up into the kitchen.

Winter in our New Environment:

Winter was long, bitterly cold, and jam-packed with blizzards from the beginning to the end. The snowbanks piled up outside the doors some nights so deeply that it became a major chore to force them open in the morning. One had to cajole the doors by pushing then scraping away the snow inch by inch from the inside as the outside snow yielded. Eventually a shovel could be brought to bear, and a path could be excavated.

The day-to-day endurance just to maintain the ordinary routine of life was something that was completely foreign to us. A fire had to be kept going in the wood stove in the kitchen to keep from freezing to death since the house had no insulation whatsoever. In spite of a roaring fire in the kitchen stove, frost formed on the inside wall of the living room not twenty feet away. I had to get up a couple of times during the night to make sure the fire was stoked to fight back the biting cold. Having a bath was a challenge. The warm water from the stove tank when combined with the supply produced by the pots and pans on the top of the stove provided the limit that was available at any one time. One of the most harsh of the daily rituals was the use of the toilet in the shed, especially on a frosty night! It was particularly telling on the children. Fortunately the bedrooms were kept moderately heated by the warm air that rose from the stove directly beneath.

Our water supply from the adjacent spring was interrupted on several occasions during the winter. The water was frozen in the pipes under the house. Consequently I spent many hours in the cramped damp basement using a blowtorch to thaw the ice in the conduits sufficiently to allow enough water to pass through to satisfy the needs of the kitchen above.

During the Summer:

My activities shifted to Frontier Lodge when the better weather arrived in the spring. A cottage, about a mile from the camp, was made available to us. Harriet and the children spent the camping season there. It was a delightful location in many ways, but it was also a lonely experience for Harriet because I was away at the camp from early morning until late at night most of the time. She could get over to the camp sometimes, but it had to be on foot and it was not easy with the two small children.

This year Frontier had the most campers and volunteer workers in its history. The spiritual results were encouraging. One of the major accomplishments we left behind was the replacement of the old farmhouse with a new fully equipped kitchen butted up against the dining hall.

The successful summer passed, and we moved back to Cherry River.

Church Life:

Some of the villagers gathered in front of the old school house

We continued our meetings in the schoolhouse throughout the winter. It was very difficult at times because of the bitter cold and the snowstorms. It was particularly distressing when it became so cold that it was impossible to keep the meeting room comfortably warm. There were times when the blazing fire in the potbelly stove in the middle of the room would be so hot that its sides would be fiery red. Despite this fact, the only part of one's body that would be warm was the part that was facing the stove.

Consequently one had to stand and rotate somewhat like a rotisserie to stay thawed for any length of time. This proved particularly awkward for the one doing the preaching and the one playing the accordion. The audience would often stand and shift around to accommodate the flow of the heat waves to be applied to the neediest part of one's body.

Regardless of the inconvenience physically, God's Spirit spoke through His Word, and many more of the Cherry River residents became believers in Jesus Christ throughout that winter. In the early summer there was another

Dr. Arthur Hill officiating at Cherry River baptism

baptism. The banks of the river were lined with people from the surrounding countryside. The crowd was a combination of those who had been baptized the previous summer plus the friends and relatives of those being baptized, added to by curious onlookers. It was another event that stirred the community.

In January we went into the bush to harvest the wood lot that had been designated to pay for the foundation of the proposed chapel. A number of the men who had become Christians joined forces and chopped the trees down, loaded them onto sleds, and hauled them out with teams of horses to a spot where they set up a circular saw to cut the logs into cord wood. It was then sold and the money set aside for the building of the chapel. We were on our way.

Villagers & David retrieving lumber from old lumber camp for use in Chapel

Also in January we broke a road through the snow to where we had dismantled the lumber camp.

After getting the snow sufficiently packed down on the designated route to remove the material, we went in with teams of horses, loaded the stacked lumber on the sleds, and dragged them several miles to the site of our chapel.

These two adventures were something I had never experienced before. I found it very challenging and invigorating.

Chapel under construction

It became apparent that we would require a considerable amount of money to complete the construction of the chapel. Steward's Foundation (a lending institution established for the purpose of helping churches finance building improvements) was prepared to lend us enough to finish our structure. I believe the payments to retire the loan were about forty dollars per month, which was a large sum for those new Christians to assume, but they did it joyfully. The church building was completed, and we held our services there instead of in the schoolhouse.

Our activities required that our means of transportation needed to be upgraded from the shoe-leather express and hitchhiking, which was our mainstay. We decided that if God wanted us to participate in directing camp, renovating camp facilities as well as preaching and at the same time constructing a church building at Cherry River, over the next months, we would need a motor vehicle.

Finished chapel

An old Buick became available via a Christian friend in Sherbrooke. It was a promising start in the direction we needed to go, but it turned out to be fraught with difficulties. It was a curse disguised as a blessing. Its main fault was a steering wheel that had to be spun halfway round before it began to have any effect on the direction the wheels would point. The result was the vehicle was not under the control of the driver when it was in motion. This did nothing for the composure of the driver nor did it increase the safety of the pedestrians or cars within striking distance.

We tried "taming" it to make it serve our minimal purposes. However, because of the slack in the steering wheel, the snow on the roads constantly grasped control of the direction of the wheels out of the driver's hands. This resulted in tedious and dangerous habitual crashes into windshield-high banks of snow. The farmers, who willingly hitched up their horses to pull us out, thought it was funny at first but, after a few calls on their generosity, agreed with us that this was an activity we could well do without. This problem along with a few other deficiencies, including a leaky radiator and a hemorrhaging oil pan, made us decide to give the car an early retirement from our employment. The task to deliver it back to Sherbrooke under the slippery winter conditions was a daunting prospect.

The day I took off for Sherbrooke at the controls of the old Buick was crisp cold and blue-sky brilliant. The brightness of the day took some of the edge off the dark fear I had relating to navigating this unreliable monster back to the stable from which it came. Some stretches of road between Magog and Sherbrooke resembled an oversized paved rollercoaster. That day, the pavement was coated with a glaze of slippery ice.

I traveled slowly and cautiously along the edge of the highway and finally succeeded in reaching the crest of the last steep slope. Suddenly one of the wheels struck a clump of snow that slid the car out into the middle of the road. I frantically tried to regain command of the vehicle but was unable. It began a deliberate spin down the middle of the thoroughfare in the face of oncoming traffic. I could see nothing but a horrific crash coming. I threw my body across the front seat and said, "Over to You, Lord!"

The rotation motion continued forever as I braced myself mentally and physically for the inevitable collision. The gyration sensation ended with a swoosh! I timidly raised my head and peeked out the window like a reluctant periscope, only to discover that the "beast" had safely deposited himself (and me) in a snowbank at the bottom of the long incline. I thanked the Lord that I was still alive and uninjured, and that no one else was hurt.

We decided to trade it in on a new Studebaker pickup truck. This required much soul searching before the Lord. We had to be absolutely certain we were on the path of God's choosing because we would be faced with a monthly payment of seventy-three dollars for the next eighteen months. This was an astronomical amount of money for us at that time given our circumstances.

God gave us the faith to believe that He would supply our need, so we proceeded with the purchase.

This reliable vehicle allowed us to devote time to the renovation required at Frontier Lodge before the start of the camping season while at the same time overseeing the building of the Cherry River chapel. Travel and physical labor demands were arduous, but they were also exciting and invigorating.

In April of 1950 a shocking event occurred in Shawinigan Falls, Quebec. A man by the name of Paul Boeda, who was the leader of a small group of Christians, was attacked while conducting a service in a rented storefront in the city. A mob broke into the building and started smashing chairs, destroying Bibles, and tossing them out into the middle of the street, where they were piled and set on fire. The Christians retreated out the back door and ran up the stairs to the apartment above. The crowd gave chase but was stopped from climbing the stairs by an occupant of the apartment who stood at the top of the stairs with a gun pointed toward the mob. He threatened to shoot unless they retreated. Fortunately they did.

During the entire episode, the police and Catholic priests were standing by watching everything. It appeared to have been planned by them and executed by the mob.

Paul made a desperation call to Arthur Hill from the suite during the encounter to see if he could get some protection for his group of huddled Christians. I happened to be at the Hills at the time and was party to all the fearful confusion. Arthur phoned the chief of police, the head of the provincial police, and Dupleissi, the premier of the province. None of them would do anything about it.

The affair received so much condemnation from the local and national press that nothing like it has ever been repeated.

In the fall Gord Warnholtz and I were asked by a couple of the men in Cherry River to work with them on a contract they had gotten from a local sawmill. Their proposal was to help them to harvest trees in the forest. They would fell the trees. Our job would be to remove the limbs and cut the logs into lengths suitable to load onto trucks that would haul them off to the mill.

It seemed like a good idea to us. It would allow us to get to know the men on a different level and also provide some additional income. We decided to accept their offer.

We purchased a power chainsaw, which was quite a new type of machinery at that time. It was an exhilarating venture. For the first while everything went well, apart from some problems that developed out of our lack of experience. However, as the days progressed, I began to become increasingly tired and felt ill. Dr. Hill thought I might be suffering from flu and treated me accordingly.

One day at midmorning I could hardly stand up. I left the job and went home. For a number of years I had been getting about five hours sleep a night and going full tilt every waking minute. Consequently I thought that might have something to do with my lack of energy. It is possible my fatigue may have reduced my resistance, but the real culprit turned out to be infectious hepatitis. The whites of my eyes and the color of my skin turned a deep yellow. I became as weak and limp as a wet dish cloth.

Once my conditioned was diagnosed, Dr. Hill told me that I had to drop all my activities. Complete and absolute bed rest was required for weeks, and perhaps months, if I were to have any chance of surviving this malady with any degree of health. It is an understatement to say that filling that prescription would turn our lives upside down.

The facilities of our home would not readily support a bedridden person, to say nothing about the physical demands upon Harriet with two small children and expecting a third. The church building was at a critical stage! The camp effort required personnel development during the winter to sustain the momentum achieved during the past two summers! There was the logging contract we had agreed to share! How could it all be handled?

Arthur and Peggy Hill offered me a spare bedroom in their home for as long as it took to recover. The two men with whom we had the contract released us from our obligation. Gord shouldered the rest of my commitments, which increased his workload considerably. Once again he proved to be the faithful and able friend I could count on.

Although Peggy Hill had many family and church demands on her life, she also became my personal nurse for the next two months. I was so feeble during the first couple weeks that my activity was limited to getting up to use the bathroom. Sleep was my primary achievement. My diet consisted of liquid, mainly fruit juices. Gradually my strength returned along with my appetite, accompanied by my desire to live and to resume my active life. It was a step-by-step procedure that stretched out to a couple months.

Chapter 21

Enlargement of Work and Family

Digest of the Times and Circumstances:

World Politics:

The North Korean forces made some gains into South Korea. There was fierce fighting between the UN troops and North Korea. U.S. general MacArthur argued openly for a frontal attack on China because it was backing the invasion of South Korea. This was in direct conflict with the policy of the United States as enunciated by President Harry Truman. The dispute resulted in MacArthur being relieved of his position and recalled to America.

Science and Social:

Remington Rand produced the first large-scale general computer. It was called UNIVAC.

Electricity was produced in the United States from atomic energy.

The heart-lung machine was devised by J. Andre Thomas.

Antibiotics were regularly used in the public at large.

Family:

It was good to get home again with my family after the debilitating prolonged illness. It was not easy for them while I was away. Little by little I assumed the responsibilities that I had to put aside for a while. After a few weeks I was up to speed again, and winter was in full force.

One of the farmers butchered some of his cattle. He offered to sell me a hindquarter at a good price. It seemed like a sound idea to me, and I agreed, providing he would cut it up into useable portions (steaks, roast, etc.). He consented to this arrangement, and the deed was done. He delivered the meat to me wrapped in separate pieces stacked in a container. The intention was to freeze the beef and then store it in our shed employing nature's natural freezer. We would use what we wanted, when we wanted throughout the next three or four months at minimal cost. Everything worked according to theory for the first two weeks of January, but in early February we had a major thaw for a couple of days. Most of the meat remained frozen. However, some on the outer edge of the pile began to melt, which we had to eat immediately.

The temperature dropped again to its usual below-freezing level, and all was well. But then we hit another extended period of warmer weather, and we had no manmade freezer to save us. This time the big melt destroyed the rest of our supply, and we had to dispose of it. What was supposed to be a huge saving turned out to be a humbling loss. We had counted on old man winter turning in the icy performance he exhibited last year, and we got fooled.

When April came we had a new member added to our family. We named him Timothy James. Before I went into the nursery to see him, Dr. Hill,

who was the attending physician, called me aside and told me that there were some problems with our son. When the nurse turned back the blankets, it revealed that both hands and feet were extremely distorted. His hands were bent back at the wrist, hugging the inside of his arms. His feet did not bend at his ankles but continued down his leg and appeared more like hands with short fingers rather than feet. I had a sinking hollow feeling as I anticipated what it might mean for him and for us as a family.

I had the task of telling Harriet about the situation before the baby was presented to her. It was a difficult moment, but we both accepted the fact that for some reason God had given us this new life for which we were to be responsible.

The weeks that followed were not easy as we tried to sort out what treatment was needed to minimize the long-term disability for Tim. The use of plaster casts was the first suggestion given to Dr. Hill. He and Dr. Klink put the first casts on, but they slid off in a couple of days. Since it was going to be a repeat process with short intervals as the limbs grew, Dr. Hill suggested that he and I should replace the casts as needed. This would release Dr. Klink because it was difficult to have both doctors available at the same time.

I consented, but it proved to be one of the most stressful and arduous activities I have ever undertaken.

My job was to force and to hold each of Tim's feet as far as they would go toward a normal position while Dr. Hill wrapped the plaster cast around them. This caused Tim great pain, and he screamed. I had to maintain a strong grip until the plaster set. It was a horrible, harrowing experience and seemed such a cruel procedure. The only thing that kept me from feeling like a callous monster was the thought that this was supposed to be good for Tim in the long run.

A specialist from Montreal came to Sherbrooke. He said to continue the cast application process on Tim's feet and the massaging of his hands. We persisted with this treatment until December, at which time the doctors recommended surgery.

We took Tim into Montreal. It was upsetting to put our cheerful little bundle into the hands of the professionals. Harriet and I had to dig deep into our faith to be able to walk away and leave him there. The intent of the procedure was to sever his Achilles tendon on each of his ankles, bend his feet toward a more normal position, and then apply a plaster cast. Theoretically, the tendon would heal in the new place and maintain the corrected angle. This process was to be repeated as many times as needed until the foot was at the proper relationship to each respective leg. This proved to be the first of many medical procedures attempted to improve Tim's ability to use his legs.

There was a cottage available near the camp. We were able to rent it. Harriet and the children spent the camping season there. It was a delightful location in many ways, but it was also a lonely experience for Harriet because I was away at the camp from early morning until late at night much of the time. She could get over to the camp sometimes, but it had to be on foot, and it was not easy with the small children.

There was a manmade trout pond a short distance from the cottage, which had been filled with small fish by the owner. This proved to be a major source of entertainment for us. There was a family of raccoons that lived in the neighborhood. They seemed to consider that the trout pond was created to provide them with their own private buffet. They could be seen whenever hunger struck, poised at strategic locations along the bank of the pond, ready to delve their deft paws into the water and flip out an unwary fish that strayed within their reach. There would be a flashing scoop, and the trout would find itself flopping around on the ground for a moment or two. It would then become a tender morsel for one of the "family."

The "family" took a passionate interest in our family. Sometimes they would follow us around; other times they would stand and stare. On occasion they would climb on the screen door and peer inside to see what we were doing! They became "stalkers," which was a little unnerving at times.

The summer passed, and we were to move back to Cherry River. The house where we had spent the previous winter was required for the owner's relatives and was no longer available, nor was anything else in Cherry River. That meant we had to search for something in Magog.

We found a place at 111 Pine Street. It was the best accommodation in which we had lived to date in the province of Quebec. While it had no central heating and we had to contend with the same kitchen stove arrangement, we had running hot and cold water and inside-toilet facilities. There were two bedrooms and a bathroom upstairs with a reasonably spacious landing. On the main floor there was a living-slash-dining room-slash-kitchen, which shared a more or less open undivided area. Star and Jonathan shared one bedroom. Tim slept in a crib on the landing at the top of the stairs.

Church:

The chapel we had constructed was a trim white building. It seated about one hundred people on pews, which we had obtained from an old church that had been renovated. We were quite proud of it in spite of its limitations. The Christians had built it themselves from start to finish. It became a symbol of the dramatic transformation that occurred since the simple message of the Gospel had been preached for the past couple of years.

Another change in the activities of the village was the discontinuance of the riotous, lustful Saturday night dance sessions that had been held for years at the hall down the street. The atmosphere of the village and the demeanor of its people had altered dramatically.

The auditorium of the building occupied the main floor. The basement supplied a kitchen, furnace room, and space for Sunday school classes. The furnace room also provided a pseudo study accommodation for me. I was able to squeeze a small table and a chair into a corner that was not covered by a giant hot air furnace and the necessary chunks of hardwood that fueled it. I built a couple of shelves on the wall that served as my library. It was here that I had a quiet corner where I did my thinking, praying, and sermon preparation.

The auditorium was small but pleasant and bright. There was a slightly raised portion at the front on which stood a modest podium. I preached from that spot many, many times and carry with me a multitude of recollections

One of my most lucid memories relates to Parker Powers. Parker, you may remember, was the man who provided the planks and boxes for us to use as seats in the schoolhouse when we first came to Cherry River. He was an old man who had spent his life in the lumber industry. He had been badly injured in his career and was arthritic and crippled at this stage of his life. He was hard of hearing and used a long hornlike gadget, one end of which he held in his left ear. It flanged out at the other end and gathered the sounds from the direction to which he faced it. The vibrations were then funneled down to his eardrum.

He always sat in the front row nearest the center aisle during the church services. The face of Parker looked straight up at me with his intense small blue eyes shining (sometimes teary), with his mouth partly ajar, revealing his toothless gums. The whole portrait was accentuated by the hearing aid protruding from the side of his head. Unforgettable!

Camp:

The camp committee asked me to be the general manager of the total camp operation as well as to direct the boys' section of the summer program. This entailed planning, organizing work parties, and supervision of construction as well as maintaining the flow of supplies needed for the various aspects of the activities. Since everyone involved were volunteers, a great deal of effort was required to contact people. This included not only the community of Christians in the eastern townships but also the city of Montreal as well. This necessitated many trips into Montreal and Sherbrooke during the winter months.

There were many night trips in hazardous blizzard conditions that had to be endured. The trips that were most memorable to me were those that I appeared to travel with only air fueling the engine of my vehicle. As I have mentioned previously, we had no stated income and no expense account from any source. We believed that if we were doing what God wanted us to do, our needs would be supplied as they arose without our having to specifically ask people for help. God seemed to put us to the test on several occasions.

A couple of those experiences involved my trips to Montreal. When I left for Montreal I had enough gas to get there but no money to buy gas for the return trip. Usually someone would give me a donation to help with my expenses, and thus I would have money to buy gas for the return trip. On these specific occasions, no one came forward with any cash. This left me with the option of asking someone for money or taking off for home trusting that God had some other arrangement. I decided I would ask only God for help.

Shortly after starting into my journey, the gas gauge pointed firmly at a big E. The E seemed to grow larger and larger with every passing mile. Most of my trip was mysteriously accomplished by energy provided from some place other than my gas tank. These incidents increased my faith in God to provide no matter what the circumstance.

The camp was well supplied with counselors and workers to meet all our requirements for the summer. The spiritual results were most encouraging once more.

Chapter 22

Back to Magog
(1952-1953)

Digest of the Times and Circumstances:

World Politics:

There were many changes in leadership on the world stage during these two years.

Dwight Eisenhower became the president of the United States, and Elizabeth became the Queen of England.

There was unrest in Egypt against King Faruk, which culminated in the army taking control and establishing a republic in place of the monarchy. In the overall shuffle, Great Britain lost a major part of her influence in the control of the Suez Canal.

At the same time, the Mau-mau Tribe rebelled against the British rule in Kenya. There was much bloodshed before an aboriginal government was established. This was to have a singular effect on the whole continent of Africa.

Joseph Stalin, the leader of the Soviet Union, died, which began a series of power struggles for the leadership of Russia, which lasted for decades. Marshall Tito became president of Yugoslavia and wrested the control of his country from the hands of the Soviets.

On the other side of the Atlantic Ocean, Fidel Castro began his campaign to overthrow Batista in Cuba, which would prove to have serious consequences for the United States and the Americas in general.

Science and Social:

The race for possession of the most destructive explosives was intensified. Britain developed the atomic bomb. The United States acquired the hydrogen bomb. A few months later the Soviet Union also manufactured a hydrogen bomb. Mankind entered a long period of what was to become known as the Cold War. The United States and the USSR tried to outproduce each other in the accumulation of weapons of mass destruction. Each strategically aimed their arsenal at the other's centers of power.

Transportation for the ordinary civilian was changed forever by Britain introducing the first scheduled passenger jet service between London and Rome.

Sony marketed the first pocket-size transistor radio. This transformed communication with the common people. Radios could be carried anywhere, anytime.

Mt. Everest, the tallest mountain in the world, was scaled for the first time ever. A party headed by Hillary and Norguay achieved this.

The first open-heart surgery was performed. Although it is now a common occurrence, at that time it was considered a daring venture.

Personal Thoughts and Memories:

Family:

Our home in Magog provided our family with a better environment than we had experienced so far in our life together. It was involvement in a large-enough community to have easy access to basic amenities such as grocery stores, schools, and a hospital. It was not so large that one had to have public transportation to travel from one end to the other. It was a reasonably happy balance between neighborliness and the maintenance of a sense of personal privacy.

Star and Jonathan found playmates in the neighborhood and seemed to adjust well to their new surroundings. However, it was also an upsetting time for them because Harriet and I had to be in Montreal often because of the medical needs of Timothy. We were fortunate that there were friends at whose homes they could stay when we both had to be away.

It was discovered that Tim had a dislocated congenital hip disorder in addition to his other problems. The doctors attempted several times to secure the hip joint but were unsuccessful. The decision was made that he would have to be placed in a cast from his hips to his toes in frog-legged fashion, with a bar placed between his heels. This would keep both his ankles and hip in the desired position for healing. There was a space left at his crotch for body-waste elimination. The cast had to be changed periodically to allow for growth.

Tim, Harriet

One of the farmers at Cherry River made a three-legged stool that had a padded seat and back, which could be maneuvered into the empty space in the middle of the cast. It was then placed an upright position, thus providing a chair for Tim. He spent hours looking out the bay window in our living room. The window was about eighteen inches from the sidewalk, and Tim waved and smiled at everyone who passed by. He became a local celebrity. He always had a cheerful, positive attitude that uplifted the spirits of all who met him.

I had a serious accident at this home. I was standing on a chair installing some curtain rods over the top of a window. The chair slipped out from under me as I was reaching toward the window with a hammer in my hand. The hammer broke through the glass, and I fell with my left arm stretched out over the jagged broken remainder of the window and landed full force onto it. My left forearm took the brunt of the fall, slashing my arm to the bone. I collapsed to the floor in a pool of blood with a mangled left forearm.

Fortunately, Mr. Milne happened to stop by just at that moment to see how we were doing. When he saw the extent of my injury, he rushed me off to the hospital. All of my tendons had been severed. I could not move any of my fingers in my hand. Happily for me, there was an excellent surgeon from Montreal in town that day. He assessed my problem and had the skill to wire together my tendons. My arm was in a sling for some time. To this day my hand has worked flawlessly.

Church:

The Christians at Cherry River were maturing in their faith. This resulted in a lessening of the overall responsibility for me as they assumed many of the tasks that had fallen to me. One of the benefits that evolved was an annual conference to which people came from all over the province. It was quite a joy to see the "Cherry Riverites" volunteering their service as their talents would allow.

This gave me more freedom to explore the possibilities of reaching out to the English-speaking people in Magog and in other localities. We already had about twenty children who were interested in attending classes. The difficulty was finding a physical location where we could meet.

After much searching, we rented a storefront that would suit our needs. However, it soon was to be snatched away from us. The Roman Catholic priest objected. He threatened to have our landlord's grocery store boycotted if he continued to rent to us. Consequently we were asked to leave.

We finally were able to lease an upstairs duplex from a Protestant Christian couple who had moved from Montreal to retire in Magog. They were free from the pressure of the Roman Catholic church and could rent to us for some time.

The Communists had taken prisoner John McGehee, the missionary with whom I had intended working with in China. He was detained for a year under poor conditions before being released to the United States. The door to China appeared closed to us. We had to reevaluate our situation; should we stay in Quebec or not? Although I could communicate in French, I was not fluent. Since there was a considerable number of English-speaking people, it seemed that we were in a position to serve among them.

Contacting people by means of radio began to loom large in our thinking. There was an English radio station in Sherbrooke that was available for programs such as we had in mind.

After prayerful consideration we launched into a Saturday night rally, which was broadcast live from Grace Chapel in Sherbrooke. It was received with much excitement and interest.

However, the idea of having a daily entrance into homes via the radio persisted in my thinking. Eventually it came together in the form of *Thoughts for Today*. This was a ten-minute combination of Scripture, music, poetry, and comments around a central theme each day, Monday to Friday, at breakfast time. It was well received.

Since there were so many new Christians in the general area of Sherbrooke, there was a hungering for a more formal knowledge of the Scripture. I was encouraged to start an evening Bible school one night a week.

All of these activities were taking their toll on my energy and time. The only way it could be handled was through the effort of competent, enthusiastic coworkers. In addition to Gord Warnholtz, whom I have already mentioned, there was his brother Fred Warnholtz, Fred's wife, Jean, Colin Anderson from Emmaus days, my friend Gord Mitchell, with whom I had been associated in youth work in Toronto, and his wife, Mary.

After the war, Gord Mitchell got his degree in accounting and was employed in Ontario. He became intrigued with the work God was doing through us in Quebec and wanted to be part of it. He was able to get a position with an accounting firm in Sherbrooke and moved his family there. He became an integral part of the Saturday broadcast, the Bible school, camp work, and other facets of my life.

Camp:

The camp continued to be well staffed, and the results showed in the increased number of campers and the good spiritual results that followed.

As the camp continued to grow, more and better facilities had to be constructed. Coincidental with our needs, God supplied a superb carpenter, named Roy Buttery, who also was a graduate from Emmaus Bible School. He moved to the province of Quebec with his family and became available to work at camp. He supervised the erecting of many additions, including a motel-type accommodation for the family members of staff and a small gym to provide cover for rainy-day activities.

Chapter 23

Finishing Our Work in Magog
(1954)

Digest of the Time and Circumstance:

World Politics:

Churchill resigned in Britain, and Anthony Eden replaced him as prime minister.

Nassar became leader in Egypt. This change in the power structure led to taking control of the Suez Canal.

Bulganin became Soviet leader.

Because of the threat of Russian aircraft carrying nuclear bombs over the North Pole, Canada and the United States planned a joint radar defense system in the north (the DEW line).

European Communist countries formed the Warsaw Pact.

Clashes between Israel and Jordan increased.

West Germany joined NATO.

Science and Social:

The U.S. Supreme Court banned racial segregation in public schools.

USS *Nautilus* became the first nuclear-powered submarine.

Dr. Salk began inoculating children against polio.

The oral contraceptive pill was introduced in the United States.

The first successful kidney transplant was performed in United States.

The first optical fibers were produced in Britain.

Personal Thoughts and Memories:

Church:

The Christians at Cherry River increasingly assumed responsibility for the operation of their church. The annual conference continued to be well attended from various parts of the province. This particular year, there were people baptized from Cherry River, Stanstead, Montreal, Sherbrooke, and Drummondville.

During the summer, a daily vacation Bible school was held in Magog under the direction of Ed Down. He was a young man who had come from Ontario to take secular employment in Magog but who was there mainly to further the Gospel. The average attendance was about seventy children. The children and their parents enthusiastically received the program. However, the Protestant and the Roman Catholic clergy took offense and protested to their congregations. It became a real bone of contention in the town. Many of the people took our side and spoke out against the criticism being leveled at us. Mr. Milne, who was one of the leading citizens of Magog, was very vocal in our defense. Finally, the town newspaper gave us a resounding editorial of support, which put the matter to rest.

Fred and Jean Warnholz took up permanent residence in Magog to devote themselves full time to Christian work. They were capable people with outgoing, warm personalities. They were heartily accepted by the Christians in the area. They devoted the rest of their lives to this work.

Radio work:

The daily program *Thoughts for Today* and the Saturday evening youth rally continued to be received well by the radio audience. This encouraged me to push further into the field of using the airwaves to reach out to more people in the province of Quebec.

Over the past couple of years I had made several trips to the New England states, primarily to Boston. I visited several churches in connection with the radio programs and to enlist support for our work in general. In the course of these visits I met a number of successful Christian businessmen who became interested in the work in the province of Quebec.

While there, I also became aware of the opportunity in the United States to have radio stations that were owned and operated by Christians. I spent some time at one of them and gained some knowledge of the operation. I was offered the job of becoming the manger of this station, but I felt I should stay in the province of Quebec.

However, it did stir some thoughts as it might relate to the province of Quebec. I learned that there was a radio station in Vermont, near the border of Quebec, just south of Montreal that was for sale. It seemed to be an ideal way to get Christian programming into the province of Quebec without the Roman Catholics or government handicapping it.

I talked with some of the men whom I had met in Boston about the idea, and they showed some interest. This spurred me on to do some further investigation. It seemed to me that the most direct way to get an exposure to the whole picture was to meet with the regulatory authorities in Washington DC. I didn't have money for transportation, so I decided that I would hitchhike and see what the Lord would do. My plan was to get to Toronto via Montreal and then to Washington. I thumbed my way to Toronto, where I stayed with my in-laws. They talked to some others about my venture, and the result was that I had enough money for bus fare to Washington. I was given some names of people in DC who willingly provided a place for me to stay while I gathered the necessary information. I also visited some of the churches in the Washington area. They gave me sufficient funds to finish my research plus bus fare to return home.

The data I gathered was informative and added encouragement to the notion of purchasing the radio station at St. Albans. I felt that the trip had been worthwhile. As always, the Lord met my needs on the way.

Family:

My dad had developed a serious case of emphysema. The medical advice he was given led him and my mother to move to Arizona. The climate was warmer and dryer and more conducive to a happier, healthier life for him. This suited my mother also, for she had always harbored a hankering to live in the desert. They stopped by to visit us in Magog on their way to Phoenix. As it turned out, this was the last time I saw my father alive.

My brother Stuart continued to serve as a pastor for a church in West Guilford, Ontario. He and his wife, Jackie, were still actively engaged in Medeba, a camp for children, which they had started. I didn't see much of them. They were busy, and we were busy, and the distance was too great for casual visits.

Tim had two more operations that straightened out his left leg and foot alignment considerably. However, he would require repeated medical attention for the foreseeable future.

Star and Jonathan seemed to be happy with their surroundings and playmates. However, we had some nagging concerns relating to the limited educational facilities for their future in Magog.

Increasingly I had the sense that our days in the eastern townships were coming to a close. There were a number of factors that caused me to arrive at this conclusion.

Montreal appeared to be the place to which we were drawn.

Tim needed to be near the medical facilities that could do him the most good and which would allow us as a family to be close to him. Better schooling would be available for Jonathan and Star. Montreal would be closer to the radio station at St. Albans should that situation materialize. I could continue my morning radio program from Montreal as well as I could from Magog. My long-term interest in Frontier Lodge was diminishing. The expansion agenda I advocated, and for which I was willing to dedicate years to develop, was not shared by others on the camp committee. The door to China was closed. To gain pioneer experience in Canada before going to China was one of the reasons I came to Magog in the first place, and now it seemed that part of our mission was concluded. We were not to go to China.

In addition to the above reasons, I had a compelling desire to be in a larger center where there would be more opportunity to live among businesspeople with the idea of presenting Christ through my life. Montreal seemed to present such a challenge.

The Christians at Grace Chapel on the west side of Montreal invited me to work in their neighborhood. They had basic accommodation for us as a family in their church building, which could serve our purpose until a more suitable house was found.

After prayerfully assessing all of these factors, including the arrival of the Warnholtzes, we decided to move to Montreal in the fall of 1954.

It was not an easy decision. Our lives had been intertwined with so many people that it was difficult to say good-bye. We had shared with them joys and sorrows, triumphs and failures. In many ways their families became our families. Two or three situations stand out for me as I look back on that section of my life.

The first wedding at which I officiated was held in the new little church we had built. They were a fine young couple, Peggy McKelvey and George Briar. It was a most joyous affair.

Peggy died during childbirth within a year of their marriage. Hers was the first funeral that I conducted in the church. It was a very sad affair. The child lived. It was a circumstance that causes one to ponder what God is about when He allows such a thing to happen.

Another mother had a baby that was strangled on the umbilical cord during birth. It was a heart-wrenching experience to have to deal with the large family whom I knew so well. The baby was the youngest at whose funeral I have officiated.

One of the most trying events that occurred while I was at Cherry River was the drowning of a six-year-old boy in the river that flowed through the village. He was an only child of two fine Christians. Somehow he had gotten away from the mother's care and fell into the water. There was great sadness in the community as he was laid to rest in the little cemetery on the hill. It was a considerable responsibility to attempt to console the parents. The mother took it particularly hard because she blamed herself for being careless.

Earlier I stated the following relating to our work in Magog:

"We found that we could trust God to meet our needs. We found that the Holy Spirit would guide us. We confirmed that it was only God's Spirit that could change the lives of people through His saving grace. We learned the wonder of being His instruments to accomplish His work."

It is appropriate to end this chapter with the same words.

Chapter 24

Montreal
(1955-1958)

Digest of the Times and Circumstances:

World:

Europe:

Nikita Krushchev became the new leader of USSR and denounced Stalin's regime as a "cult of personality."

Anthony Eden was the new prime minister of Great Britain and was eventually succeeded by Harold Macmillan. Eight European countries joined the Warsaw Pact. USSR crushed a rebellion against Communism by military force in Hungary. Charles De Gaulle was elected president of France.

Vice President Richard Nixon of the United States and Krushchev exchanged visits in each other's countries. The Middle East became a cauldron of activity. Nassar was elected president of Egypt and took control of the Suez Canal. France and Great Britain immediately challenged this action with military power and were joined by Israeli troops. They attacked Egypt. The United Nations resolved the situation by inserting soldiers to keep the peace.

Egypt, Jordan, and Syria formed the United Arab Republic.

Iraq's King Faisal was assassinated in a military coup.

John Deifenbaker became the prime minister of Canada.

Fidel Castro established a Communist government in Cuba.

Science and Social:

The first optical fibers were produced in Britain.

Martin Luther King led the march against segregation in the southern United States.

Transatlantic telephone service began.

The USSR sent a probe to the moon and photographed the dark side.

Personal Thoughts and Memories:

Business:

While the main purpose of my life was to spread the message of the Gospel, I felt that I should become active in commerce as well. One of the employment choices available to me was some manner of sales. It had to be something that would allow me the freedom to work at my own tempo so that I might be able to have the flexibility that I required to use as much of my time as possible to be involved in Christian activities. Selling life insurance seemed to be one of the better prospects. One of my Christian friends worked for the Sun Life Assurance company, and he recommended that this would be a good thing to consider. I applied to this company and was hired. I received their training and was assigned to the downtown office branch.

I reasoned that if I were going to make a success of this endeavor, I would require clients that had money and the need for this product. It seemed to me that such a group would be the CEOs and presidents of commercial enterprises. I set out to meet these people by locating their names and addresses in financial publications that were available.

One of the people I met during this process was a Mr. H. C. Flood. He was the principal in a brokerage firm that bore his name. I asked for and got an appointment to present to him some ideas about business insurance. He requested me to put together some more information and return to see him. On my second appointment he asked me to consider working in his sales department. He offered me a job as a bond and stock salesman. I explained to him that I could not because I had committed June through September to Frontier Lodge, a children's camp.

This was in May of 1955. He told me that he would pay me a salary of five hundred dollars a month starting immediately until the end of September if I would come to work at his firm at that time! This was a substantial amount of money for a starting wage in those days. It meant that I would have no financial concerns for my family during the summer. I had already indicated to Frontier Lodge that I would not be continuing in my capacity there beyond that point.

In the course of daily business, one had to be aware of what was happening in the world, and in Canada in particular, since the value of the product we were marketing was affected by current events. This was a different experience for me because until this point, I spent my time, for the most part, studying the Bible and its application to the people with whom I dealt from day to day.

I quite enjoyed it and matured into one of the better bond salesmen in the company.

In the course of doing business I became aware of how much politics affected the daily life of everyone. My interest was piqued and would have a bearing on some decisions I would make a few years later.

Church:

I preached regularly at Grace Chapel and attempted to rejuvenate their approach to reach out to the neighborhood through renovating their physical facilities and revamping their public programs to meet the need of present day society. There was some compliance, in that some physical changes to the church facility were permitted, but the enthusiastic support of the older Christians was lackluster at best. Opposition materialized when suggestions were made to change the Sunday morning service to accommodate visitors from the surrounding area.

In addition to the work at Grace Chapel I became active in the Youth for Christ in the city of Montreal. This was an effort to reach out to the youth of the city through the joint activity of a number of different churches that represented several denominations. I was vice president of the organization for some time but resigned when the total of my other responsibilities became more than I could handle.

David, Stan Mackey, Malcomb Spankie, leaders of Montreal YFC

Later, when we moved to a new location as described below, one of the additional activities that I felt was important was to start a Sunday school in our neighborhood. I was permitted to use the space in the new school building across the street. There were many families moving into the new development. The parents were delighted to send their children to our classes. Grace Chapel eventually continued this project. Some years later they sold their building and moved their location to Cote St. Luc.

Family:

We moved to Montreal without having a home in which to locate. Grace Chapel had some extra rooms where we could sleep, and we used the general toilet facilities and kitchen for our other needs.

We had a harrowing experience while we lived at Grace Chapel. The floor of the sanctuary was refinished one evening, and the rags that had been used to apply the stain to the floor were left in a pile under the only stairs to our family sleeping quarters on the second level. In the middle of the night, the rags spontaneously burst into flames. Fortunately for us the caretaker, who had an apartment on the upper level on the other side of the sanctuary, saw what had happened. He yelled and awakened me. When I realized the situation, we got the children out of danger and were able to put the fire out. A few more minutes and our whole family could have been trapped and likely burned to death.

Another memorable occurrence that looms large in my mind took place in the kitchen of the church. As a family we went to have our evening meal, and as we entered the room, there appeared a huge rat. Harriet and the children scrambled to get off the floor and onto the counters. I grabbed a broom that was handy and attacked the rat. It was quite a duel (however unequal). The rat and I were the gladiators, and Harriet and the children were the cheering spectators. The good guy finally won and deposited the dead rat in the garbage. I felt like a conquering hero.

We lived for several months in less-than-ideal conditions, but there was hope ahead for something better. A new residential development was being constructed in the western part of the city called Cote St. Luc. We were able to buy a newly built home for ten thousand dollars. Since I had no established income that the bank would accept, one of the Christians in the congregation cosigned the mortgage for us that made it possible to complete the purchase. We were still living with no stated salary from any source.

This home proved to be the best accommodation that we had had as a family since the day we were married. It was a semi-detached dwelling. There were one thousand square feet of space on the main floor with hardwood floors throughout and a high undeveloped basement containing another one thousand square feet. There was no garage, but it had a driveway alongside the building. I constructed shelving for some tropical fish aquariums along the walls of the basement as well as a large wooden tank. My purpose was to breed them to sell in my spare time so that our income could be increased.

There was a brand-new elementary school erected across the street that was ideal for our children to attend.

Jonathan, Tim and Star in front of school across the street

We had more normal consistent family relationship than we had experienced so far. We were located in an English neighborhood. I had a daily work regimen. The children were going to the school nearby. We were able to take care of Tim's medical needs at local hospitals.

We also got a pet dog named Beaver. He was a Welsh corgi that contributed some spice to the children's lives. We had him when there were still construction workers busy in the area, and they teased him quite a bit, which caused a commotion. He also objected to the postman delivering mail and made his displeasure known by barking and charging at the door. As a result, he developed a strong dislike for anyone in work clothes or uniforms. This tendency was destined to get him into serious trouble.

One of those times occurred when a policeman was in our neighborhood, and for some reason, he approached Tim. Beaver was Tim's protectorate and consequently kept the cop at bay. The policeman pulled his gun and was going to shoot the dog. The situation was explained to the officer, and he left with no bad result.

Camp:

I decided that my major time limitation given to camp would be the summer following our move to Montreal. The camp committee did not share the expansion and far-reaching vision that I had for Frontier Lodge, and therefore, I felt that I could not invest any more of my life to this endeavor. I gave notice that I would not be available beyond September. This ended my contribution to Frontier Lodge.

Radio:

I continued my broadcast of *Thoughts for Today* from Montreal. However, after a couple of years, I had to discontinue the program because there were not sufficient funds to maintain payment to the radio stations.

A man by the name of Stan Mackay conducted a radio broadcast each Saturday morning from People's Church, which was in the center of Montreal. It was called The Sunday School of the Air. Our whole family became participants in the program.

The purchase of the radio station in Vermont did not materialize because the people who were the financial backers were concerned that some of the sponsors who were under contract sold products that were not acceptable (such as alcoholic beverages). I felt that we could wait until their contracts expired, but the fear was that this aspect of the venture might tarnish the reputation of the Christians involved. They found this unacceptable.

Move to Ontario:

By 1959, Camp Mini-Yo-We had grown so large that a general manager, in combination with directing the boys' camp in a more intensive manner, was required. I was offered the post.

The camp committee agreed to pay me five hundred dollars per month if I would take on the responsibility. Additionally they did not object if I took on other activities to supplement my income.

A bonus at my work supplied several thousand dollars at the same time, which, taken together with the sale of our home, would provide enough money to meet our moving expenses as well as sufficient funds to buy a home in Toronto.

It appeared to us that the Lord was indicating that our time in Quebec was coming to an end. The radio work had faltered, and the Christians at Grace Chapel were interested in assuming the responsibility of maintaining the Sunday school we had started at Cote St. Luc.

Chapter 25

Toronto
(1959-1968)

Digest of the Times and Circumstances:

World Politics:

The continent of Europe experienced a huge change in its political and social structure during this decade. The politicians realized that their countries needed to become more unified if they were to have any strong place in world trade and international influence. The superpowers, Russia and the USA, plus the emerging Chinese colossus, presented gigantic forces that dwarfed them as individual entities, but if united, they could compete on a more equal footing.

Great Britain endured a downsizing of breathtaking proportion. It was diminished from an empire on which the sun never set to a cluster of islands off the European coast. Country after country in the empire rebelled against the control of the British government. Generally, England resolved these insurrections with governments that were democratically chosen by the people within those countries. The net result was that most of those concerned remained within what became known as the British Commonwealth. The net result of this reorganization left Britain with severely reduced influence in world affairs. Because of the link historically, culturally, and linguistically, Britain became more allied with United States on most internationally important issues.

The USSR and the USA became increasingly fierce antagonists throughout the entire world. Russia pushed forward its influence through propaganda, trade, and military action from Vietnam to Cuba. The USA responded in kind, from financial support to forces that opposed Communism in

Vietnam to military support of an invasion of Cuba by Cuban exiles living in the United States. The invasion called the Bay of Pigs failed. Castro continued his allegiance to Communism and received from Kruschev, the leader of the USSR, a missile base in his country. The United States learned of this and set up a naval blockade to prohibit Soviet ships from reaching Cuban ports with missiles to aim at the United States.

The outcome was a competition between communism and capitalism as represented by USSR and the USA throughout the nations of the world. The struggle became known as the Cold War. Both counties had nuclear bombs loaded onto rockets that could reach each other's territory. Although open warfare was not engaged between the two opponents, there were many side struggles that summarized how fierce and emotional the issue became.

One of the most outstanding was the partitioning within East and West Germany. In the course of the aftermath of WWII, part of Germany was ceded to Russia and part to the Western capitalistic nations. West Germany became a democratically governed territory, and East Germany remained under the Communist ideology. West Germany prospered dramatically, and East Germany was a dismal economic failure. The consequence was a surge of East Germany citizens into West Germany to enjoy the good life. To counter the outflow of its people, the government of East Germany placed a guarded fence around the entire land with instructions to shoot to kill anyone attempting to escape to West Germany. The flash point of the scheme, which drew the attention of the world, was a wall that severed Berlin. This city had also been equally apportioned between East and West as part of the settlement of the war.

Despite the dangers of crossing the wall, hopeless people were willing to risk their lives to attain freedom. Many of them lost their lives in the attempt by being shot down by their countrymen as they tried to escape. Some, however, were successful and reached freedom by scaling the barrier safely and others by daring weeks and months of planning and digging under the wall. The action related to the wall drew the attention of the world and threw the Communistic approach to life into a bad light compared to Western capitalistic accomplishments.

John F. Kennedy was elected president of the USA. It was under his direction that the Bay of Pigs fiasco with Cuba occurred. It was also under his administration that the courageous stand against the USSR blockade relating to the missile bases in Cuba happened. The struggle against the expansion of Communism intensified in Vietnam with an increasing U.S. military presence. Racial tension in the USA heightened under the nonviolent leadership of Martin Luther King. Kennedy tried to have the Congress pass legislature to alleviate the situation, but he was unsuccessful.

In 1963 Kennedy was senselessly assassinated by a lone gunman who killed himself before giving any explanation for committing the act.

Vice President Lyndon Johnson was sworn into office immediately. He occupied this position for the balance of the term and was reelected in his own right in 1964. Under his time in office, Congress passed legislature that attempted to assuage the racial anxiety in the land; however, it became increasingly vehement, culminating in vicious riots.

Furious tumults challenging the Vietnamese conflict flared up over the entire nation. There was a huge divide in the population over the war. Because of the unpopularity of the conflict and the manner the public perceived it to be handled by Johnson, he declined to run for reelection and retired from politics.

Egypt, Jordan, and Syria united to attack Israel with the intent to obliterate it as a nation. To their chagrin, they were summarily defeated in a matter of six days. This counteraction resulted in Israel seizing and occupying the Sinai Peninsula, Golan Heights, Gaza Strip, and the east bank of the Suez Canal. The outcome of this audacious action caused many of the Palestinians to vacate these areas and crowd into land still under the control of Palestinians. This condition was fought by the formation of an organization that called itself the Palestinian Liberation Organization (PLO). This would prove to be a contentious situation over the succeeding decades.

Canada celebrated its centennial. Expo 67 was held in the city of Montreal.

Science and Social:
Major steps forward in several scientific categories altered the social structure of the entire world.

Medical:

Surgical repairs to the heart were developed, including the pacemaker, artificial heart, and human heart transplants. These procedures revolutionized the approach to life expectancy and gave hope to critically ill people who previously would have died of the illness.

Space:

Regardless of the loss of life in the operation, the USSR and the USA put the first humans in space to circle the globe. Satellites were placed in space to continually orbit the earth.

Communication:

The silicon chip was patented in the United States, which made possible the evolution of the word processor and the computer for the masses. The orbiting satellites were used to relay TV images and telephone conversations worldwide. They were also employed to determine weather patterns and distribute the information internationally.

Nuclear Arms:

The fear aroused by the constant increased in production of nuclear-armed intercontinental missiles by the USSR caused the construction of a large number of family bomb shelters throughout North America.

Personal Thoughts and Memories:

Family:

The situation for us as a family seemed ideal as we started out life together in Toronto. We had a brand-new house. It had three bedrooms, a bathroom, a combined living-dining room, and a completely equipped kitchen adjacent to a comfortable eating nook. There was a full undeveloped basement with roughed-in plumbing for an additional bathroom. A compact efficient gas furnace provided central heating.

We had sufficient surplus funds from the sale of our real estate in Montreal to furnish our house in a tasteful manner.

Newly constructed primary and secondary schools were within a short walking distance. Educational opportunities for the children and excellent medical facilities were within easy reach.

We created a recreation room in the basement, complete with a television set. Compared to some of the places we had lived, it felt quite grand.

The first year or so after our move to Toronto, we were all engaged as a family with a new church that was meeting in one of the school buildings in addition to our responsibilities at Camp Mini-Yo-We.

We had a couple of wonderful holidays in Florida and the intervening states between Toronto and the Everglades.

Soon, however, Harriet became unfulfilled by the activities of family, church, and camp and wanted to once again have a business experience of her own. She had had a satisfying and successful venture working in a bank before our marriage and wished to join the workforce again. She did so and became a salesperson at the Bay department store.

As time progressed, Star and Jonathan became teenagers complete with quirks of that age group. This resulted in a rupture in relationship between Harriet and them that produced a lack of harmony in our family life. The situation was intensified because I had taken a position in national politics, of which Harriet was not in favor. She became vindictive toward me and made life intolerable by her verbal personal attacks and criticism every time I crossed the threshold of our home. This condition intensified over about three or four years.

In the middle of all this, my father died. Although he had been ill for a long time, the end came tragically and suddenly. He and my mother were on vacation some miles from their home in Arizona. He had emphysema and collapsed in their motel room after a tiring day of travel.

There were opportunities presented to me that would allow me to be away for periods of time. This seemed a good idea to permit some space to be found between Harriet and me with the hope that a better relationship could be established. This, however, did not occur.

We drifted further apart. The entire circumstance became untenable and rapidly deteriorated into a condition where our family was on the verge of breaking up. The situation was resolved in the divorce court. The court awarded me custody of Timothy and Jonathan. Star was of age and, upon being employed by Air Canada, had previously moved into an apartment of her own.

Sadly our union of twenty-three years came to an end in 1967. For me, the years leading to this event were painful and lonely. It extinguished many of the spiritual activities that had filled my life. An event such as this was not tolerated at that time in the religious society in which I moved.

Harriet had never enthusiastically personally participated in the church pursuits in which I had engaged over the years, but she had stuck with me despite the difficulties through which my endeavors led us. She also was an excellent mother to our children when they were younger, this despite the fact that her own ambitions were thwarted and subdued by mine. Many years later she told me that she should have continued her career and not gotten married. This is probably correct since she had a very good mind and had a passion to manage other people. A major part of our problem was this very fact. She wanted to manage me. I wouldn't allow it.

We sold the house. Harriet moved into an apartment of her own. I had custody of Tim and Jonathan, and we three moved into an apartment nearby so that there would be continuity of schooling for them.

Jonathan, Tim, and I carried on with family activities as best we could. We celebrated Christmas, etc., and even managed another trip south where we had some interesting adventures along with some good fun.

In 1968 Tim, Jonathan, and I moved to Vancouver, British Columbia. My political involvement had come to an end. There was no church or business association that required me to remain in Toronto.

Early in the decade my political activity took me to Vancouver for the first time. It was a clear sunny day in March that I flew across a continent that was completely blanketed with snow. The aircraft approached Vancouver over the Fraser Valley, which was carpeted with lush green grass. The contrast was startling! The drive from the airport to the Vancouver Hotel added to the enchantment. The well-kept lawns provided backdrop for the luxuriant blossoms that permeated the grounds of the residences along the route. It was most impressive! I thought to myself, *This is the place to live!*

Over the years my political responsibilities caused me to spend a good deal of time in Vancouver, which allowed me to experience it in summer, winter, and fall, rain and sunshine, fair and foul. My initial conclusion that this was the place to live had not changed. Since my circumstances now made it possible, I made the move for Tim's and Jonathan's sake as well as my own.

Camp:

I directed Camp Mini-Yo-We from 1959 to 1964. There was much to do during the winter as well as the summer.

In addition to being responsible to obtain and train the staff during the winter, means of contact had to be provided with the boys who had attended camp the previous summer. This took several different forms. There were boys' clubs throughout the province for which activities had to be generated. This ranged from meeting in homes near to where they lived to ski weekends, which were jointly planned with Ethyl Lee, who was the director of girls' camp. Father and Son banquets were also a popular affair held once a year.

In the summer, as general manager of the whole operation, my duties started in the springtime with the supervision of any new construction that was underway and continued through July and August overseeing the maintenance. In July I directed boys' camp as well.

Politics:

During my time in the investment business in Montreal, I had become aware of the enormous influence that politics in Ottawa had on the everyday life of the individual people in the country. When I returned to Toronto I had an understanding with the committee of Camp Mini-Yo-We that I would have the freedom to be occupied in other things in addition to camp activities. When the initial work relating to my responsibilities at camp were in hand, one of the things to which I devoted my attention was to learn more about the national political parties that controlled the decision making in Ottawa.

The two major parties were the Liberals and Progressive Conservatives. There were two lesser parties, the New Democrats and Social Credit.

I set out to discover the principles for which each of them stood and how they operated.

I had some connections with people from my high school days, which had become involved in politics. One was a Liberal, and the other was a Conservative. I contacted them and told them of my interest and asked them to take me to some of their meetings and give me some literature so that I could have some idea for what they stood and how they went about doing their business. I met many of the top people in both parties and attended several meetings.

The result was disappointing to me. I concluded that neither party was founded on basic principles underlying decision making that guided their thinking when planning for the future of the country. Both seemed to have the attitude that they would do or say anything to persuade the electorate to vote them into power. Once in power, they would legislate according to the expediency of the moment. This was completely foreign to my nature and the practice of my lifetime to that point. It seemed to promote power at any cost both within the parties themselves and, what is more damaging, the people of Canada. I concluded that neither organization offered a vehicle that satisfied the requirement of my primary approach to life.

I then set out to examine how the other two parties arrived at their belief systems upon which they would determine legislative action.

I concluded that the New Democratic Party was based on a set of principles and that their attitude was to implement those principles in a manner, which in their judgment would be in the best interest of Canadians. It did not appear to be a power-hungry group of people. The problem for me was that their beliefs ran counter to what seemed right to me. The underlying tenet they held appeared to be that the state should control the social and economic life of the country—in a word, socialism. I believed then, and do now, that individuals lose their personal initiative when they are stripped of the need to fend for themselves and become totally dependent on the state. It is debilitating for the person, and the accumulated outcome is a weak international presence as a country.

This left me with one other party to examine to see if there was some organizational avenue in Canadian politics that could accommodate what I believed that I had within me to contribute. That was the Social Credit Party of Canada.

I did not like the name of the party because it used two words, social and credit, that appeared to indicate the very things that I was against. However, upon further investigation of their literature, I learned that they stood for something far different from the name would suggest. They held that all the citizens contributed to the aggregate value compiled by country, and that should be recognized by each member of society receiving a monetary dividend periodically, which would represent their portion of the net worth of the whole, hence the name Social Credit. This did not make sense to me because of the complication of establishing such a value. I did not think it was workable. Fortunately it was not in the forefront of their platform and was not adhered as a major pillar of their approach. As I soon learned, most of the influential people in the party were of the same opinion as I.

The principles upon which they did base their approach to government were (1) to have as little government as possible to create an atmosphere in which private initiative would be encouraged and rewarded; (2) the general public would not be dependent on the handouts of the state; (3) those who were handicapped mentally or physically would be supported in a suitable manner that would preserve their dignity and personal worth; and (4) taxation would be kept as low as possible so that more money would be in the hands of the people rather than the government. This was a framework within which I felt I could be comfortable.

It appeared to me that this party held some possibility for me if I were to become interested in participating in politics. However, there were other considerations that would come into play before I could make such a move. I would have to be satisfied that this was something I should do as a Christian.

There was a strong feeling among some Christian circles at the time that politics was an arena in which Christians should not be active. It was a conclusion that I did not share. My belief was that Christians should be in positions of influence that have the possibility of improving the life of the masses.

Social Credit had strength in the West (it formed the governments of Alberta and British Columbia). It was quite well known in Quebec but not in eastern Canada. In Ontario it was little known and generally was ridiculed and reviled.

The lack of acceptance of Social Credit by the people of Ontario, combined with the disapproval of many Christians, would draw much personal criticism if I were to associate myself with this party. Consequently I took a harder look at the people in the organization to help me ascertain what the right thing was for me to do.

I found that there was a mix of characters, which had different agendas, but there were also a great number of Christians. The leader of the party, Robert Thompson, and the premier of Alberta, were prominent Christians in their own right. I felt an immediate bond with them. In the end, after much consideration, I believed that God could use me in some capacity in this organization. I decided to join the party and contribute what I could and ignore whatever criticism might be thrown my way. In doing so, I felt that I should take out my Canadian citizenship, which I did.

It wasn't long before I was asked to organize an office in Toronto. A

David Wilson and Bob Thompson

businessman in the city offered to pay the rent for the use of a suite in the King Edward Hotel. This became our Toronto headquarters and was manned by Elsie Dawson, an older lady who was a friend of Robert Thompson. She was a Christian and proved to be a stalwart aid for much of the time I was in politics.

After working in the Toronto area for a few months, Bob Thompson asked me to be his executive assistant. This occurred after a meeting in our Toronto office. Another Christian, who was a friend of Bob's and also of Premier Ernest Manning, was present. His named was Jim Clemenger. He and I became fast friends, which lasted until his death some years later. The three of us discussed the ramifications of this new undertaking and if it was something I could handle. It would require being in Ottawa most of the time when the House was in session, it would entail engaging the press, overseeing the Ottawa staff, and be a general consultant to the leader. We prayed together about it, and I said I would let them know.

I felt this could be worked into the schedule of my camp activities. It seemed that my absence from home for some of the time might help the relationship between Harriet and myself. I felt it might be an opportunity to influence the decision making of Parliament if somehow I had a small part in it. It appeared to be a door that was opening before me, so I took on the responsibility.

I commuted between Toronto and Ottawa for some months. I found the work interesting and challenging although at times I felt I was called upon to perform beyond what my previous experience would warrant. Despite this, I proved to be a fast learner. This was confirmed by the fact that the national committee of the Social Credit Party asked me to be the executive director of the national party.

I had some concern about accepting this offer because although the party had made great strides across the country under the leadership of Bob Thompson, it had also accumulated a significant debt. I did not want to be in a position of leadership unless the deficit was brought under control. I finally accepted the position, providing that I would also be the comptroller of the organization and that no money would be spent without my signature. In addition to this, I agreed to be responsible for the raising of funds to meet the obligation of the organization. The committee concurred with my counterproposal, and the deed was done.

This placed the general underlying operation of the party squarely on my shoulders.

The first thing I did was to go to Allen Lambert, the president of the Toronto Dominion Bank, and ask him for a loan of half a million dollars to pay our bills and to give us some operating capital. I had met him before, along with Bob Thompson, and believed he was sympathetic to our cause. He looked at me for what seemed a long time and then said yes, providing I could get enough people across the country to sign personal guarantees that would cover a significant amount of the loan if it were not repaid. I agreed, and he handed me a stack of forms to be signed by people who believed in our effort.

I immediately traversed Canada. Two or three weeks later I returned with the required indication of support. There were signatures of businessmen, politicians, cabinet ministers, and ordinary folk. Each had accepted an amount that they thought they could handle. The sums ranged from five thousand to twenty thousand dollars. Mr. Lambert was satisfied and took me down to the assistant manager of the main TD branch and told him to open an account for the party and to deposit the money we needed.

Now I had to raise the funds to pay back the loan and set the party on a sound financial footing.

This required travelling from one end of the country to the other. I contacted the CEO of every corporation of any significance from St. John, Newfoundland, to Victoria, British Columbia. I asked them to contribute to the party. We were looking at an election in the near future, and I had to raise the funds to pay for our election expenses. My message to them was simple: "We stand for private enterprise, and you need to have private enterprise represented in the House of Commons." Bob Thompson was doing a great job of presenting this point of view to the country. As time progressed, the party was gaining credibility. The corporations responded. We were able to pay off our bank debt and finance the expenses of the election campaign of 1962.

I was asked to be the national campaign manager in the election of 1962. This position was the most demanding and relentless devourer of my time and energy each day, of anything I have experienced in my life. It covered working with the press, setting up meetings for the leader, travelling to key meetings, briefing ad agencies, deciding what ridings we had a chance to win and which should get more money. Arising out of all this, I had to deal with telephone calls from all the different time zones throughout Canada any hour of the day or night. It was exciting but terribly exhausting.

That election resulted in the Conservatives eking out a minority government, with the Liberals having one hundred seats, and Social Credit jumped from zero to thirty seats, and the NDP increased from eight to nineteen seats. Social Credit had the balance of power.

This made Social Credit a force that had to be taken into account by the rest of the parties and the country in general. The press did not easily accept this. They set out to do everything they could to tarnish the reputation of Social Credit and to diminish the contribution the party could make in the country.

John Diefenbaker, the leader of the Progressive Conservative Party and the prime minister of the country, took personal affront with Bob Thomson because he felt that Thompson had robbed him of a majority government. As a consequence, in addition to being an ineffectual and bombastic chief executive officer of Canada, he had a personal vindictive approach to any constructive suggestion presented by Thompson to help parliament run more smoothly.

During his tenure as prime minister, Diefenbaker proved to be a petulant man who trusted scarcely anyone, even the members of his cabinet. He would permit none of his ministers to make decisions without his personal authorization. He was a person who seemed to be incapable of making timely decisions on his own. These characteristics taken together resulted in a backlog of business decisions of great import to Canada. The languishing accumulation of inaction formed an ever-growing blight on his administration.

This situation fostered a wave of foment among ministers of the various departments of the government, which eventually swelled into a rebellious tidal wave.

The PCs were divided and could not get their approach to parliamentary business in order. They became the laughingstock of the country as they sunk ever deeper into the morass of their own incompetence.

It became so bad that many of the members of cabinet were about to resign.

This had a marked effect on the conduct of parliament. It became a shambles of shouting, catcalls, and vindictiveness. Part of my responsibility was to sit in the gallery to observe in order to present my thoughts to our leader. I found it to be a juvenile exhibition, unbecoming to the major institution of the government of Canada.

Thompson tried his best to make this session succeed but received no cooperation from the prime minister. With great reluctance, Social Credit decided to vote to defeat the government, which in turn resulted in the call of a new election.

For the election of 1963 Social Credit presented the strongest slate of Social Credit candidates in the history of the party. Bob Thompson as the leader and Real Coauette as the deputy leader traveled the country extensively. We had high hopes that Social Credit might form the official opposition.

Again I was asked to be the national campaign manager. In addition to the other duties I had performed in the last election, I traveled extensively with Bob Thompson. He wanted to have the daily input of my reactions to the events as they unfolded. It was a time of excitement, bustling activity, and challenge. There were moments when the press talked of Social Credit forming the government, which drew ever-increasing attention to Bob Thompson.

When the dust cleared, after election night, it resulted in the Liberals having 128 seats, the Conservatives 96, Social Credit 24, and the NDP 17. This gave the Liberals a minority government and Social Credit holding the balance of power once again.

Mike Pearson, the leader of the Liberal Party, was chagrined that after several tries, he had not been able to secure a majority government, and Diefenbaker was furious that he had lost power.

Because of the closeness of the count, it left room for speculation as to whether one of the smaller parties might form a coalition government with one of the larger parties, thus achieving majority control of the House. Diefenbaker did not concede defeat for four days. This left everything hanging in midair.

Social Credit met as a caucus and decided that they would not make a move until either the Liberals or Conservatives indicated their response to the circumstance.

The Liberals were active behind the scenes. A high-ranking Liberal Party member in Quebec was busy contacting six French-Canadian Social Credit members. They were offered twenty-five thousand dollars each if they would cross the floor of the House and sit as members of the Liberal Party. In a secret agreement, which was sworn to by the six Creditistes (which was the name Social Credit had in Quebec), the announcement of the deal was made public. It had the effect of giving the Liberals control of Parliament.

Ottawa was in shock, most particularly the Social Credit Party. Thompson held a caucus meeting, and the six Social Credit members were condemned. Three of them disavowed their action, stating that they were mislead and did not understand the implication of what they had done. The other three completed their arrangement with the Liberals, but it still left the Liberals in a minority position and Social Credit with the balance of power.

Coauette was less than enthusiastic in the condemnation of the actions of the people who had made private deals with the Liberals, much to Thompson's distress. Eventually this event culminated in the open split between Thompson and Coauette. There had been a lack of the acceptance of the authority of Thompson by Coauette ever since Thompson defeated him for the leadership of the party. Matters were worsened when there were more Social Credit MPs elected from the province of Quebec than Western Canada. This fact was constantly played up by the press and inflated Caouette's already considerable ego. The sentiment overflowed into the public arena, which led to the division of the Social Credit members in the province of Quebec. Some remained under the leadership of Thompson, and Real Caouette led the others. The two groups sat independently in the House of Parliament.

Prime Minister Pearson was a genuine man of peace. He was willing to use his authority and power to do what he could in world affairs and in Canada to try to achieve it. In this mode he was ready to meet with Bob Thompson to listen to any of his ideas and to use his talents despite the fact that Thomson was in opposition to his government. This trait of Pearson's led to some very interesting ventures for Thompson. One of them was a trip to Africa in October 1965.

With Bob Thompson and dignitary in Addis Ababa

The Congo was in the midst of a revolution, and eight hundred foreigners were held captive. Thirty-eight of them were Canadian. The whole continent was in transitional upheaval at the time. They were in the process of throwing off the subjugation of the countries of Europe that had maintained military, political, and economic control over them for decades.

After WWII, Thompson helped Ethiopia to become reestablished following the occupation of Italy. He became a favored and revered person of Emperor Hailie Salassie and his people. During this period he was exposed to and became knowledgeable about much of the concerns of the other nations in Africa. The prime minister was aware of his background and felt that he could play a valuable role in seeking the release of the eight hundred hostages being held in Stanleyville. A secret mission was arranged with the Canadian Department of Foreign Affairs for Bob to work with them in meeting with some of the leaders of the various African countries to attempt release of the hostages. Bob asked me to accompany him. Although I would travel under Canadian diplomatic coverage, my expenses were to be paid by Canadian businessmen. I was to sound out the commercial people in each country we would visit.

It was a most interesting and venturesome experience for me. The three countries in which I spent the most time were Ghana, Kenya, and Ethiopia. I met many interesting people, including Nkruma (the dictator of Ghana) and Hailie Salassie (the Emperor of Ethiopia). We were in Africa for three weeks. I returned home via Paris where I had the opportunity to spend a few days.

The trip did not achieve the release of the hostages diplomatically; however, shortly after our departure, United States planes flew Belgian paratroopers into Stanleyville. The rebels fled. The hostages were rescued, released, and flown to safety.

Back in Canada our party was in disarray. The PCs were floundering because of the lack of confidence in their leader Diefenbacker, and a small number of Liberals, whose convictions were more conservative than the current trend of the Liberal Party, were discontent. Some clandestine meetings were held and some public discourse relating to the formation of a new party, which would reflect a conservative base that would accommodate all the dissident MPs of the various stripes. The Liberals also had some scandals that they were anxious to put behind them.

With all this happening, the prime minister was convinced by some of his frontbenches to call an election before it was required. He went to the country with the plea that a majority government was needed. It was also the election that he brought the "three wise men" into the Liberal

Party from Quebec. They were Trudeau, Marchand, and Pelletier. This trio would have far-reaching implications for the future of Canada.

The result of the election of 1965 left Social Credit with only five seats in Parliament. Two were from Alberta and three from British Columbia. It was a disheartening and discouraging situation. Caouette retained some seats from the province of Quebec under the banner of Creditistes. None of the MPs from the province of Quebec who remained loyal to Thompson were reelected.

David Wilson & Premier Manning

My travels throughout Canada during the past number of years had convinced me that there was a real need of leadership of the caliber of Earnest Manning, the premier of Alberta. Businessmen constantly asked me if there was any possibility that he would respond to such an undertaking.

I talked to him about it, and he indicated that if the conditions were right, he would consider it. Bob Brown, a prominent citizen of Alberta and the CEO of Home Oil Ltd., took it upon himself to discuss the matter personally with the premier.

Manning suggested that an intermediate step might be to form an independent organization specifically designed to study and to speak out on national issues. Then, when he retired from Alberta politics, he would become the spokesman for the group. Perhaps this might result in political leadership at the federal level in Canada. Brown asked him who should direct this organization in the interim. Manning suggested that I was one in whom he had confidence.

Brown contacted a good friend of mine, Ron Clarke, who was an architect in Edmonton. I was in Halifax, NS, on Social Credit business when Ron telephoned me. I had been locked in there for three days because of fog that had shut down the airport. He wanted me to fly directly to British Columbia and meet with Brown at his summer home at Qualicum Beach on Vancouver Island. I agreed, and as soon as the fog lifted, I flew across the country for consultation.

Brown asked me if I would consider undertaking this venture. I said I would but that I needed time to resolve my present activity with Social Credit.

I returned to Ottawa to a hopeless situation as far as I was concerned. Caouette had not been kept in check, and some of his members eventually became organizers of the Separatist Movement in the province of Quebec. I felt that Social Credit had no future and the best chance for the country was for Manning to provide direction. I also felt that Thomson could best serve as a member of the Progressive Conservatives if he wanted to stay in politics. All this I related to Bob and told him that I had been asked to be part of this new foundation and that I wished to resign.

I left the Social Credit Party of Canada with all the bills paid, a budget for a year, and the cash in the bank to pay for it. Unfortunately no more money was raised, and the party eventually fell flat.

National Public Affairs Research Foundation:

The new association was called the National Public Affairs Research Foundation. It was incorporated under a federal charter. A paragraph in the brochure we printed explained some of our goals:

"An important purpose of the Foundation, and a primary function, which is intended to be carried out by its members, is the conducting of systematic research into national public affairs. The results of such research will be devoted to the cause of public awareness. The particular spheres in which it is hoped to stimulate public interest have to do with the responsibilities of citizens, organizations, and governments and their relationships one to another. It is further intended to promote discussion and understanding of the basic principles of economics and government."

The Board of Directors was as follows:

R. A. Brown Jr., President, Home Oil, Calgary
C. McLean, Chairman, British Columbia Telephone, Vancouver
Renault St. Laurent, Barrister, Quebec

Ron Clarke, Architect, Edmonton
R. J. Burns, Barrister, Calgary
M. Shoults, President, James Lovick, Toronto

I was named the executive director of the foundation and was given a posh office at the corner of King and Yonge streets in Toronto. I had access to a chauffeur-driven car, an open-ended expense account, and travel privileges. My responsibility was to get some studies done on subjects that were of national interest. I was also given the freedom to be active in other unrelated business activities.

*David Wilson
named exec director*

Initially it was our intention to remain quiet and not to make a splash in the media. This was achieved for a while, but eventually I was confronted by Peter Newman, who was then a reporter for the *Toronto Star,* who told me that he had information about our activities. He asked me for an interview to reveal what we were all about.

I had given Peter time during the period when I was executive director of Social Credit, and our association was congenial. I told him that we were not ready to go public and persuaded him to forego publishing anything now. I told him that when the time came I would give him a head start on the story. He agreed to wait. He waited for some time but called me one day and said that the story was circulating in the rumor stage and that he would have to print what he knew unless I would give him the facts.

I realized that it was a sensitive issue because many of the people who were on the board of the foundation did not want to have publicity. I phoned Bob Brown, who was in London, England, and related to him the situation. He advised me to grant the interview and to let the facts be known. This I did, and Peter conveyed a true representation of our discussion. The article in the *Toronto Star* carried pictures of all the members of the board as well as myself, including a description of each person's background. However, the damaging part of the piece was the headline given to it by the newspaper's editor. It indicated that we were a "new right-wing group," which of course we were not. Several of the members of the board were incensed, especially

Renault St. Laurent, who was the son of the former Liberal prime minister of Canada. I was accused of being a publicity seeker. It was a difficult moment for me, but with time it passed.

The foundation was instrumental in distributing copies of Premier Manning's published thesis "Political Realignment" and Preston Manning's studies on Indian affairs.

Toronto office

Premier Manning's stand on politics drew attention from some of the important figures in the United States. I was contacted by them to try to arrange a meeting with him in California. He agreed to go, and I was also included, as was his son Preston. It was an interesting trip, and many contacts were made. Among those that I met were leaders in the industrial space giant TRW. This proved helpful to me in that TRW wanted to have someone who could open doors for them in Canada. They paid me a retainer to aide them to meet people who might further their enterprise. This association also made it possible for me to recommend Preston Manning to be employed by them in California, which proved to be a timely venture for him.

Bob Brown made life easy for me and provided the opportunity to travel to many of the places where his business took him. It was an exciting life in many ways, and in other ways it took away much of the initiative I personally possessed because everything was provided. He supplied all of the expenses of the foundation and at the same time exercised control over its actions. I became a temporary figurehead. This was not good for me in the long run.

The time came when Earnest Manning retired. He called me into his office and told me what he had in mind. He was pleased with what I had done in relation to the foundation but was leery of the fact that one man controlled it. He thought that it was unwise for him to place himself in such a situation. His wife was also at our meeting, and she pleaded with me to let him retire since he had served the public for so many years and deserved to be out of the limelight. He wanted to be excused from his commitment to assume the leadership of the foundation on the basis of these two arguments. I understood his feeling and accepted the reality of the case and realized that the foundation's days were numbered. I conveyed the information to Bob Brown, and he proceeded to close down the organization.

The situation presented a predicament for me. I was left hung out to dry, and all that I had to show for it was the car I was given to drive as executive director. It was a 1968 Thunderbird.

That was when I moved to Vancouver.

Sermons from Science:

The city of Montreal was awarded the World's Fair concession for the year 1967 and named the project Expo '67. The world's attention would be focused on the city at that time, and visitors were expected to flood into it from all over the globe. Some Christians in Montreal wanted to take advantage of the event. Their desire was to establish an exhibit that would draw the public's attention to God the Creator. They formed a committee to develop the idea. My friend Stan Mackay was the leading force in the group and was named the chairman.

Stan and I had a close relationship when I was living in Montreal. We had great a deal of mutual respect for each other. They were looking for someone to give leadership to fund raising and input to the thrust of their concept. He asked me if I would help them in this regard. I said I would. They gave me the title of executive director.

My first responsibility was to help select the type of program that would be at the center of the endeavor. This entailed going to Los Angeles with Stan. We reviewed and selected a series of films done in time-lapse photography, which emphasized the God of Creation. It was very impressive.

Some people of national recognition were needed to be on the board to give the project acceptability across Canada. I asked Bob Thompson, the leader of the Social Credit Party, and Paul Hellyer, a member of the cabinet of the Liberal Government, to serve. They were both well-known Christians who believed in the proposal and enthusiastically allowed their names to be connected to Sermons from Science.

The World's Fair was being held in New York City at the time. The Billy Graham Association had a pavilion with the idea of reaching out to the people attending the fair. The board of Sermons from Science thought it would be wise to get some advice arising from their experience that might be applied in Montreal. They asked me to go to New York to bring back some data. I went, met some encouraging people, and brought back material and suggestions that were helpful in our stage of development.

Unfortunately, the problem I was having with Harriet was getting to the point of no return. For me to hold a position of such prominence would do untold damage to a Christian activity, such as Sermons from Science, if a divorce were to occur. I reviewed the circumstances with Stan, and we concurred that I should resign.

This happened at the same time as the position at the National Public Affair Research Foundation was being offered to me. Therefore, my move to this organization was given as the reason for my resignation rather than my personal problems. I knew another individual whom I felt would be supremely fit to take my position at Sermons from Science. I suggested the contact to Stan, and he followed through. His name was Keith Price, who went on to do an outstanding job with Sermons from Science.

Jones Morris Wilson:

My contacts in the business world presented many opportunities. One could take advantage of the situation if a suitable corporate vehicle were available, providing it did not conflict with the other activities in which I was engaged.

There was a person in Montreal who had some experience in securities and whom I had come to know when I lived in Montreal. His name was Frank Jones. Through Bob Thompson, I met another person who lived in British Columbia who was a businessman and an investor. His name was George Morris. Both of them were interested in forming an alliance to find businesses that were for sale or that required money for expansion. For a fee, we were to match them with appropriate partners. The company was Jones, Morris, Wilson. I was the executive vice president and carried most of the responsibility. Our office was in Toronto.

We chased a lot of intriguing stuff, but none of it materialized into dollars in the bank for us. Many of the projects would have meant large sums of money in our pockets. One of the more fascinating ones involved the government of Antigua in the Caribbean.

The Canadian government established a fund to help some of the undeveloped countries to improve their standard of living. Several Canadian companies ventured into these countries to use their expertise in engineering, construction, and various other talents to help them upgrade. Ron Clarke, my friend in Edmonton, went to Antigua and got agreement for his architectural firm to construct a school for the children. He was of the opinion that a consortium of Canadian companies should make a proposal to Antigua to modernize their sewage, streets, and electric power in their capital city, St. Johns.

A consortium was formed consisting of Calgary Power, Montreal Engineering, and Diamond, Clarke Architects. Jones, Morris, Wilson was asked to try to put this deal together and to explore other opportunities in the Caribbean Islands.

I went to Antigua several times and met with the president of the government there. They were very interested in proceeding with the program. However, a problem arose when we were about to conclude the deal.

Antigua had been part of the British Empire. When they got their independence, it only applied to the control of their internal arrangements, not one that involved other countries. It so happened that a British organization was interested in providing the same service we were offering. Antigua had to defer to them, and we lost out.

I traveled to many of the other islands but ran into the same situation. It was all very fascinating and educational but not profitable financially. When I moved to Vancouver, Jones, Morris, Wilson was dissolved.

Global Consultants Limited:

I formed this company soon after I moved to Toronto. It was registered under the Ontario charter. The purpose of this action was to have a vehicle to incorporate myself so that I might have clarity in handling the income from my various activities and the expenses entailed. The stated intent of the charter was broad enough that it permitted me to participate in a wide range of activities. I retained Global Consultants when I moved to Vancouver and found it useful for several years.

Summary:

This was a decade in which I rose to the heights and sank to the depths. I was exalted and I was abased. I had great hopes and found despair. Now I was travelling across Canada with my two boys in two cars, a Valiant and a Thunderbird, with some furniture trailing in a van somewhere behind. I did not know what might lie ahead. In spite of all the turmoil, I still sensed the hand of God upon me for good.

Chapter 26

Vancouver
1968-1970

Digest of the Times and Circumstances:

World Politics:

The world continued to be in turmoil as the two superpowers struggled to make their own ideologies supreme on earth. The primary current bloody battleground was Vietnam.

Soviet troops crushed freedom fighters in Czechoslovakia.

Yasar Arafat became PLO Chairman.

Golda Meier became prime minister of Israel.

Arab commandos hijacked three jets bound for New York from Europe.

The United States of America:

Johnson was the president of the United States and bore the wrath of the American citizens, particularly the young men that were slated to be drafted into the military. Riots broke out at some universities. This, along with the failure to bring the Vietnam War to an end, caused Johnson to lose the presidency to Richard Nixon.

Martin Luther King and Robert Kennedy were assassinated which increased the trauma in the nation.

Canada:

After Pearson's retirement, the Liberals chose Pierre Elliott Trudeau as their leader. He went on to win the general election of 1968. He led the Liberals to dominate the government of Canada for most of the period from 1968 until the early 1980s.

FLQ kidnapped British commissioner James Cross and kidnapped and murdered Quebec cabinet minister Pierre Laport.

The Canadian Cabinet responded by invoking the War Measures Act, temporarily suspending civil liberties in Canada.

Trudeau was a determined opponent of Quebec separatism. Instead he promoted a bilingual and bicultural Canada. He passed the Official Languages Bill in 1969.

Science and Social:

The hippie movement began earlier in the 1960s and increased to reach a plateau in the "summer of love" in 1967. It consisted mainly of people in their teens and twenties who considered themselves freethinkers who deemed they were not responsible to society and not responsible for society. They abandoned the normal behavior of ordinary citizens and lived on the streets and parks day and night. They set up camps in cities such as Los Angeles, San Francisco, and Vancouver, Canada. The net result was the creation of an upsetting element in the lives of many families and community life in general.

In Canada the hippie movement was condoned by Prime Minister Trudeau by saying that Canada was a rich country and that people should be able to live in any fashion they want. This had a detrimental effect on the lives of many young people, causing them to forfeit positive roles in society for much of the rest of their lives.

Pope Paul VI banned artificial birth control.

A treaty was signed by sixty-two nations limiting the military use of outer space.

The Concord supersonic airliner made its first flight.

Three U.S. astronauts circled the moon and returned to earth.
Survey 7 landed on the moon without a crew on board.
Apollo 11 landed on the moon. Neil Armstrong became the first man to walk on the moon.
Mariner probed space and sent back pictures from Mars.
The University of Wisconsin announced the first complete synthesis of a gene.

Family:

Upon landing in Vancouver, the first line of business was to find a place to live. The west end of the city was a logical location to try to locate a residence. There was a high school and many apartment buildings in the area. A new one had just been completed at the corner of Bute and Harwood that seemed ideal for what we wanted. I rented two side-by-side one-bedroom suites on the top floor. The boys occupied one and I the other. There was parking for the cars underneath the structure. And so we began our life in Vancouver.

Mabel in our boat

There was another person who was a key element in our family life because of the fact that she had become a beacon light for me during the years when my marriage had fallen apart. I met Mabel Midbo at a time when my marital situation was hopeless and had disintegrated beyond repair. It was three years, from the time we met until my children had arrived at a point when our marriage could come to an end without too much catastrophic damage occurring to them.

From the very beginning Mabel was very leery of having anything to do with the breaking up of a marriage. She brought this subject up on many occasions. I had to assure her that it was only a matter of time before my present circumstance would have to be resolved. The delay was only because of concern for my children, their schooling, and their future. Now that we were living in the same city, she became an intricate part of my life and the boys.

Mabel had her widowed mother living with her. She had a colostomy condition as well as a disintegrating eye malady. Mabel felt a deep compassionate responsibility in the situation that she could not treat lightly. This was something that had to be considered in any future we might have together.

High on my list of priorities was to be able to get out on the water again. I wasn't in Vancouver very long before I bought a small outboard powered boat. I kept it in a marina in False Creek. It gave me my first taste of fishing for West Coast salmon. It was a thrill that I never really got over. The first boat led to a bigger one, and that one led to another one more powerful and larger. By this time, I had gotten a mooring spot at Thunderbird Marina in West Vancouver.

I have a multitude of cherished memories of my boat time in British Columbia. Because of the many years I had already spent on or near the ocean, I had a profound respect and awe for the majesty, serenity, and raw power of the sea. Of the many mental videos I have stored in my mind, I will mention two.

The first one Mabel and I shared together. We started out at Secret Cove on the Georgia Strait side of Sechelt Peninsular. I kept my boat there for part of the summer months at a place called the Jolly Roger. A friend of mine owned it, and he let me use it for free. I did so because it was near some of the places I liked to fish. It was quicker getting there by car and ferry than by boat.

From Secret Cove we went north up the coast via Malaspina Strait to Jervis Inlet and then into Princess Louisa Inlet. It was a smooth sunny trip ending at one of the most naturally beautiful spots I have seen in all my life. We were both enthralled to be in the middle of one of nature's jewels. At the time we had no idea that we would one day have a daughter, who would play a leading role at Young Life Camp that was placed at the entrance of this magnificent inlet.

On the other journey I traveled alone. Again I went north from Secret Cove up the Malaspino Strait, keeping to the mainland side of Georgia Strait, in behind the many islands, up to the mouth of Bute Inlet, finally making my way into Johnson Strait.

I was threading my way, as a tiny soul, through the impressive, massive grandeur of God's handiwork. Nights I anchored in fiords where the stillness was accompanied by the serenading of gentle creature sounds that soothingly saturated my spirit. All the while, the surrounding blackness was pierced by diamonds across the sky, whose sparkle had left their source light-years ago especially to reach me at this moment.

Johnson Strait took me by surprise as I turned south to return home. It was quite a wide expanse of water, and yet there were very large threatening whirlpools formed all over it during the tide change. I was once again impressed by the power of the sea in motion. It was somewhat scary to be alone surrounded by liquid sinkholes. I was happy to have a strong engine to pull me through.

As much as I enjoyed my boat and being out on the water, there came a moment when the cost of owning it exceeded the time I could in good conscience spend on it. Mabel put up with me and my boat but was never fully inspired as I was. Consequently I sold it and took up golf instead.

Back at the apartment, I was the chief cook and managed this job by dedicating about one day a week to making casseroles, spaghetti sauce, salads, and similar things that could be kept in the freezer or the refrigerator and pulled out to meet the demand during the week. The rest of the meals were fast foods of some type or other. We survived, but it was not an extravagant gourmet lifestyle.

Jonathan finished high school and wanted to take an engineering course at UBC. I didn't have the money to pay for the tuition. However, I did have two cars, and I decided to sell the Valiant to raise the needed funds. However, it was imperative that Tim have a car to get around because of his disabilities. Buying a Toyota Corolla on credit for Tim solved this.

Before the end of the first term at UBC, Jonathan decided that this was not for him. He then took a course to be a steelworker and found that he didn't like heights and quit that career. He asked me what he should do, and I suggested that he go to Fort McMurray and get involved in the real estate market. I had been there and knew that it was going to be a boom economy. He took my advice and eventually moved. He has lived there ever since.

After leaving high school, Tim became involved with some friends in a secondhand store. He also had many adventures travelling. He finally acquired a farm in the interior that he used for many purposes, including a camp for children with disabilities.

The time came when Mabel and I felt that we had taken care of our responsibilities and could have the freedom to be married. That is the story of the next chapter.

Business:

When I moved to Vancouver, the only income I had was two retainer fees. One was from TRW, the U.S. space and electronics giant, and the other was from a group in Ottawa who, in effect, were lobbyists. Both groups wanted me to be their eyes and ears in business and politics in western Canada.

While I participated to some degree in politics, I was more intent on getting into productive business endeavors.

The extent of my political activity was to be the campaign manager for Herb Cappossi and Evan Wolf when they ran for reelection in the west end. They lost, and that was end of politics in BC for me.

I had participated in some exploration companies in Ontario and was asked by a group in Vancouver to become involved in raising funds to finance in their search for minerals. I did this for a while, but it led nowhere.

One day both of the companies that were paying me the monthly fee sent me a note saying that they were terminating their retainer fees. They were not satisfied with the quality and quantity of information that I was sending them. This left me in a real dilemma.

I had the two boys to care for and no income. As I reviewed my situation, I came to the decision that I had been trying to sort things out without any recourse to God and He had brought me to an abrupt stop. I immediately asked for forgiveness and sought His direction. About three days later, Premier Harry Strom phoned and asked me if I would consider raising money for him to fight the soon-to-be election. He had taken over when Manning retired as premier. I took the next convenient flight to Edmonton to work out the details with him.

This began my travelling back and forth across the country again. I called on the CEOs that I had come to know over the years in national politics and received a lot of money for the coffers of the Albert Social Credit Party.

Harry Strom was a wonderful man with whom to work. We got along very well. He told me that if he won the election, he would make me the czar of industrial development in Alberta. I would report directly to him.

When the election neared, the poles were indicating that Harry was going to be defeated by Peter Lockheed. At that time, the deputy minister of Industrial Development suggested that I should be his assistant and become a civil servant and thus continue to use my contacts for Alberta. I felt this would be an act of treason against Harry, and I would not do it. Besides, I wanted to be in British Columbia with Mabel.

Harry was defeated, and I had to rework my employment schedule. But that is the story of the next chapter.

Chapter 27

A New Life
(1970-1975)

Digest of the Times and Circumstances:

World:

The Vietnam War remained in the forefront of the contest between the Communist nations and the Western nations in the struggle for world supremacy. By 1975 North Vietnam occupied Saigon, and the U.S. forces evacuated the peninsula.

Mainland China was admitted to the United Nations. President Nixon flew to China to meet with Mao.

Turmoil in the Middle East among Jews and Arabs contributed to the general malaise throughout the globe. Arab terrorist massacred eleven Israeli athletes in West Germany.

United States:

President Nixon resigned as president of the United States to avoid impeachment as a result of the cover-up of Watergate. Gerald Ford replaced Nixon as president.

Canada:

By the late 1970s, the bilingual policy had become a strong source of resentment in English Canada, contributing to a decline in Trudeau's popularity. The question of separatism was revived when a separatist party in Quebec won the 1976 provincial election and passed several measures to strengthen the movement. Under a controversial law adopted in 1977, the provincial government greatly restricted education in English-language schools in Quebec. The bill also changed English place-names and imposed French as the language of business, court judgments, laws, government regulations, and public institutions. (Future court decisions, including a 1984 Supreme Court ruling against Quebec's schooling restrictions, would limit the scope of the law.)

The Canadian economy experienced tremendous growth during the Trudeau years, sometimes despite the government's policies. The 1970s were boom decades in which Canadian farm products and minerals were in great demand on the world market. Long with this growth, however, came high inflation. The measures taken by the government to deal with the problem—controls on rising prices and wage increases—angered the labor movement. At the same time, Trudeau's advocacy of greater government intervention in the economy lost him support among business leaders.

Science and Social:

USSR soft-lands a space capsule on Mars and Venus.

Family:

Mabel and I were married in the United Church on Burrrard Street. It was the church that she and her mother attended and which I also attended with them when I first arrived in Vancouver. It was a simple dignified service held in a delightful little chapel that was incorporated into the main church. Reverend Cunningham was the minister at the time. We had a wonderful honeymoon in Hawaii and returned to British Columbia to begin our lives together.

We rented a three-bedroom apartment in the west end of Vancouver. The boys moved in with us. Tim went to Toronto at Christmastime to visit his mother and was to return by train. I was concerned about the trip back for him and phoned Star to see if she could travel with him. She was able to, and while here she intended to see a friend of hers who had moved to British Columbia. Having the three of them together was like the old days. Among the memorable events was the celebration of my birthday at the Bayshore Inn. As it turned out, Star remained a permanent resident of British Columbia.

During the next couple of years, my children went their separate ways and Mabel and I moved into a one-bedroom apartment in the same building.

An outstanding event happened! I became a grandfather! Star had been living common-law with Ralph Ajas. They had a son whom they named Harley David. They lived in the interior of British Columbia in the small community of Beaverdell.

About a year later, Mabel told me that she was pregnant. Heather was on her way into the world. If ever a child was conceived out of deep passionate love, it was Heather. It was 1973. It was the crowning moment of eight years of tenaciously clinging to each other through countless barriers and obstacles. A new and different life was about to begin!

When living in the above-mentioned one-bedroom apartment, we met a mature lady who did some of the cleaning and drapery changing in the building. Her name was Maria. We were struck with her buoyant, cheerful, competent, responsible demeanor. She took a liking to our little new daughter, and the result was that she became Heather's babysitter when Mabel or I were not able to be with her. She was an intricate part of our lives until the day she died. Maria introduced us to another lady named Esther, who was of equal quality as Maria. Between the two of them, they were substitute parents for Heather when necessary.

It was a period when new condominium high rises were being constructed in the west end. We bought one at 1725 Pendrell Street. It was the first place that we felt was our home. We brought our new baby to live there. It had a swimming pool, and our wee girl splashed and learned to enjoy the water, which, as it turned out, was to play an important part through many years of her life.

One day, when the three of us were out for a walk, we happened upon a new building of condos, and since it was an open house, we entered and inspected it. We liked what we saw, and the result was that we sold the one we had purchased and bought an apartment in this one. The address was 1816 Haro Street. It was here that Heather would grow from a baby to a young girl.

As time went on, Mabel was able to take longer flights because I was in Vancouver to maintain a stable environment for Heather. We complemented each other in all phases of our lives. One filled in the gaps for the other, which tended to cement our relationship even more solidly.

Mabel had a great pride in what she did. She felt honored to work for Air Canada. At that time, employees of Air Canada displayed the same esprit de corps. She took Heather and me to many of the places to which she flew. Japan, Hong Kong, New York City, London, and India were some of the stops we made. Mabel was highly thought of by Air Canada and was selected to be on the crew of exceptional flights involving the prime minister of Canada and special trips around the world. She was remarkably competent at what she did. She had the knack of making everyone feel comfortable in any situation. Through her whole life, she was never pompous or boastful of any of her accomplishments or the accolades she received. She had a graceful humility that was authentic and attractive.

Business:

Up until now, my business activities had taken me away from home much of the time. I determined that I was going to change my way of earning a living so that I would not have to travel. This was particularly important because Mabel's occupation demanded that she be away a great deal. I could have used the connections I had across the country to develop Global Consultants, but this would demand more travelling.

One of the things that would work for me was to enter sales in the real estate market. Consequently I got my license to sell real estate. I wanted to be as qualified as I could to advance in the industry, so I continued my education to obtain my agent's license. This would allow me to own or manage a real estate company. This entailed taking a crash course at UBC in contract law. In order to do this, I had to attend lectures every day for three months, Monday to Friday. In addition to this I had to complete assignments daily. It was a demanding time, but Mabel was right there in support of this activity. The combination of Mabel, Maria, and I managed to take care of Heather.

I began my career in residential real estate by being employed by Royal Trust as a salesman in their office on Cambie Street in Oakridge.

Chapter 28

A New Career
(1975-1979)

Digest of the Times and Circumstance:

World:

India exploded a nuclear device, thus expanding the number of nations having the capacity to develop a devastating bomb. This caused increased fear in other countries, notably Pakistan.

Civil war between Christians and Muslims broke out in Beirut that involved Syrian and Israel, causing increased tensions and unrest in the Middle East.

Chou En Lai and Mao Tse-tung, the leaders of the Chinese Communist reign, died. This initiated a struggle for control of the government in China.

Riots against apartheid tore apart the inhabitants of South Africa. It caused a reaction throughout the nations of the world and brought wrath upon the white government of the country.

United States:

Carter was the president of the USA. He led the country into a state of discouragement and lack of confidence. During his administration the interest rates rose to over 20 percent, which caused the failure of many companies and projects, including some in which I had personal involvement.

The Ayatollah Khomeini led a revolt against the shah of Iran and took over the government. Students attacked the U.S. embassy and captured the staff. Carter sent U.S. troops via helicopters to attempt a rescue and failed miserably. The embassy staff was eventually released by subtle means by the Canadian ambassador.

Carter arranged peace accord between Israel and Egypt.

Full diplomatic relationship between China and the USA was established.

Canada:

Resentment over bilingualism and the economy, led by Joe Clark, formed a minority government that fell after only six months as a result of foreign-policy missteps and opposition to his federal budget. Although Trudeau considered resigning his party leadership after his defeat, he was again named prime minister in 1980.

Trudeau demonstrated his continued opposition to separatism by campaigning in Quebec against a May 1980 referendum called by the provincial government. The referendum gave Quebec voters the opportunity to decide whether the province should become an independent country. The referendum was defeated.

Trudeau was successful in bringing the constitution of Canada home from Great Britain.

Family:

We had several happy years living at 1816 Haro Street.

It was within a couple of blocks of Stanley Park. This location afforded us the luxury of a front yard full of swings, slides, pools, beaches, and an old fire engine to climb on. It had a pond full of ducks, majestic swans, and sassy Canada geese to feed as well as an aquarium chockfull of all sorts and sizes of sea animals, right up to killer whales. If all that was not enough, there was the Vancouver zoo with a variety of animals from monkeys to wolves to wild cats and bears and many other species.

The seasons came and went. Each time of year our neighborhood gave us something special. In the spring and summer we were inundated with fragrant and magnificent flowers, added to by special events such as spectacular firework at English Bay. Almost every evening in July and August the nighthawks put on a sensational aerial show for us as we sat on our sixteenth-floor balcony. In the fall there were colorful leaves that we could pile up and jump into and a grove of mighty oak trees that produced plump acorns for us to gather. Most winters, Lost Lagoon provided a magical coating of ice on which we could run and slide and skate.

We had a couple of favorite restaurants within two blocks that we visited on Sundays, McDonald's (where Heather always had a hamburger) and the Roosters Quarters (where we had Montreal smoked meat sandwiches or barbecue chicken and french fries).

We had an unexpected addition to our family while we lived in this apartment. One day Tim arrived with a distinguished gift for Heather. It was a pure white gentleman cat, who immediately took command of everything and everyone. We named him Snowball. He became Heather's beloved pet for many years.

A part of Heather's life she seemed to enjoy immensely was preschool at the West End Community Center. Soon, however, she became old enough to attend regular school. We did not feel confident in the public school system and considered sending her to a private school. We investigated and decided to enroll her at Crafton House. It was located in the same general area as my office. This made it possible for me to have the privilege of driving her to and from school for many years. The daily time spent with her became very precious to me because we shared much of life in our conversations. By the time high school years arrived, the lure and prestige to travel by bus overruled the mundane and immature "Dad-transport." I lost my star passenger for much of the time.

Mabel and I felt that apartment living had served its purpose very well, but as Heather grew a little older, we wanted her to have a neighborhood of single-family homes to be part of her life. We decided to look for one near where my office was located. It so happened that a fellow who worked in my branch had developed heart trouble. He decided that he wanted to retire and move to the interior. He offered to sell his house on Fifth Ave in

Point Grey to us. It had three bedrooms and two bathrooms up and two bedrooms and one bathroom down. It was more than we needed, but it was a perfect location for us.

Church:

I had not actively participated in any church since moving to Vancouver. As I mentioned in the last chapter, I attended the United Church on Burrard Street with Mabel and her mother. Geof Still, a Christian with whom I had a church relationship in Toronto, moved to West Vancouver. He became a member of West Vancouver Baptist Church and invited me to join him. Mabel, Heather, and I did that for some time.

I wanted to have an association with a church closer at hand so that as a family we would have a better opportunity to become involved in the activities of the church. As a result, we went to First Baptist Church on Burrard Street.

Roy Bell was the pastor. Both Mabel and I appreciated his ministry. We encouraged Heather to participate in the children's activities on Sunday.

Roy Bell was appointed dean of Carey House, a Baptist college on UBC grounds. Rev. Croucher was recruited from Australia as the senior pastor at First Baptist. He was an outgoing individual who had become a leading church personality in one of the major cities in Australia. I was impressed with the way he was accepted in the city of Vancouver at large and his approach to the ministry at the Church in particular. I made a point of seeking him out, and we became friends as did our wives and children.

I was interested in exploring how I could become more involved in the activities he was promoting. However, just as that was coming into focus, there were some in the church who were unhappy with him and began to take steps to have him removed. The board of the church abruptly fired him and refused to give a reason, either to the church or to him. They just stated that he held some beliefs that would be detrimental to the long-term well-being of the church if he were to continue.

My observations led me to conclude that there were two things that he demonstrated by his actions that caused the church to take the action it did: (1) from time to time, he had other members of the church preach on Sunday while he sat in the audience. He believed that other gifts in the church should be used and developed; and (2) he accepted that all believers in Jesus Christ were members of the local church they attended and that they should be recognized as such without formal registration required.

I think that the board did not overtly make these charges because they realized that their position was nonbiblical and could not be substantiated in Scripture. They chose to bitterly uphold their traditions and were willing to sacrifice a valuable servant of God who had the potential to be used mightily in this city.

This was a great disappointment to me. I could not continue to associate with a group of Christians who could be so cruel, pharisaical, and despotic.

Years ago, when I was executive director of Sermons from Science, a Vancouver architect came to Montreal. He had produced an outstanding booklet called God and His World. The theme of Expo was "Man and His World," and this publication was a superb use of the time and circumstance. His name was Will Wilding. Will and a few others had started a church in Vancouver called Marineview Chapel, and it had prospered. I decided that we should visit the church and see if it was something that we might fit into as a family. It was a neighborhood assembly consisting of many families as well as students from UBC. We felt at home and began to attend regularly.

There were three services on Sunday to accommodate the number of people in the limited seating capacity. It soon became apparent that more spacious quarters were needed.

A shrinking United Church congregation decided to vacate a building located on the UBC grounds. Part of the Marineview Congregation started a new church named University Chapel. We decided to move with the group to University Chapel because it was closer to our home on Fifth Avenue.

Business:

Working at the Royal Trust office in Oakridge was a good introduction to the real estate business, but it was not in the part of the city that I wanted to concentrate my activity. My plan was to develop an operation in the Point Grey—Dunbar—Kerrisdale sections of the city. Consequently I looked for an office in that area that seemed to meet this situation. I offered my services to Canada Trust, the location of which fulfilled the requirements that I had in mind.

Soon after making this move, a friend that I had known for some time while I lived in Toronto, moved to Vancouver. He and his family had attended Hilltop Chapel, which I had a part in establishing. His children and mine had also been friends at that time. It was Geof Still that I mentioned above. He made a point of finding me and offered his friendship. I was pleased that he took this action. His reason for moving to Vancouver was to be the president of the real estate company A. E. LePage, British Columbia. This was a very large corporation in Ontario. It was expanding across the country by purchasing other real estate organizations located in other provinces. This was fortuitous for me since they were looking to open new offices and would require people who had their agent's license to manage the additional branches. This presented me the opportunity of being on the inside track if he were interested in offering me the position.

He did offer me such a proposition, and I accepted. Opening another office on the west side of Vancouver had been suggested in their expansion plans, and I was asked to pick a location and state the reasoning behind such a proposal.

It happened that a new building was being constructed at the corner of Dunbar and Sixteenth Ave. It was situated almost perfectly in the area into which I had planned to put my effort. I presented the case to Head Office, and they concurred that it would be an ideal location. While the construction was in progress, I needed to be occupied in sales. The most convenient office for me was in West Vancouver because it was just across the Lions Gate Bridge from where we lived in the west end of Vancouver.

Opening day of the A.E. Le Page office
(Heather and Mabel 3rd from left)

When the construction was finished and the office furnished, I had to get my staff together. Many of the people who joined me consisted of people with whom I had worked in Royal Trust and Canada Trust. It was an exciting time. The grand opening was a gala affair with the lieutenant governor of British Columbia being present as well as many company dignitaries from British Columbia and Ontario. Among the guests were my two favorite ones—Heather and Mabel. This was a complete change for me. I would now come to the same office every day for many years. I would have the responsibility for overseeing the activity of a couple of dozen people instead of being accountable only for my own actions and myself, which had been the case for most of my previous life.

Chapter 29

Branch Manager
(1979-1985)

Digest of the Times and Circumstance:

World:

Margaret Thatcher became the prime minister of Great Britain and took a firm hand in dealing with national and international affairs. She and Ronald Reagan became partners in their approach to world affairs during the last few years she was in power. The Russian's dubbed her the Iron Lady.

Israel singlehandedly destroyed an Iraqi nuclear plant to remove the threat of an attack.

United States:

Ronald Reagan was elected president of the USA. His positive attitude and legislative accomplishments restored the national confidence left void by the previous administration. He and Prime Minister Thatcher presented a united front opposed to the advancement of Soviet power in the world. He strengthened the U.S. military might and made it possible for the Russian rule to collapse.

Canada:

Trudeau was still prime minister during the first part of Reagan's presidency in the United States. They did not get along well.

After a brief period of Turner as prime minister, Brian Mulronney was elected to the office.

Reagan and Mulronney got along famously which, among other things, resulted in a Free Trade Agreement between the USA and Canada.

Mulronney obtained the right for Canada to mend its own constitution.

Family:

Our home in Fifth Avenue in Point Grey provided everything that we had hoped it would. The lane between Fifth Avenue and Sixth Avenue had family homes on either side. In some ways it was a village without stores and traffic. Friendly people, varying in age from little children to seniors, were the occupants. It was ideal for youngsters to play games, to coast their scooters, and to ride their bikes. It was a pleasant neighborhood. Some of the events and the stuff of life as I remember them follow:

It was here that Heather graduated from a bike with trainer wheels to one that she had to balance. Her first crash was into a telephone pole, but she got up and mastered the beast. It was not long before she was a pro, cruising along on a racer.

When we first moved into our house on Fifth Avenue, Mabel's mother joined us. She was becoming less able to carry out her activities on her own, and we wanted to make it easier, both for her and for Mabel, by having her in closer proximity. It wasn't long before she had a stroke and passed on. It was a devastating blow for Mabel.

Snowball took to the expanded landscape (after the confines of the apartment at 1816 Haro) as if he were released into the African wilds. He was still just an overgrown kitten, but he moved through the block-long neighborhood like the king of beasts. Soon after arrival he decided to demonstrate his prowess by climbing a large pine tree. He was fearless up to about twenty feet, where he clung to a branch, afraid to move either up or down. After letting him remain frozen in a scared position for several hours, we got a long ladder and the boy next door rescued him. Snowball never tried that again.

One of Heather's new playmates had a cat that had a fresh litter of kittens. One of them was offered to Heather, and she brought it home with a

dramatic plea to have it become our second pet. As usual she melted our hearts, and a little black-and-white girl ball of fluff named Suzy challenged Snowball for control over his newly claimed territory. Neither of them ever capitulated to the other as long as they lived. They agreed to disagree but just the same managed to live under the same roof for many years.

Our backyard consisted of a driveway into a carport and a small patch of grass. This small patch of grass enticed me to plant a garden. I had almost always planted something wherever I had lived in the past. I divided the space up so that it could contain a plum tree, raspberry bushes, tomato plants, lettuce, beets, carrots, radishes, beans, and peas. It didn't produce a huge quantity of anything, but it was delicious to have a taste of something from the garden that was freshly picked. The only thing that did produce a large amount of fruit was the plum tree. We always had lots of plums to satisfy our own appetites and also to share with our neighbors.

The roof over our carport was also a deck that was adjoined to our kitchen. It was a very spacious outdoor area that we used quite frequently. It had one detriment: the stairs that led from the deck to the backyard garden had deteriorated and needed to be replaced. My son Tim was at this time working with the provincial social aid department. He had several teenage boys who were estranged from their families for one reason or another. One of the boys had had some carpenter experience, and Tim brought his crew and replaced the stairs. It was an experience that I remember because of Tim's desire to help me and the fact that these youngsters were so willing to participate in such a venture.

Family Thanksgiving celebration David Star Tim Grandma Mabel
(holding Wilson)Heather Harley Bob

When we lived in the apartment, there was a sauna. I had made a habit of using it. I found it very relaxing, and when we moved I missed it. We had room to have one in our home, and so I had one installed. This was a great bonus for me. Every morning I would rise at about five AM and shave in the sauna, followed by a refreshing shower before facing the activities of the day. It was an invigorating addition to my busy life.

Christmas was a very special time for Heather. She constantly planned and dreamed about it all-year long. When the time approached for the celebration, she could hardly contain herself until the day arrived. On December 26 of every year, she began the process all over again. It was a time we all enjoyed immensely.

The province of British Columbia has so much to offer in terms of magnificent combinations of rivers, lakes, mountains, and forests. They tantalized me constantly to see more of them. I proposed to Mabel and Heather that on our summer holiday we should rent a camper that would provide sleeping and eating accommodation for us whenever we stopped. This would allow us to travel and not be concerned about hotel rooms, etc. It would enable us to move on back roads and venture into the unknown. We leased a suitable vehicle and planned our adventure.

Tim was staying in a place called Christian Valley at a spot where he was hoping to build a log cabin. Star was visiting at Edgewood, a village on Lower Arrow Lake. We decided that we would visit Tim first and then stay on the same road that passed his location and proceed to Edgewood.

Tim said he would put a hat on a stick on the roadside to indicate his spot. We found the road but never did see the hat on the stick. We decided to keep on going and head for where Star was located. The map indicated that the route was paved for several miles and then turned into a secondary unpaved road but leading to a highway that would take us to Edgewood.

We proceeded merrily along the asphalt until it turned into a well-kept two-lane gravel road. It was a sunny day, and we were happily enjoying this new venture. The two lanes shrunk to a one-and-half lane, and the roadway began to escalate to higher ground. The climb began to be steeper, and the road became two ruts. Instead of clean gravel, dry dirt was the pavement. As the vehicle moved across the dirt, it blew up as dust and invaded every nook and cranny of the camper. Breathing became difficult, and our nostrils were caked with a dry powdery crust.

We had seen no people, houses, or animals for miles. We were in the midst of a forest surrounded by trees, trees, and trees. Then we came upon a carcass of a dead bear. Mabel and Heather started to cry, thinking that we were hopelessly lost. The map said that were we headed in the right direction and should soon come out on a highway that was paved and which would lead us to Edgewood. Despite the fears and tears of my passengers, I pressed on relentlessly. Finally, to the relief of all (especially me), we burst out of the woods and landed on the blessed highway we had been promised.

The dust no longer plumed into our noses, and the rush through the clean air whisked away the layers of sediment that adhered to the exterior of the camper. With great relief we arrived at Edgewood, and Star got us settled into a pleasant spot beside Lower Arrow Lake. However, a monumental task still lay ahead. The interior of the camper was not livable because everything (including the bedding) was coated with the powder we had collected off the dirt road in the forest. We had no vacuum cleaner, so cleaning demanded manual effort—shaking, sweeping, cloth wiping.

All the dishes needed washing, which meant removing some from the camper. I had to change the location of the camper, and I didn't notice that Mabel's prized Tupperware bowl was in my path. I backed into it, producing a hole.

To say the least, I was not the most popular fellow in our family at the end of that day.

In spite of everything, we had a very pleasant visit with Star and an enjoyable stay of several days beside the waters of Arrow Lake.

The time came to depart. We decided to take another secondary road that appeared to be more substantial than the one we had followed a few days ago. More than half of it showed to be asphalt. It went over Mt. Faith and came back on primary highways at Grand Forks. It seemed to be the type of route we had planned to travel. Everything went as anticipated as we climbed the mountain, and when we reached the top, there was a place to pull off the road. We did so, thinking that we would have some lunch on the high ground and then move on down the mountain to Grand Forks. As I backed off the road, my right back tire hit something. It was a broken jagged bottle that had pierced the tire and produced a hole from which air slowly hissed. I had no time for lunch now and started down the incline to get to the town below as quickly as possible.

We had not gone far until the road narrowed to accommodate the width of only one vehicle. On the left there was a sheer rock cliff up, and on the right there was a sheer rock cliff down, with no guardrail. The roadway had been blasted and carved from the surface of a rock bluff, leaving no room for error. Occasionally there was passing space if one met another car. It was a nerve-rattling, nail-biting plight to be in with a collapsing tire.

After what seemed to be hours of white-knuckle steering, the road became tame again. It widened and was paved with asphalt. It emptied us into the town. We proceeded to the nearest garage and got the tire repaired while we caught our breath and prepared to head for home.

We had other family tent-camping adventures, but I could persuade no one to invade the wilderness of British Columbia via camper again!

Mabel's nephew, Tom Midbo, wanted to study criminal justice. There was a course offered in Langara College in Vancouver. Harold and Edith, Tom's mother and father, asked if Tom could stay at our home while he took the course. We agreed, and he came to live with us. He stayed for two winters and then changed his mind as to what career he wanted to pursue. Instead of criminal justice, he decided to become a teacher and he continued his education in Alberta. It turned out to be a good choice for him. The years have proven him to be an outstanding educator. Mabel became a mentor to Tom from the time he spent with us until she died. He gave the eulogy at her memorial service.

Heather wanted to earn money so that she could save for continued education and enjoy some extra things in life as a teenager. She got a job making and selling candy in a shop on Tenth Avenue. It was an excellent experience for her learning to deal with people and to handle money of her own.

Heather pursued training in the Red Cross swimming program that gave her qualification to become a lifeguard or a swimming instructor. This proved to be a good source of income for her during the summers at children's camps and at the local family Arbutus Club. These activities helped to pay for the expenses of her university education.

My mother came to visit us several times when we lived at this location. It was pleasant to have her. I had not been able to visit with her over the years very often, but our home and the environment on Fifth Avenue provided the ideal circumstances to accommodate her. Mabel and Heather came to love her dearly, and they had many enjoyable outings together.

LePage, the company for whom I worked, had purchased a condominium unit in San Diego, California. The purpose of the acquisition was to make available to managers within the corporation vacation accommodation at no charge. My time came for two weeks' vacation there. Mabel, Heather, and I had an unforgettable experience at this lovely city.

One of the places to which we were able to travel with Mabel was India. Mabel's assignment was from Vancouver to London, with a layover of two or three days and then on to Bombay, India, the name of which has since been changed to Mumbai. This was one of the most interesting and informative ventures we had.

We had several trips to India, and as a result, we were able to spend some time in London as well as Bombay. We saw many of the historic and current places of interest in London.

The exposure to the Indian society was educational and at the same time shocking. To see such wealth and poverty living side by side was revolting. There were millions of people who were born, lived, and died on the streets of the city while extremely wealthy people, as they traveled to work in the morning, stepped over corpses of the poverty-stricken who had died the previous night. All this was a result of the remnants of the class system prevalent in the country.

On one of those trips, I continued on to Singapore, where I stayed for a week with Peter and Donna Jordon, who were conducting a program to train YWAM volunteers. The atmosphere of Singapore was different from any other city I have visited. The city was strict in its laws in order to keep it free from illegal drugs. To participate in drug trafficking could lead to the death penalty. It was against an enforced law to litter on the streets, including spitting out gum. As a result, the streets were immaculate. However, by contrast, I remember dining in a kind of outdoor food fare, which consisted of a number of separate kitchens that prepared a variety of different foods that one could purchase and then take to outdoor tables and benches to eat. The drawback was that there were ditches nearby that were inhabited by very large rats that competed for any scraps under the tables dropped by careless diners.

Mabel had several assignments to New York City during the time we lived on Fifth Avenue. It was a city we both enjoyed visiting. It was my homeport for several years during my U.S. Navy days in WWII. I found it exciting then, and my interest had not diminished over time. It was Mabel's top-of-the-list place to go as well. As a consequence, we took advantage of the privilege we had to use passes on Air Canada to occasionally spend a few days in the Big Apple. We stayed with Mabel in the hotel during her airline layover at no cost to us. This made it possible for us to go to New York City for dinner and a Broadway show over a weekend.

On one of these adventures, our six-year-old Heather became an instant Broadway starlet. We went to see the play Annie. In the story, the moment arrived when Annie was going to leave the orphanage. All the orphans in chorus loudly pleaded with Annie not to go. There was a dramatic silence as all waited for Annie's answer. Immediately Heather jumped up on her seat and shouted at the top of her lungs, "Don't go, Annie! Don't go!" It brought the house down with a happy blend of cheering, clapping, and laughing! For a fleeting moment, adoring fans surrounded our Heather.

Mabel and I believed that if possible everyone should have some exposure to music as a child. To bring this to pass as far as Heather was concerned, we purchased an electric organ. We arranged for her to have lessons in Richmond. This continued for a number of years. She became quite proficient, and I, for one, really enjoyed listening to her play. She tried to get her music teacher at Crofton School to become interested in her and her instrument, but the teacher discredited her and her instrument to the point where she gave it up completely. I was furious to say the least.

Star and Ralph Ajas dissolved their relationship, and Star became a single mother. She moved to the lower mainland and met Bob McBride, whom she married. They had a son they named Wilson.

Jonathan visited periodically from Fort McMurray. I had tried to encourage him to return to school to become qualified in some activity that he enjoyed. Eventually he enrolled in Malispina College on Vancouver Island. He lasted a week or so and left because he felt he knew more than the teachers.

He came to our home on Fifth Avenue. I was disappointed he had once again walked away from a chance to gain qualification in a specific area that would be helpful to him. I came home from work one day, tired and stressed out, and he was there in a quandary as to what he should do next. We had a heated discussion, and out of strain and impatience, I blurted, "The only time I hear from you is when you want something." He walked out the door, and I have never seen him again. We have communicated by letter a couple of times but have never met face-to-face. Despite my efforts, true reconciliation has never happened.

Mabel felt that our present home was larger than we needed and more than she wanted to care for. A smaller townhouse became available on Sixth Avenue in Kitsilano to which we moved.

Business:

There were many aspects of managing a real estate office that I enjoyed and found challenging. One of them was the overall need to assess what was happening in the business world as it applied to the real estate industry. I liked having a part in helping people to find a suitable home. It was also interesting to me to encourage the salespeople who worked in my office to progress in their lives in general and to achieve good results in their careers. I also appreciated having a lot of the perks that came with the job.

However, the business was one of big money, and with it came greed and vicious behavior between salespeople and also clients. I found this side of the occupation undesirable and distressing at times.

Working under the command and restrictions of a large organization was something that I had never experienced before. I found it quite constraining to have to conform my action to accommodate the greater policymaking of upper management. The entire thrust of the company was to make a profit. The method they used was to exalt the salespeople who produced and to make those who had lesser production feel inferior, despite the fact the lesser producer may have finer business and human qualities. Hotshot action that materialized monetary results drew all the accolades.

The approach to commerce that appealed to me was to provide the best honest service, consistent over a period that would result in adequate return on the total investment of energy, time, and money.

Eventually this difference of attitude ate away at my enthusiasm for the business over the years until I finally left management in 1985 and became a salesman again. Ultimately I resigned from the business at the age of 69.

Church:

Mabel, Heather, and I attended University Chapel. UC became an instant success as far as size of congregation was concerned.

At the beginning there was a fruitful effort to reach out to the students at UBC on the part of a number of the members of the congregation. However, when students graduated, they went to other parts of the world and did not remain in our congregation. This seemed like an operation that would continue forever and not produce growth in the congregation. As a result, interest in this effort diminished and practically ceased.

University Chapel became a place for Christian secular professionals to meet on a Sunday to taste some biblical morsels suitably seasoned for their conditioned palates. We then returned to our jobs on Monday. There was little or no united attempt to portrait the love of God to the adjacent community. I was certainly part of that lethargic group.

My mother, my brother Stu, and his wife, Jackie, lived in Tucson, Arizona. We visited them several times over the years. It was always a pleasant affair. Most of the time we traveled by airplane, but a couple of times we went by car. On one of those occasions, we drove down the interior route through Oregon and California. We stopped overnight in San Diego, continuing to Arizona the following day. After our stay in Tucson, Heather and Mabel had to return to Vancouver by plane to keep schedules that were already in place. I drove back by myself and chose to go by the coastal route. I wanted to see some different scenery and to have some time alone to think some things through. This was a good opportunity.

I had become dissatisfied with my lack of participation in spiritual activities for the past few years and felt that I had to spend some time confronting this fact. I wanted to have God's guidance in the time ahead of me in life.

I planned to stop over in San Diego and some place in Oregon on the way home. Most of the time driving and overnight was spent in attempting to be open to God's guidance. The net result was my attention was drawn to Luke 4:18. The passage is concerned with Jesus at the beginning of His ministry. He read from Isaiah and applied it to Himself.

"The Spirit of the Lord is upon me, He has appointed me to preach the Good News to the poor; he has sent me to heal the broken hearted and to announce that captives shall be released and the blind shall see, that the downtrodden shall be freed from their oppressors, and that God is ready to give blessing to all who come to Him" (the Living Bible paraphrase).

This was His mission statement in brief. As one of his followers, I should fit better into what He was about. I meditated on these words for many hours while the beautiful coastline of the Pacific came and went as the highway meandered northward.

To what part of this magnificent announcement could I possibly contribute at this time of my life with the training, experiences, knowledge, and failures that composed my history to date? I spent hour upon hour thinking, praying, and absorbing these words, examining each clause before God.

The phrase that became magnified and personalized was "He has set me to heal the broken hearted." I had dealt with people in all stages of life and in all strata of society, in health and illness, in wealth and poverty, educated and unschooled, rural and urban, those who had succeeded and those who had failed. I had a comprehensive and practical grasp of the Bible, the truths of which are the source of all comfort and wisdom. I therefore concluded that my future activities should be among those who were in emotional, physical, or financial despair.

After arriving back home and prayerfully evaluating the practical application of what I should do to implement what seemed to be what God was telling me, hospital visitation was an obvious place to begin. This is the course of action that I took.

The hospital that was closest to where we lived was at UBC University Hospital. I began by volunteering as a visitor. The chaplain of the hospital assigned persons with whom to visit at the extended care unit. As a rule, I spent some time every week with someone who was not only ill but facing a difficult future.

I invested eight to nine years in this activity and met a wide variety of people. One of them was a man by the name of Gord Mowat. He was in a wheelchair and was difficult for the staff to handle at times because of his independent spirit and temper outbursts. Years ago he was in a car accident in the wintertime in northern Ontario. He was unconscious, lying on the front seat with his legs hanging outside through an open door. Before he was discovered, both legs had been frozen. As a result, they had to be amputated above the knee. He was in constant pain and was confined to a wheelchair for the rest of his life. Because some of his children lived in British Columbia, he was transferred here and he was assigned to the extended care facility at UBC. I was asked to include him in my visitation schedule.

I soon learned that he had become a Christian early in life and had not lived a pattern becoming a Christian but still was a believer in his heart. I spent seven years visiting Gordon. We became good friends and shared many ups and downs of life. The time came when he was passing from this life. I was called to his bedside. He was raving and irrational and did not know me. I quoted Psalm 23 aloud, and he calmed down peacefully. His whole faced relaxed, and he passed into eternity.

The staff wanted to hold a memorial service for Gord in the hospital, and they asked me to preside at the service. There were many people present who worked in the institution. Gord's daughter and her family also attended. Despite his idiosyncrasies, the people who knew him best loved him. I look forward to seeing him in heaven.

I learned there was a need for volunteers in the city of Vancouver for people to visit terminally ill patients as part of a hospice endeavor. I applied and was accepted. I added this to my hospital visitation.

There were two aspects to this activity. One involved going to the hospice section of the general hospital once a week, and the other was to be assigned to a person who was not in the hospital but who had an ailment that was terminal.

Most of the patients in the hospital had cancer and generally were close to the end of their lives. The duty of a person in my position was to visit any or all of the patients to do what we could do to make their situation more bearable. It might be just having a conversation with them, getting some coffee, or doing an errand for them outside the hospital. This led to my meeting many, many people over the period of four to five years. It was a heart-rending experience. I saw cancer victims of different ages with horribly deformed anatomies that made daily existence for them a harrowing ordeal. More often than not, I would visit with someone, and when I returned the following week, they would have passed into eternity. On a lot of occasions we had the opportunity to contact their families to try to provide some consolation.

The other part of the program dealt with people who were not in the Vancouver General. For the years I participated in this section of the hospice agenda, I met primarily with one man. His name was Ralph Knox. When I first met him, he was in an extended care facility in the west side of Vancouver. Ralph was a very large man who had lost the use of his legs and was confined to a wheelchair all day long. At night he would have to be lifted into his bed by a crane. There he would stay until the crane lifted him out in the morning and placed him back into his chair. He had the use of his arms, hands, and most of his upper body. He could breathe easily and talk. He had a power wheelchair that he could maneuver very well with his hands. He could get to the table and feed himself. He had a pleasant disposition, and conversation was easy.

Ralph had Lou Gehrig's disease. He was walking along one day when his right leg collapsed, and he fell to the ground. Testing revealed that he had ALS for which there was no known cure. It would progressively attack all his muscles until it terminated a vital organ and he would die. He was in his forties.

I visited with Ralph at least on a weekly basis for about four years. We discuss everything—life, business, politics, and God. Ralph became a believer in Jesus Christ, and we had the joy of sharing together some of the promises of God that accompany membership in His family through Jesus Christ.

Ralph didn't have relatives in Vancouver and not many acquaintances because he had not lived here long before becoming ill. I became a brother and friend to him.

His health deteriorated over time until he lost the use of his arms and hands and could no longer operate his wheelchair with them. He then perfected the use of a kind of electronic stick that he held in his mouth and was able to negotiate the power chair into the smallest spot, backward or forward. He amazed me.

By this time, he had been transferred to Lions Gate Hospital in North Vancouver. It was not long before he could not use his mouth and could not speak. He could hear and see and blink his eyes, so we communicated by my saying things and he would blink his eyes: once for yes and twice for no.

One day I visited him, and the nurse told me that he was refusing to have any nourishment. I asked him, "Are you going home?" He blinked once.

On my next visit, as I was entering the hospital, one of the nurses who knew Ralph and my association with him said, "You better hurry, his lungs are filling with fluid." I got to his ward, and I entered the curtain around his bed. His eyes were closed, his breathing rapid and shallow, but his was face was relaxed, peaceful, and at rest. The space in that little cubicle seemed to glow with the presence of the One Who is the Light of the world. Ralph had escaped the confines of a crippled body and was released into the boundless expanse of eternal life. Ralph was safe at home. He is another one whom I look forward to seeing in heaven.

There were some businessmen that came into my sphere of contact during this part of the ministry that God gave me. I will relate the story of one of them.

His name was Ron Brown. He was the brother of the president of Home Oil, who was the chairman of National Public Affairs Research Foundation of which I had been the executive director. I had met Ron during my days in politics. He lived in Vancouver. When I moved to Vancouver, I maintained contact with him.

Ron was a wealthy man who knew everyone who was anyone of social status in the city. He was a renowned member of the prestigious Vancouver Club and lived in a penthouse on the edge of Stanley Park.

Unfortunately he lost everything in a bad move on the stock market. He not only lost his money, he lost his prestige, he lost his posh penthouse, he lost his family, he lost most of his friends, and he became an alcoholic. A provision was left in his sister's will that his rent was to be paid for as long as he lived. This allowed him to retain a small apartment in the building where he had once occupied the penthouse.

There was much to like about Ron. He was pleasant, knowledgeable, intelligent, and affable although at times cantankerous. We spent many hours together over several years. There were no topics that we excluded from our conversation. Religion, God, and Jesus Christ was examined and debated from every angle. He rejected it all.

He lived until he was eighty-two. At the end, his health deteriorated rapidly. He was hospitalized in St. Paul's Hospital. I was the only one by his bedside at his death. His ex-wife said there would be no funeral since he believed in nothing. I arranged for his cremation, and his daughter came out from Calgary to receive his ashes. At her request, I prayed as she spread the ashes at the base of a tree in Stanley Park just outside the apartment where he had lived. A dismal and sad ending to a life that once was full of promise.

Chapter 30

Retirement
(1985-1995)

Digest of the Times and Circumstances:

World:

Mikhail Gorbachev became leader of USSR in 1985. He and President Reagan met and immediately found mutual respect for each other. This led to further exchanges. On a visit to Berlin, Reagan challenged Gorbachev by saying in a speech carried around the world, "Mr. Gorbechev, tear down this wall."

Gorbachev began a radical revamping of the USSR that led to a more democratic form of government even though he lost power in the process.

U.S. spacecraft *Challenger* exploded in midair after takeoff en route to the international space station.

United States:

George H. W. Bush was elected president of the USA. During his administration, the wall in Berlin came down and East and West Germany became united. The USSR disintegrated, leaving Russia standing alone.

Iraq invaded Kuwait and took over her oil reserves. Under United Nations sanction, Bush formed a coalition of military forces from a variety of countries and routed Iraq.

After one term in office, Bill Clinton replaced Bush as the U.S. president.

In the first two years of the Clinton administration, he led the country to a position that was far left of what the people wanted, and he lost control of the House of Representative in the midterm elections. He shifted his approach under pressure from the Republican House and balanced the budget, reduced taxes, and revamped the welfare system. These steps produced a buoyant economy, and he was granted another term as president.

Some missteps in Clinton's second term, coupled with other longstanding questionable activities, led to impeachment hearings, which drained the life out of his administration even though he was not impeached.

Canada:

Brian Mulronney became prime minister of Canada in 1984 and was defeated by Jean Chretien in 1993. His downfall was caused by poor management of the finances of the country and the introduction of the general sales tax, which was hated by the Canadian electorate.

Jean Chretien stated if elected he would abolish the GST, and he reneged on his promise.

The Reform Party was formed in 1987 under the leadership of Preston Manning and became the Official Opposition in 1997. Preston Manning used his power as the leader of the Official Opposition to force the Liberal government to achieve a balanced budget that provided a sound financial base for the country to move forward. Paul Martin was the finance minister at the time and took credit for it.

Family:

Our home in Sixth Avenue was one of two separate structures connected on the exterior but not joined in the interior. One of the buildings faced Sixth Avenue, and the other was directly behind. We occupied the one in the rear. There was an access walk from the street to our residence. A lane ran beside the property and behind it. A garage off the lane belonged to us. Between our house, the garage, and lane was a pleasant patio bordered by a patch of earth that we promptly planted with an apple tree, a plum tree, and many lovely flowers. It was a pleasant outdoor space that we thoroughly enjoyed. Our plum tree prospered and gave us and the neighborhood fruit for years. The apple tree, however, did not do so well in that it needed to be sprayed and was not. As a consequence the fruit was full of worms.

The interior of our home composed of two bedrooms and a bathroom up and living-slash-dining room, kitchen, and bathroom down. A fireplace was in the living room. All in all it was a cozy, comfortable place to be.

Our two cats, Snowball, and Suzy, embraced the new surroundings and happily lived there for the remainder of their lives.

We quickly established warm relationships with the neighbors. A young Jewish couple by the name of Rose occupied the other duplex on our land. They had a young boy. Mabel babysat him often, and the two of them became very attached to each other. Mabel also took under her wing two elderly widows that lived across the lane. Each of them lived alone in single family houses side by side. One of them, Dorothy Morrison, received Mabel's careful attention on a daily basis for several years until Dorothy died.

We bought a fancy new barbecue with the thought that Heather would have her friends come to our pleasant patio and have a good time cooking all sort of goodies. As it turned out, this type of culinary art was out of fashion with her group at the time since the food prepared in this manner was deemed to be unhealthy.

Mabel retired in 1991. By this time the airline had drastically changed from the organization of which she was so proud to one where the sense of doing a great job became one composed of people who were interested only in what was in it for them. The unions had corrupted the employees and had stripped them of their esprit de corps. They were diminished from being an outstanding company to mediocrity. As a result, Mabel was ready to retire and leave the unpleasant environment. When a suitable package was made available to her, she happily accepted.

I too retired in 1991 at the age of sixty-nine. About this time, Preston, the son of Premier Earnest Manning, was forming what would be named the Reform Party and would eventually become the Official Opposition in Ottawa. He pressed me two or three times to help him with this endeavor, but I declined because I wanted to use my time in hospital—and church-related efforts. Also I was in good health and played golf as often as I could and had done so since about the age of fifty. I wanted more time to enjoy this sport.

Golf to me was a great form of relaxation and social exchange. I found that walking through the beautifully manicured courses was spiritual therapy since I was plunked right in the middle of a sample of God's handiwork. Also I enjoyed the relationship with other golfers, some of whom became close friends over time.

My mother passed into eternity in 1989. The cause of her death was cancer, which at the end gradually sapped the life out of her. She lived with my brother Stuart and his wife, Jackie, in her final days. They gave her every comfort possible. I visited with them a short time before she died, and it was an experience of sweet sorrow. We talked about many things, including the wonderful future that she was about to embark upon. The morning that I was to depart, I went into her room, and she was sleeping. I was reluctant to waken her, but Jackie insisted I say good-bye. When she awoke, we had a few precious moments. The room seemed to fill with the presence of the Light of the world. There was hope and peace. It was similar to the time I have mentioned when Ralph Knox left this earth. My mother gave me much of the foundation that formed my character when she and I were buddies when I was so little.

The years Heather spent at Crofton had whipped speedily by, and we had arrived at graduation. It seemed only days ago that Heather, Mabel, and I sat in the principal's office, asking and answering questions, attempting to determine if this was the place we wanted our little girl to be and the school assessing if they wanted her or not. The answer was yes on both sides, and a journey of many years began, and now it was coming to an end.

When we started out, we had the financial resources to pay for the first year but had no assurance beyond that. We decided that we would push ahead semester by semester. Some of the years were more difficult than were others as tuition fees increased and we were faced with additional financial hazards of life in general. But we made it!

All the sports days, the father-and-daughter dinners, the science-display events, the choral and musical performances, etc., were all shuffled into a disorganized jumble of delightfully fragrant memories and stashed into an ethereal album of the mind. It was over. But yet it was just beginning.

At the dinner-dance celebration of the graduation, we as parents were invited to attend. It was a night that I remember with deep emotion. The climactic moment came when Heather asked me to dance. The song that was playing was "Wind Beneath My Wings." She told me that I had been the wind beneath her wings all these years. She suggested that this should be our song. She has since referred to this on birthday cards down through the years. I periodically read the words to this melody and draw encouragement from it.

After considering many alternatives, Heather applied for and was accepted by UBC to study for a degree in occupational therapy.

Before starting out on this next educational excursion, she wanted to have a year off and, among other things, become a crewmember on a training cruise on a sailing vessel with a group of young people. We encouraged her and gave her our approval but told her that she would have to pay for the cost of the venture. She worked at lifeguarding and swimming instruction to earn and save the necessary funds.

The time finally arrived for her to board the vessel. The Christian organization that sponsored the enterprise planned a trip around the world that was divided into segments. One could buy into many of the segments or choose one. Heather chose the part of the voyage that would travel the Caribbean, stopping at various islands.

Mabel, Heather, and I flew to Miami, where the ship was docked. We checked into a hotel and then found the pier where the *Swift* was located. We boarded the ship and met the people in charge. They escorted us through every corner of the vessel, even to the place where Heather was to bunk.

The time came for the *Swift* to depart with its new green crew. It was with a sense of deprivation that we watched as the lines that moored the ship to the shore were dropped and the gap of water began to widen between us and our precious cargo. Mabel and I ran to our rented car and raced to the channel through which the *Swift* had to pass to get to the open sea. We drove along the levy as far as we could and waved and stared as the top of the mast of the *Swift* was swallowed by the blue horizon. She would be gone a month.

I stood there with a hallowed feeling, occupied with the thought that my daughter would be on the very same waters that I had sailed in pursuit of the dreaded wolf pack of German submarines and where I had that blessed intimate night encounter with God so many years ago.

Mabel and I returned home. We had been given a schedule indicating where the *Swift* would be and on what day. We pacified our concerns by attempting to enter into the travel experiences she would have, moving from island to island. We also got some phone calls and letters from Heather.

The month soon passed, and we made our way back to Miami to collect our voyager. There she was—tanned, healthy, happy, packed, and ready to tackle the next step on life's calendar.

I should mention a horrible, frightening thing that happened to us when we were in Miami. We were driving along in the line of traffic next to the curb on one of the main streets. We were behind a bus. Traffic lights ahead of us turned red, and all the vehicles stopped. We were trapped in that spot until the light turned green. I was driving, and Heather was in the passenger seat in the front. Mabel was sitting behind me with her purse on the seat beside her.

A young man standing with a group on the curb held something in his hand. He hit the curbside rear window and smashed it. He reached in, grabbed Mabel's purse, and ran away with it. Heather wanted to chase after him, but I stopped her. When the traffic moved, I drove around the block to see if we could see any sign of him but could not. By the time we got back to the corner where it had happened, the group of young men had disappeared. A man was there who had seen the whole thing, and he called the police. The police could not do anything. They told us that this was a usual occurrence. People with rental car licenses are targeted. From then on, we felt very insecure in that city.

Apart from catching cold quite easily and a moderate struggle with high blood pressure, Mabel's health was robust. However, that was about to change. One day she began to have pain in her abdomen. We went to the emergency at University Hospital, where appendicitis was diagnosed. Her appendix was removed, and during the procedure, her blood pressure shot up unacceptably high. The surgeon found that a cyst that had been formed on her kidney had caused it. The condition was unusual in medical circles, and Mabel became a center of interest among the medics at the university. The surgeon recommended that the cyst should be removed. Mabel agreed because her high blood pressure was of concern to her.

The doctor had the choice of a simple operation through her back or a major intrusion through her abdomen to look around (as he called it). Without any discussion with us regarding the implications or side effects, he decided to look around. He was a teaching professor at UBC, and he used Mabel as a living sideshow for his students and confreres. He ripped her abdomen open from her waist to her crotch in the shape of a gaping flap in order to prod around her insides.

I was expecting the process to last about an hour and a half max, and it continued over five hours. I was filled with anxiety, thinking that something untoward had happened. Finally a swarm of students burst out of the operating room, laughing and guffawing. Mabel was taken to the intensive care, where I found her unconscious and wiped out. She remained in intensive care for several days.

I was furious that such a thing could have happened to her when we thought that we were putting her in hands that cared. I was in the position that I dare not say anything to her or to the hospital because I was desperate to have her recover at all costs and did not want in any way to jeopardize that possibility. It took some time for her to regain her strength. She never did recapture her limitless vitality, spontaneity, and venturesome spirit. That physical episode robbed her of many of the characteristics that made her so exceptionally special to me. However, despite that horrible experience, she remained the solid person I had come to love and respect.

Life had barely returned to normal when Mabel developed pain in her chest. After examination, it was determined that she had a cancerous tumor. The suggested treatment was chemotherapy and radiation. This came as a blow that was difficult to take for the both of us. We decided that we would do two things: (1) leave everything on the hands of God, and (2) think and act positively.

It was a trying time where we learned to support each other even more than we had before. We went together when she had to take the chemical therapy sessions. This was applied over many weeks, which she tolerated very well although she progressively lost weight. The next step was radiation, which had devastating effects on her constitution. She literally was reduced to skin and bones over the course of the treatment. She constantly maintained a strong mental and spiritual attitude, and the tumor shrunk and disappeared. We were thankful that God granted this to happen. Determination and tenacity returned her to reasonable physical strength again.

During this period Heather was attending UBC, receiving her first year of instruction toward her degree in occupational therapy. When the time came for her to move into her second year, she felt that she needed to have a change of environment and applied for entrance in the same course at the University of Alberta in Edmonton. She was affirmed and moved there. It was rather lonely without her, but we accepted the fact that it was probably good for her to have some experience being on her own as she moved toward adulthood.

Heather found the venture in Edmonton difficult in many ways. The weather was so very cold in comparison to British Columbia, where she had spent most of her life. She formed close relationships with some of her fellow students, but the absence of Vancouver family and friends left a gap in her life. As a result she stayed only one year in Edmonton and returned to UBC to finish her studies.

Tim had acquired a farm in the interior and used it for many projects, among them a camp for disabled children. I was very proud of him because despite his physical handicaps, he pressed on to achieve many things against odds that seemed insurmountable. His ingenuity and tenacity was outstanding.

Star was busy raising her family, but she found time and energy to establish a refuge for battered women. I was pleased that she would devote her talents to such a worthy endeavor.

Delightful and pleasant as our home was on Sixth Avenue, it had one disadvantage. There were stairs to climb. After Mabel's illness, it became a major consideration. We were both advancing in age, and having a two-story home did not seem wise. Consequently we began to look for an apartment that would meet our changing requirements. We found one on Eighth Avenue on the border between Point Grey and Kitsilano.

Church:
The pastoral positions at University Chapel had several changes as time went by. I had tried to encourage an increased participation in the neighborhood but without much response from the leadership or the congregation. I continued with my hospital and hospice work. I was asked to become part of the staff to participate in general visitation in the church.

There was dissatisfaction with the senior pastor leadership, and the church found itself without a person in that position. I was asked to fill some of the responsibility on a temporary basis until another person could be found.

Chapter 31

Major Life Changes
(1996-2007)

Digest of Times and Circumstance:

United States:

George W. Bush became the president of the United States after Clinton. He was the son of the former president Bush. Shortly after he became president, the twin towers in New York City were attacked by members of an organization composed of an offshoot of the Islamic religion. Commercial aircraft were hijacked and flown into the buildings, and another one was flown into the Pentagon and yet another crashed into an area in Pennsylvania after being recaptured by passengers aboard it. This was considered an act of terrorism, and the president declared war on the perpetrators. A Saudi Arabian by the name of Bin Laden was deemed to be the individual behind the action. He was in Afghanistan, and as a consequence, the USA attacked and drove the prevailing government out. Bin Laden was not taken captive, and the search for him continues.

Iraq was again a threat because they claimed to have weapons of mass destruction and would not give the inspectors from the United Nations free access to search for any sign of them. Because of the strategic position of the country as a producer of oil and located in the middle of others who were also producers of oil on which the world depended, President Bush, along with other countries, decided to subdue Iraq. This was done, and a lengthy procedure began to reestablish Iraq as a democracy.

After eight years in office, Barack Obama, who became the first African-American to rise to that position, replaced Bush.

George Bush ran an administration that increased the debt of the United States to an unacceptable level and lost the confidence of the people. Obama also lost the confidence of the people in his first two years in office and ran the country many times more into debt. Additionally he operated a government that increasingly passed legislation and instituted regulations that put more and more power into the hands of the federal government. At midterm elections, the people turned against him and put control of the House of Representatives into the hands of the opposition.

At time of writing, the USA, and the world is in the midst of a deep recession. The United States is in dire straits and could possibly go bankrupt if drastic steps are not taken to remedy the situation.

Canada:

The Reform Party was formed in 1987 under the leadership of Preston Manning and became the official opposition in 1997. Preston Manning used his power as the leader of the official opposition to force the Liberal government to achieve a balanced budget that provided a sound financial base for the country to move forward. Paul Martin was the finance minister at the time and took credit for it.

Paul Martin replaced Trudeau as the Leader of the Liberal Party and became prime minister in 2003 until Stephen Harper defeated him in 2005.

The Reform Party was not able to form the government and attempted to revamp itself. In the process, Preston Manning lost the leadership of the party, and eventually, Stephen Harper became the leader and formed an amalgamation with the Progressive Conservative Party. The new party was named the Conservative Party of Canada.

Stephen Harper was elected prime minister of Canada in 2005. The world fell into a deep recession in 2008, and the Harper government guided the country through it very well until the time of writing.

Family:

Our next residence at 209 3788 West Eighth Avenue was ideal for us in many ways. The location was near bus transportation, stores and restaurants of all types, parks, and the waterfront of English Bay. Everything was within easy walking distance on flat land.

The building itself was a unique design. There were three stories with irregularly scalloped parameters having generous outdoor patios and balconies. The variable exteriors made it possible to have a variety of floor plans for the living spaces within. There were no apartments exactly alike. It was composed of two structures joined on the main floor by a common room incorporating a self-contained suite that was available for use of the owners to accommodate visitors. There was secure parking and storage space in the basement. The finishing such as carpeting, wallpaper, doors, and landscaping were of good quality.

Our apartment was ideal for us. We could drive into the underground parking area, enter into the elevator, and travel to our floor level. If we wanted to, we could park on the street and reach our living space by mounting a few steps. There were two bedrooms, two bathrooms, kitchen, dining-slash-living room, an office space, and a wraparound spacious balcony. We were very happy. Mabel said that she would like to live there the rest of her life (which she did). Heather stayed with us while she continued her education at UBC.

After graduating from UBC, Heather worked at the G. F. Strong rehabilitation facility, where she specialized in rheumatic hand disability. She also worked occasionally at Mary Pack rheumatic center as well as lectured at UBC. After some years she was appointed to the Children's Hospital rheumatic treatment assessment program.

During the summer breaks she worked in the waterfront activities of summer camps in British Columbia. One of them was Young Life Camp at Princess Louisa Inlet, where Mabel and I had boated so many years ago. Another one was Anvil Island, which was located in Howe Sound. It was there that she met Ken Best. This acquaintance consummated in marriage after an on-again-off-again relationship over a period of three to four years.

It was a delightful wedding held in a chapel on the UBC campus. The Best family provided a fabulous celebration dinner in their home in North Vancouver, and the weather cooperated throughout the affair with balmy, sunny fall days. Mabel and I were pleased that they were married. We felt that they both brought something of great value to contribute to each other in building a new family.

In 2001 Mabel and I traveled to Toronto to have a bit of a change and to visit some of the homes where I had lived during the time I spent in that city. We also stopped by at some of the places we were together so many years ago. Elinor and Earl McNutt lived north of Toronto, and we stayed with them. Earl had been a pastor who was in retirement but supplied interim service for churches that were temporarily without a pastor. He provided this activity for University Chapel during a period when the church was searching for a permanent minister. Mabel and I had become close friends with them while they were in Vancouver. Toronto was their home, and they invited us to stay with them on our visit to that city.

Mabel's father had left her mineral rights on the family farm. She leased it to an oil exploration company that drilled and found natural gas. This produced additional revenue for a short period that allowed us to do many things we had not been able to do up to that point in our life together. One of the things we did was to take Heather and Ken to Arizona. We rented a posh villa near where Stu and Jackie lived. It was an experience of a lifetime, which we all greatly enjoyed.

I had not spent much time with Star and Tim in recent years. They were both single and living on the farm that Tim had acquired. I thought that it would be a good idea if the three of us went away together somewhere. I had not seen the Oregon coast and suggested that perhaps that might be a place that we could go. Tim got busy and found a house we could rent right on the beach on the Pacific Ocean. It turned out to be a terrific time together that I hold in fond memory.

In 2003 began a series of health problems, which dramatically changed our lives. Upon arriving home one afternoon, my right leg felt a bit strange. As the evening progressed, it continued to have an increasing unusual sensation. I slept through the night, and when I woke in the morning, there were some muscles in my leg that would not respond. I could not walk without assistance. Mabel drove me to emergency at the University Hospital, where Heather joined us. I was given a multitude of procedures (by a Dr. Oger, a neurologist)—MRI, CT scan, ultrasound, and blood tests, all of which did not produce a definitive reason for my condition. It was a Friday, and the doctor wanted to hold me over the weekend, but there were no beds available. I went home.

I returned the following Monday, by which time some muscular control had been restored. Subsequently there continued to be improvement, but I never recovered the full use of my leg. The medical people concluded that I had had a spinal stroke. I could still drive a car and play limited golf, but my activities were considerably curtailed.

Over the next number of months I developed some bowel problems that proved to be the result of a cancerous growth near my rectum. The doctors, including the surgeon, held out very little hope for me but recommended that I have a colostomy procedure followed by radiation and chemical therapy.

I had the colostomy operation from which I recovered reasonably well. Except that when I was fitted for the receptacles to adhere to my skin to receive the waste material, my skin erupted and would not tolerate the adhesives that were employed. There were weeks of tortuous experiments trying different manufacturers to find one that my system would accept. I finally found one!

Concurrently I was visiting the British Columbia cancer clinic for radiation. These were followed by chemical treatments. I had a pump that was battery powered attached to my waist that pumped chemicals twenty-four hours a day through a catheter that ran from my armpit in a blood vessel to just above my heart. Sleeping and having showers were a challenge.

Simultaneously I applied powerful magnets, concentrating on the location of the cancer. I had benefited from the use of magnetic therapy in other instances; therefore, I decided to see if it could be useful in this circumstance. There seemed to be nothing to lose since the medical opinion did not offer hope to eliminate the cancer.

The next step was to have the operation to remove the cancerous growth. This also entailed the reconnection of my lower intestine to my rectum, thus eliminating the need for my colostomy. It was a complicated process that would require five to six hours to complete. In the midst of the procedure, the stitching machine broke down, which resulted in the doctor deciding that it was too risky to reattach the intestine.

The second night after my surgery, my digestive system plugged up, and I commenced to vomit large quantities of bile-like fluid. The doctors concluded that I needed to have a stomach pump installed. This required that a tube be inserted in my nose, down my throat, and into my stomach. This was an awkward and uncomfortable process. It was finally accomplished, and the tube was attached to a pump, and the liquid accumulated in a container. There were about two liters of fluid removed in the next couple of hours. This rig remained attached to me day and night for the following eight days. I immediately developed hiccups, which continued twenty-four hours a day. I had to take my fluid, nourishment, and medication intravenously. There was a further complication in that my veins were not conducive to the acceptance of needles. As a consequence, my blood vessels at the point of insertion would burn out, and a new location would have to be found. In the search for a new location often, several veins would be burnt. The cumulative result was that my forearms and the back of my hands were black and blue and covered with needle punctures. Both limbs were irritated and uncomfortable.

After many x-rays and scans, the doctors were still unsure how to correct the digestive problem. I lay in this state for a week as they waited for the condition to rectify itself. Day followed day and night followed night of unending revolving pain, gnawing discomfort, and disconcerting uncertainty, punctuated by a hiccup with every breath. I had no restful sleep and remained in a semiconscious dazed mode most of the time. On the eighth night, somehow I must have gotten tangled in the tube coming out of my nose and wrenched it loose. When I came to my senses, the nurse was removing the remainder of the tube from my body. The doctors decided to leave it out and try giving me some liquid food. My system digested it, and they switched to more solid nourishment that was also accepted, and everything got back on track.

Mabel, Heather, and Tim spent many hours by my bedside doing what they could to make me more comfortable. Their companionship, which meant a great deal to me, could only go so far. I constantly would fall into a semiconscious mode. Most of the time I had very little restful sleep and experienced isolated loneliness. My prayers seemed to be unheard, and I could not feel the presence of God. There were long intervals where I seemed to be completely forsaken. These sessions would end abruptly as I would become aware that despite my feelings, the strong everlasting arms of the God of the universe encompassed me, bringing warmth, security, and hope. These incidences repeatedly occurred throughout the week that I was attached to the stomach pump.

I regained enough strength to return home. The net result of all of this effort was that the cancerous cells had been killed and removed, which seemed miraculous after the medical prognosis to the contrary. The downside was that I would have to live with a colostomy situation for the rest of my life. In addition, the radiation treatment had damaged my bladder, requiring that I use a catheter constantly.

Mabel and I had planned to do a lot of travelling on the passes to which she was entitled from her years with the airline, including two trips first-class anywhere in the world. However, the limits of my physical condition made that impossible.

Heather and Ken had two wonderful children. The first one was a boy, Graham David Best, and the second one was a girl, Lucie Anna Best. It was a delight for Mabel and me to have the privilege of sharing the care of them, along with Ken's parents, Grace and Lee Best, for a portion of each week while they were at work. Even though my physical disabilities limited my capacity to play with them as I would want, it was a special fulfillment to have them nearby and to share the joy of watching them learn and grow.

Mabel was a superb gramma who anticipated every need and whim. The large share of the responsibility of our babysitting fell on her shoulders because of my limitation. The children adored her.

With the passage of time, I observed that she increasingly found it difficult to regain her energy after the children's visit or other activities.

She quickly became noticeably weaker, and her breathing was very shallow when she slept. Finally she went to the doctor on a Friday afternoon, and he sent her to the lab across the street from his office for chest x-rays. The technician sent her back to the doctor with the report, and the doctor told her that if her breathing became more difficult she should go to the emergency room immediately. He offered to drive her home, but she insisted that she could drive her own car. When she arrived home and told me the story, I wanted to take her to the hospital right away, but she declined.

The next day she said she was ready to go to the hospital. I phone Heather and explained the situation. We left for the General and parked on the street, and Mabel walked on her own steam to Emergency, where Heather met us. She was examined and admitted to the lung section of the hospital.

I stayed with her every day from midmorning to early evening. It was difficult to see her increasingly losing vitality. She had no appetite and could not and would not eat food no matter how much I tried to persuade her. They finally put her on intravenous.

The medical staff examined her with all the equipment and tests that they had available and could not diagnose what was causing her lung cavities to fill with fluid. Her lungs were drained of the accumulated liquid several times, but on each occasion they refilled.

Every day she became weaker and weaker. On the tenth day she didn't have the strength to go to the bathroom on her own. Despite her lack of energy, with great difficulty she managed to put a few hairpins in her hair. I left her in early evening. It was her habit to phone me to say good night just before she went to sleep. About eight PM she called, and we each said, "Love you. See you in the morning." That was the last time I heard her voice.

The phone rang about midnight. It was the hospital, telling me that Mabel was very ill and was on life support. I dressed immediately and went to the hospital. When I got there, I couldn't see her just yet, but they showed me to a room that had reclining chairs and suggested that I use one of them. Heather had been informed of the circumstance. She arrived and took a chair beside mine.

After a while a nurse came and told us we could see Mabel. We were informed that she was heavily sedated and that she would not show any response but that people in that state could possibly hear what was said. Heather and I approached the apparatus on which Mabel lay. There was a breathing tube forced into her mouth that completely distorted her face. The sound of the machine that provided air to her lungs produced a harrowing sound that I will never forget. I noticed that the pins she had put into her hair yesterday were still there.

Heather took one of her hands and I the other. We told her we loved her and thanked her for all she meant to us and that we were right with her. We had no indication she heard. It was a heart-rending, heart-wrenching, sad, and empty moment. There appeared to be no hope for her survival.

Mabel's brother Dick lived in Surrey. They were called and given the chance to see Mabel because of the dire circumstances. He and his wife, Florence, and their daughter, Kim, arrived. They were devastated when they saw Mabel's failing condition.

I was faced with a terrible decision. Should I continue the machinery to keep her technically alive or not? Was there any hope that she would ever again have anything that would look like a normal life? She and I had discussed this type of event, and we both promised each other that we would not let the other one suffer but would terminate the artificial means and let nature take its course. That is the action I chose.

By this time, Ken, Heather's husband, was with us. I told the small group what I intended to do. I would tell the attendants to disconnect Mabel from the apparatus, and we would gather at her bedside and pray as she passed into eternity. Dick and his family decided to leave before that happened.

And so Heather held one hand and I the other with Ken beside us. The breathing tube had been removed from her mouth. The nurse had tried to spruce up her appearance, including removing the pins in her hair and fluffing it up. We each thanked God for her life and what she had meant to us individually. She left us at noon November 21, 2007.

The doctors were baffled by her case and asked permission to do an extensive autopsy to try to discover what caused it all to happen. Her illness was so sudden and so unexpected. I agreed and signed the papers to authorize it.

Life had abruptly changed for me. I just lost my soul mate, my common sense compass, my steadfast caregiver, and my reliable friend. Given my own debilitating physical problems, it presented quite a challenge.

David Booker, who had been the senior pastor at University Chapel, arrived shortly after Mabel died. He went home with us, and we had lunch together. His presence was much appreciated.

Heather and Ken asked me to go home with them to spend the night at their place. I welcomed the invitation and joined them. During the evening we spent some time discussing what should happen in the future.

They suggested that we pool our resources and find a place that would suitably house their family and me. I agreed, provided we could find accommodation that would allow them to function as a family without my interference and at the same time permit me to have separation of time and space to pursue my own activities.

Star phoned and offered to stay with me in the apartment until things got sorted out. This was a tremendous relief. She became an indispensable resource of problem solving in daily matters and a comfortable conversational partner. Her unselfish attitude in her approach to the whole situation was gratifying.

We wanted to have Mabel's life celebrated by those who knew her over the years. We needed to get a suitable space to hold a memorial service followed by a tea reception afterward. The Baptist church at Sixteenth and Fir had the accommodation that we required and was available on Saturday, December 1, 2007.

This did not leave much time to make preparations, give notification in the press, and to make phone calls to key people, particularly to those out of town. Ken and his family and Heather's friends, especially Terra Bentall, were indispensable in their assistance. David Booker agreed to be the moderator and speaker at the event and organized that department. Tom Midbo and Mabel had a special relationship over the years, so I thought it fitting that he should give the eulogy at the service. I asked him, and he accepted. My brother Stu came from Arizona to be with me at the memorial service.

A couple of days before the event, I developed a severe case of diarrhea that caused major stress on the colostomy bag adhered to my abdomen, which could result in the adhesive giving way, causing the feces to escape. I had to be vigilant at all times to avoid this catastrophe from occurring. This problem persisted on Friday. Added to this, I had a high fever, which triggered periods of violent shaking. I felt I could not attend Mabel's memorial with the possibility of either or both of these happening and causing a huge disruption. I told Heather the problem, and she phoned my GP, Dr. Barrett. He said that I should go to emergency immediately. I was admitted. I remained there for the entire month of December.

Saturday came, and with it a blizzard of snow that lasted the whole day. Despite the weather, a good number of family and friends participated in the memorial for Mabel. Unfortunately for me, I was not there. Tim, who had come into town for the memorial, remained with me. David Booker, Heather, Ken, family, and friends made it all happen in fine form.

Meanwhile, back at the hospital, my condition was diagnosed as blood poisoning of some type, and a regimen of antibiotic was applied. By late afternoon my fever had subsided and my periods of shaking stopped. My family members and David Booker came back to see me after the memorial service was over. They all returned home early that evening.

Soon after they left, my temperature started to rise again, and I could sense that the shaking was on the verge of returning. I asked for more Tylenol to reduce my fever, and they told me that I had enough and would not give me any more. Soon I was violently shaking and could not make it stop. The tension grew in my entire body as the waves of shivers increased in tempo and intensity. My chest was squeezed to the point where I could hardly breathe. I kept fading in and out of consciousness. I foolishly lost all confidence in the doctors and nurses who were trying to help me and kept telling them to get my daughter Heather.

After a while Heather arrived, along with Ken, Star, and Tim. Tests were taken, and it was determined that I had had a heart attack. They moved me to the cardiac emergency center and hooked me up to the monitoring machinery. After I became stabilized, my children returned home again.

Heather and Ken stayed at my apartment to be near the hospital. Shortly after going to bed, Heather began to have severe chest pains. Ken took her to Emergency, where she remained for three days since there were no beds available to admit her. We were both in the same hospital at different locations. I was not told about the Heather's situation but was informed that she had the flu and did not come to see me because of the fear of transferring it to me. She had a terrible time. The final diagnosis was a major case of heartburn.

My condition continued to deteriorate. The head cardiologist in the department told me that I was in a very dangerous condition because a large amount of acid was in my blood, and that I might not survive. He said he wanted to introduce me to the life-support doctor. This he did. This man asked me if I wanted to have my heart started again when it stopped. I told him yes. He then asked me if I wanted to be attached to the life-sustaining equipment. I said, "Yes, but not for an extended period." I explained to him that two weeks ago I had to make the decision to remove my wife from that machinery and why. He then walked away.

My brother Stu had to return to Arizona, so he came to say good-bye. We wept, believing that this was the last time we would see each other on earth.

Little by little I improved. My heart rate slowed down, and my blood returned to a more normal chemistry. After several days, I was returned to the room I originally had upstairs. I regained enough strength to be able to sit up in a chair. One day I was doing this, and as I was returning to go back into bed, my heart malfunctioned and I nearly collapsed on the floor. The nurse was at hand and got me back into bed. I was immediately rushed to the cardiac section again, where I remained for several more days.

In the meantime it was suspected that I had a bleeding ulcer in my stomach. To confirm this, they moved a large apparatus into my room at the cardiac department to take pictures of the interior of my stomach. There was a team of about six people involved. I was given a light anesthetic after which a camera was thrust down my throat into my stomach. There they found the bleeding ulcer. They determined medicinal chemicals had caused it and that it would soon heal.

After a few days I was returned to my room again. I was weak and not able to do much for myself. I had the complication of needing to periodically have my colostomy bag changed. I found this difficult to do lying in bed and therefore had to rely on nurses to do it for me. It was a procedure with which most of them were not familiar. One day the dreaded thing happened. The colostomy bag broke loose from my skin, and a flood of liquid feces went all over the bed and me. A nurse grabbed me and dragged me to the shower room and cleaned me up while she was giving commanding orders to the assistants who were changing the bedclothes. I could hardly stand, and she held me with one hand and the shower with the other. She was a wonder.

I found that the health caregivers in the hospital were beyond excellent. Most of them were from the Philippine islands. Until I got into this hospital routine, I had not met many from that part of the world and did not know what quality people they were. I know now and am very grateful to them.

At the end of December, I felt that I had gained enough strength to return home to the apartment. I was not strong, but as long as I watched my every step, I was able to get around from room to room. Star and Heather were absolutely essential to me. I had daily help from homecare people.

The time had come to try to plan for the long-term living situation. I had accepted Heather and Ken's invitation to pool resources and find joint accommodation that would provide for their needs and mine. I would sell my condo and put up to five hundred thousand dollars for one-half interest in a property, and they would earn one-half interest by being 100 percent responsible for any mortgage that was involve. Our properties went on the market, and after some confusion, they sold. Real estate was in a disorderly state at the time. Properties were being snapped up as soon as they appeared, and it became very difficult to deal for desirable situations. We searched for homes in many areas that were within striking distance of Heather and Ken's work and also provided suitable neighborhoods for Graham and Anna. In the end, North Vancouver seemed to be the most appropriate.

Ken worked for a firm that did home remodeling. There was a neighboring house beside the one on which he was working in North Vancouver that looked promising. He placed a note in the mailbox of this house, indicating that he was interested in this property should it become available. A Mr. Brown, who lived there alone, passed the note on to his son. The following day, Mr. Brown died and his family contacted Ken. It was a three-bedroom building on a large-enough lot to add a self-contained apartment where I could live. A price was negotiated, and we took possession. Heather, Ken, Graham, and Anna moved in.

I was still living in the apartment with Star until the purchaser's possession date. I needed a place to live while my new residence was completed. It so happened that Ken's employer owned a two-bedroom self-contained bungalow near our newly purchased land. The occupant had given notice, and we rented it with the intention that Star and I would move in.

Before all of this took place, I was physically struck down again. It was night, and I was in bed sleeping when suddenly excruciating pain emanated from my spine, shooting through the right side of my torso. It pulsated in waves and prohibited me from getting out of bed or turning. Star was away for the weekend, and I used my phone to call my neighbor in the adjacent apartment. He helped me stand up, but the pain still persisted. The ambulance was called, and I was transported to emergency at the Vancouver General. It was the middle of July 2008.

I was in emergency for two to three days while the doctors tried to determine what was causing the pain that would attack for a couple of minutes and then subside for a short time and then repeat. I have endured many types of physical suffering, but none that came close to the intensity of this encounter. If there were not breaks in the painful periods, I do not think I could have kept my sanity. Eventually two stress fractures on the vertebra of my spine showed up on the x-rays. I was admitted to the hospital.

A number of different medicines were used to reduce the pain, but none were effective. There was only one remedy that was suggested, and there was no assurance that it would work. It entailed squirting a kind of cement into my spine that would seal up the fractures. They gave me a light anesthetic and completed the procedure. Within a couple of days I felt some improvement. As long as I stayed perfectly still, the pain would not occur. However, if I moved, it would recommence. Finally two woman doctors, who were pain specialists, were called into my case. They advocated heavy doses of morphine. There was immediate positive reaction. As long as I moved carefully, I was pain-free.

I had been in the hospital for two weeks, and I was anxious to get out. During the time I was in the hospital, Star and Heather moved the furniture from the apartment into the bungalow we had rented in North Vancouver, so the ambulance delivered me there.

In the absence of Mabel, Star assumed some of the babysitting responsibilities for Heather as well as increased care for me. We stayed in the bungalow while the new addition for me was being constructed. While there, the provincial social worker arranged for help to come in every day to aid in assistance for me.

I became stronger and increasingly able to provide for myself in daily living. Ken worked hard to design and to supervise the construction of my new home. It was ready for my occupation on Friday the thirteenth of March 2009, and I moved in. Star continued to live in the cottage. She and Heather went to Christian Valley and retrieved Star's furniture. Star kept helping me with cleaning, shopping, etc., as well as babysitting for Heather. My provincial aid was decreased to one person coming to my home every Saturday for two hours.

The winter of 2008 was very cold, blustery, and snow filled. It produced the kind of days that one was happy to be inside. Fortunately for me I could remain indoors most of the time because of the help that others gave me. Beside my daughters, one of the people who rendered great assistance was Ken's father, Lee Best. He is a jack-of-all-trades and was and is a person who gives of himself to others. I was and am one of the recipients of his generosity.

Because of the length of my recovery time and the consequence of dealing with inclement weather, we had not interred Mabel's remains after the autopsy. While there was no definitive cause established for her lungs to be filling up with fluid, there was a serious untreatable late-stage cancerous liver problem discovered, which could have affected the situation. Mabel was reluctant to discuss her interment preferences with me, even though I had tried several times to talk about the subject in later years. The decision was left for Heather and me.

I had officiated at a funeral a long time ago for a man whom I had known from Quebec and who had moved to North Vancouver on his retirement.

His family had arranged for a service to be held at Boal Chapel in North Vancouver. My memory of this place was very positive even after the passage of time, so Heather and I looked into it. In the middle of the cemetery, verdant bushes, trees, and flowers surrounded a delightful placid pond. The pond was covered with lily pads. We thought Mabel would have approved the location. We made the necessary arrangements and chose the middle of May for the time of the interment ceremony.

It was a lovely day, with the lilies in the pond blossoming profusely and the supporting vegetation blending in harmony. There was a pavilion that jutted out into the water that was large enough to accommodate the people who were there. Among them were Stu and Jackie, who combined a holiday trip to be with me. David Booker was the moderator. Those present were given the opportunity to tell of their remembrances of Mabel. It was a touching time for me to hear uplifting words about the one I loved and with whom I had shared so much of life. We placed her remains in a niche in the rock with a place beside for my remains when the time comes. The caption on the outside of the door enclosing the space says, "See you in the morning," the last words we said to each other.

The interior of the main house where Heather, Ken, and family lived needed to be thoroughly renovated, which required them to move out. It took several months for the work to be done. Fortunately friends and family made several locations available to them for temporary residency. With great difficulty and strategic planning, it all happened, and they moved back in February 2010.

Grace Best, Ken's mother, was an intimate part of every member of her family. She was highly esteemed and loved by everyone who knew her, including me. Her contribution to the lives of her children and grandchildren, in particular, was vital to their everyday activities. She truly had the servant attitude that Jesus Christ held in such high regard. Grace became ill with untreatable cancer in the latter part of 2009 and passed on in early 2010. Her passing has left a huge gap in the lives of many and especially Heather, Ken, and their children.

I am going to end my story here. It is November 2010. I am living in very comfortable surroundings with every convenience I desire although I have a daily struggle with the physical disabilities that I have acquired which are compounded by advancing age.

I am thankful to have some part in the daily lives of Star, Heather, Ken, Graham, and Anna. I also get to see my grandson Wilson, who married Amber, who had two previous children. At time of writing they have had

two other delightful girls, Miley and Kaylee, which are my two great-grandchildren. I see them once in a while.

My son Tim has moved to Rosedale, British Columbia, and I hope to see him occasionally. My son Jonathan still lives in Alberta. I haven't seen or heard from him in decades.

Star still lives in the cottage in North Vancouver to which we moved a couple of years ago. She has assumed a greater role in the care of Graham and Anna, following the death of Grace. She is a constant source of help and comfort to me.

Church:

We attended University Chapel as a family since its inception. I had participated in supporting roles most of the seventeen years that I was there. Unfortunately Mabel was not made to feel welcome by some of the people who were members of the church, and she switched to First Baptist for the last two or three years of her life. I remained at UC because I felt that I had a responsibility.

There was a period when we were without a senior pastor that Earl McNutt came from Toronto to be a temporary supply person while the church attempted to find a suitable senior pastor. He was a fine warm Christian as was his wife, Elinor. Mabel and I had a very friendly relationship with them.

I was asked to be part of a pastoral search committee. This committee settled on David Booker from Toronto and moved him and his family to Vancouver to assume this position. There were members of the church that did not accept him from the beginning and set out to discredit him. After about three to four years, they finally succeeded in removing him. I was so thoroughly disgusted with the whole process that I left UC and joined Mabel at First Baptist, where we stayed until Mabel's death.

David Booker became a pastor of a church in North Vancouver where he was appreciated and where he is at the time of writing. After my illness, I was unable to go to church for a long time, and he regularly has come to visit me. This he continues to do since I have moved to North Vancouver. His fellowship means a great deal to me.

I do not go to church services now even though, with considerable effort, I could. I like to hear the old hymns of the faith and find that that is missing these days. I am an old guy from a different era. I enjoy a program on Sunday morning that has been broadcast for many years called *Day of Discovery*. Outside of that, my spiritual activity is limited to my own Bible study and meditation. When I finish this book, I will spend my time putting my thoughts down in *As It Seems to Me*.

Chapter 32

Retrospect
Fall 2010

It has taken me over a decade to complete this review of my life because I have worked on it only sporadically. During that time, I was busy with other things. Also I suffered several illnesses, which required lengthy periods of recuperation that took me right out of daily activities.

One of the reasons I undertook this project was for my own benefit. I wanted to look back on my life and see the hand of God as I spent the time He had given me. One of the sermons I preached to others went something like this:

"God has given us a life to live. It is like having pockets full of coins. The denominations of the coins are called minutes, hours, days, months, years. Every day we must put our hands into the pockets of our lives and start spending. When all the coins are gone, our life is over. The question is, 'What have I bought with all that money?'"

The Bible tells us to lay up treasures in heaven. I wonder what my account looks like.

One thing I do know is that I have put the security of my eternity into the hands of Jesus Christ, and because of that, I have been born into God's family. I can look forward to experiencing the fullness of life that God intended from the beginning. However, I also know that as a Christian, I will have to stand before the Judgment Seat of Christ. This is where He will evaluate how I spent the minutes, hours, days, months, and years here on earth. The fire of truth will refine the eternal value of my actions during my life. Will it be wood, hay, and stubble or gold, silver, and precious stones? I will be rewarded, or not, over and above the blessings of eternal life.

It seems to me that there are six significant events in my adult life on which much of my activity turned:

1. I had the encounter with God while in the USN on the ship on the Caribbean Sea. This permeated decision making for the rest of my life.
2. Making the choice of either being permanently employed by Goodyear Tire or volunteering to go to China as a missionary. This led to all of the years in Christian camping and the time in Quebec.
3. The day I had to leave my family in Magog and go to direct camp at Frontier Lodge. This was a huge test to see if I could trust God to meet my needs if I put Him first. The ramifications of this incident affected immensely everything from that point on.
4. Accepting Bob Thompson's offer to be his executive assistant. This opened the door to my years in politics.
5. Becoming the executive director of the National Affairs Research Foundation. I was given everything with little or no effort on my part. This was not good for me spiritually or psychologically. It triggered a period of a less-than-intimate relationship with God.
6. The trip by myself from Arizona along the Pacific coast to Vancouver, where I received a fresh start before God. This opened the way for me to participate in hospital visitation and hospice care. It also prepared me for the emotional and physical testing that God allowed occurring to me personally over the ensuing years.

I have lived through a world that has been in constant turmoil, where mankind plotted evil against mankind. I have seen science develop amazing improvements: in transportation (from horse and wagons to spaceships), in communication (from hand-rung, wall-hung telephones to pocket-size sound and image-bearing satellite-fed cell phones, and yes, the Internet), in medicine (from pasteurization to heart and lung transplants), and in science (magnifying glasses to the Hubble telescope). But the heart of man has remained the same. There is a desperate need for a close relationship with God if humans are to have the internal peace that God intends for us.

The unbroken strong cord through all of this has been the abiding personal faithfulness of the God of the universe to a speck of life named David Wilson. He has always been there despite the fact that I often ignored Him and went my own way. I look forward to the time when I will pass into His presence—never to leave it again.

The following are some of the sayings that have had meaning for me as I mingled among my fellow mankind. Many are direct quotes from the Bible, and most of the others have their roots in the Bible:

"The truth shall make you free."

"Only what is done for Christ will last."

"God gave us two ears and one mouth. Listen to others twice as much as you talk."

"Self-praise stinks."

"The most blessed occupation of a human being is to love the God of the universe unconditionally. Then everything in time and eternity will come into focus."

"Humble yourself under the mighty hand of God, and in due time, He will exalt you."

"God upholds all things by the word of His power."

"One person plus God is a majority."

"With God, all things are possible."

"Inch by inch, everything is a cinch."

"Listen much, speak little."

"A great forest can be set on fire by one tiny spark."

"The tongue is a flame of fire."

"Much can be done if we don't worry about who gets the credit."

"The greatest is the one who is a faithful servant."

"Never quit."

"Tenacity in adversity."

"What a man is within himself is more important than what a man has."

I am going to finish with a poem and an old hymn. Between them, they broadly cover the summary of my life and my testimony.

The Ship that Sails

Anonymous

I'd rather be the ship that sails
And rides the billows wild and free;
Than be the ship that always fails
To leave its port and go to sea.

I'd rather feel the sting of strife,
Where gales are born and tempests roar;
Than settle down to a useless life
And rot in dry dock on the shore.

I'd rather fight some mighty wave
With honor in supreme command;
And fill a last well-earned grave,
Than die at ease upon the sand.

I'd rather drive where storm winds blow
And be the ship that always failed
To make the ports where it would go,
Than be the ship that never sails.

Immanuel's Land

A. R. Cousin

The sands of time are sinking,
The dawn of heaven breaks;
The summer morn I've sighed for,
The fair sweet morn awakes;
Dark, dark hath been the midnight,
But dayspring is at hand,
And glory, glory dwelleth
In Immanuel's land.

Oh Christ, He is the fountain
The deep sweet well of love;
The streams on earth I've tasted,
More deep I'll drink above;
There to an ocean fullness
His mercy doth expand,
And glory, glory dwelleth
In Immanuel's land.

With mercy and with judgment,
My web of time He wove,
And aye the dews of sorrow
Were lustered with His love;
I'll bless the hand that guided,
I'll bless the heart that planned,
When throned where glory dwelleth
In Immanuel's land.

Shalom!